The Poetics of Digital Media

For Caroline, Gefen, Tomer and Nitzan

The Poetics of Digital Media

Paul Frosh

polity

The right of Paul Frosh to be identified as Author of this Work has been
asserted in accordance with the UK Copyright, Designs and Patents Act 1988.

First published in 2019 by Polity Press

Reprinted 2019

Polity Press
65 Bridge Street
Cambridge CB2 1UR, UK

Polity Press
101 Station Landing
Suite 300
Medford, MA 02155, USA

ISBN-13: 978-0-7456-5131-6
ISBN-13: 978-0-7456-5132-3 (pb)

A catalogue record for this book is available from the British Library.

Library of Congress Cataloging-in-Publication Data

Names: Frosh, Paul, author.
Title: The poetics of digital media / Paul Frosh.
Description: Medford, MA : Polity, 2018. | Includes bibliographical references
    and index.
Identifiers: LCCN 2018022728 (print) | LCCN 2018038836 (ebook) |
    ISBN 9781509532681 (Epub) | ISBN 9780745651316 (hardback) |
    ISBN 9780745651323 (pbk.)
Subjects: LCSH: Mass media–Philosophy. | Digital media–Philosophy.
Classification: LCC P90 (ebook) | LCC P90 .F7614 2018 (print) |
    DDC 302.2301–dc23
LC record available at https://lccn.loc.gov/2018022728

Typeset in 10.5 on 12 pt Sabon by Toppan Best-set Premedia Limited
Printed and bound in the UK by CPI Group (UK) Ltd, Croydon

For further information on Polity, visit our website: politybooks.com

Contents

Acknowledgements

This book has emerged slowly, some might say sluggishly, over several years. My colleagues at the Department of Communication and Journalism at the Hebrew University of Jerusalem have sustained me throughout with continual friendship, good humour, inspiration and intellectual fellowship. I cannot think of a better, warmer, more stimulating and supportive place to work. I am particularly grateful to Nik John, Zohar Kampf, Ifat Maoz, Amit Pinchevski, Limor Shifman and Keren Tenenboim-Weinblatt for their insights and comments on different sections of the book: yes, you are mainly to blame. I am also indebted to the organizers and participants in a variety of forums where the book's ideas, in different stages of gestation, were ruthlessly inflicted on the innocent: the Freie University of Berlin, Haifa University, the Hebrew University of Jerusalem, the University of Leeds, the London School of Economics and Political Science, the University of Mainz, the University of Michigan, Northwestern University, the Open University (UK), the Open University (Israel), the Sigtuna Foundation, Stockholm University and Tel Aviv University, as well as in various panels at the annual conferences of the International Communication Association. My editors at Polity have been paragons of patience, encouragement and efficiency (virtues which do not always easily combine). I would especially like to thank Mary Savigar and Ellen Mac-Donald-Kramer, for their exemplary stewardship of the manuscript into publishable form, and the reviewers for their enthusiasm and extremely helpful suggestions.

I would like to thank several individuals and organizations for permission to reproduce their images: Guardian News and Media (Figure 3.2); Yedioth Ahronoth (Figure 3.3), with particular gratitude to Yacov Netzer for his help; Murad Osmann (Figures 5.1 and 5.2); Noa Jansma (Figures 5.3 and 5.4); and the USC Shoah Foundation (Figures 6.1 and 6.2). An earlier version of chapter 2 appeared as 'Indifferent Looks: Visuality, Inattention and the Composition of Strangers', in G. Rose and D. P. Tolia-Kelly (eds), *Visuality/Materiality: Images, Objects and Practices* (2012), Ashgate: Farnham, pp. 171–90; of chapter 5 as 'The Gestural Image: The Selfie, Photography Theory and Kinaesthetic Sociability' (2015), *International Journal of Communication* 9: 1607–28; and of chapter 6 as 'The Mouse, the Screen and the Holocaust Witness: Interface Aesthetics and Moral Response', *New Media & Society* (2018) 20(1): 351–68.

Last, but really first, there is family. Caroline: my closest companion, love of my life. It would be boring, and lonely, and far too chaotic without you. Gefen, Tomer and Nitzan: my sources of delightful distraction, deepest pride, cool cynicism (mainly about the signified's relation to the signifier) and occasionally useful information (see the notes). This book, you may have noticed, is dedicated to you all.

Author's Note on the Cover Image

I would dearly love to claim that the reasons for choosing the cover image of the blue flower were plain to me as soon as I saw it, but in this case intuition definitely preceded understanding. The flower, marketed by stock imagery company Shutterstock and created by photographer and illustrator BoxerX, was an inspired suggestion made by Clare Ansell (art director), Andrew Corbett (graphic designer) and Mary Savigar (Senior Commissioning Editor) at Polity. I was immediately struck by its enigmatic beauty on the cover mock-up, and by its hazy connotation of 'the poetic'. I also quickly associated the interleaving of petals and the openness of the flower with the ideas of world disclosure and mediated palpability that appear in the book. It was only later that memory involuntarily supplied another connection: Walter Benjamin's comment, itself rather enigmatic, about 'the blue flower in the land of technology', which appears in his famous essay on artwork in the age of mechanical reproduction (1992 [1936]: 226).[1] The 'blue flower' refers to a symbol in German romanticism (traced mainly to Novalis) of yearning for the infinite, union with nature, and of poetry itself: 'the unattainable object of the romantic quest, the incarnation of desire' (Hansen 1987: 204). However, in Benjamin's essay, the idea of the 'blue flower *in the land of technology*' follows a complex discussion of how cinema's technological intervention into reality (fragmentation of the studio space through the multiplication of camera viewpoints, and especially the reconfiguration of viewpoints through editing) constructs a new reality, whose 'illusionary nature is a nature of the second degree' (1992 [1936]: 226). While Benjamin's essay certainly critiques the alienating consequences of this artifice (summarized, roughly, as the 'loss of the aura'), it also contains crucial moments of what Miriam Hansen calls 'redemptive criticism', whereby technologized second nature discloses itself through a medium whose mimetic qualities register 'sediments of experience that are no longer or not yet claimed by social and economic rationality' (Hansen 1987: 209).

Benjamin's comments resonate in multiple ways with the image of the blue flower used on the front cover of this book. The picture is computer generated; it is an image of nature germinated in a digital ecosystem that populates our surroundings with such an abundance of objects that they form a primary experiential habitat, a lifeworld of mediated existence. Furthermore, the palpable detail of the flower in simulated close-up makes the mimetic powers of digital technologies manifest as world-producing forces. Finally, the flower is a stock image – another serendipitous connection, given my earlier research on stock photography. Verging on cliché and kitsch, designed in order to be resold many times for myriad uses and appearing in Shutterstock's online catalogue in numerous versions (with, for instance, backgrounds of different colour), it is perhaps the most generic, commodified and alienated type of cultural product, here fulfilling its destiny in social and economic rationality – a commercial destiny – through adorning and promoting this book. And yet, I hope, it also exceeds that destiny. As the blue flower is plucked for this book from the 'natural' habitat in which it was seeded and cultivated – the digital stock archive – it becomes an emblem of the mediated lifeworld: a sensuously and symbolically condensed incarnation of 'the land of technology' itself and of the possibilities – offered but never guaranteed – for meaningful life within it.

Prologue

Monsters, Inc. as a Poetic Manifesto

Night-time in a child's bedroom. When I was very young, I occasionally believed, like many other children, that there were monsters under my bed. I would be safe from their teeth and claws, I imagined, if only I could keep my limbs from extending into the darkness beyond the edges of the mattress until morning, by which time the monsters would have left, dissolving into the daylight. Curled into a ball which I was too young to describe as foetal, I would spend what felt like hours, but was really only a matter of minutes, furiously wishing away the fearsome phantoms I had conjured out of the night of my own bedroom, hardening my body against the unseen dangers of the dark even as it relaxed into sleep and dreams.

Marcel Proust and Maurice Sendak jointly minister over this scene, shaping its emotional structure as a modern cultural trope.[1] Proust's famous 'Overture' to *In Search of Lost Time* does not describe monsters lurking in a child's imagination but rather the experience of being on the brink of sleep and the oscillation between waking and slumber, world and bedchamber, consciousness and memory, that links the sensations of the adult narrator with the child's bedtime anxieties on being separated from his mother. Maurice Sendak's illustrated classic *Where the Wild Things Are* lovingly depicts the dreamlike metamorphosis of a child's room – as with Proust, following the hero's temporary removal from his mother's affection – into an entire world of monsters; like Proust's wakeful sleepiness, the experience involves the mutation of physical space far beyond the bedroom's boundaries, performing spatial and sensory transformations that Gaston Bachelard (1994), in his analysis of the 'poetics of space', calls 'intimate immensity'. Beyond and against these works is another, older image of darkened inner space – Plato's famous parable of the cave, which is Proust and Sendak's archetype as well as their inherited critique: we are deceived by the worlds we conjure, even as we are undeniably moved by the reality we grant them.[2]

Yet perhaps the richest contemporary elaboration of this scene of world transformation is accomplished by a less canonical text: Pixar Studio's animated film *Monsters, Inc.* (2001). *Monsters, Inc.* vividly dramatizes the power of human imagining; but it also tethers that power to modern media, in particular to their 'poetic' capacities, their ability to disclose and produce worlds. Night-time in a child's bedroom comprises the film's opening sequence – a sequence that utilizes the familiarity of childhood experiences and their dissemination through folk culture and literature, only to confound the expectations of viewers several times as it unfolds.

The scene begins, like Proust and Sendak, with separation from parental protection and affection, as the off-screen voices of a child's mother and father say goodnight, the light is turned off and the bedroom door is closed. The parents' footsteps recede, and the camera pans down slowly from a shelf full of toys to a sleeping boy in his bed, followed by a series of shots of the moonlit interior, the wind wafting the curtains, the clock ticking, and other suspenseful vignettes. The boy wakes briefly and sees the cupboard door ajar. An arm emerges from it; but he returns to sleep when he realizes that it is only his bathrobe stirring in the breeze. A shadow passes across the bed covers. The camera pans down again towards the floor, below the bed. Two eyes glow there, glaring out of the darkness. And here is the first surprise for viewers: for there *is* a monster under this child's bed and, as it rises, many-tentacled, to its full height by the bedside, the child wakes, sits up and screams.

Immediately, there is another surprise: the monster becomes infected with the boy's terror. Responding to his fear-distorted features, the monster screams in turn, wheels away in panic, falls backwards over a ball and finally tumbles – rump first – onto some sharp-edged toy jacks on which it bounces for several startled seconds of pain and distress. Horror gives way to slapstick.

Then follows the most radical blow to viewers' expectations: we hear the shrill sound of an alarm, the lights go up, and an astonishing scene is disclosed. Not only is the monster confirmed as diegetically real – real within the world of the film and not a figment of the boy's imagination at all – but the human child is shown to be artificial: a mechanical upper body lying in a bed, watched in turn by other monsters, all situated in some kind of laboratory-cum-studio. The narrative explanation for this revelation is marvellously inventive. We, the viewers, are not onlookers in a child's bedroom after all but are observing a special facility designed to train monsters in the apparently perilous art of scaring children.

The mechanical child and his artificial bedroom are part of a general apparatus of simulation and training set in what we later discover to be a central power station (owned by the eponymous power company, Monsters Incorporated), itself located in a conveniently English-speaking monster world: the city of Monstropolis. Indeed, given the implied location of our viewing situation, we observe the scene *as monsters*, peering, with our compatriots, over the shoulder of the trainer at the control desk and through a glass barrier into the simulated child's bedroom. The scene is comic and engaging not just because of the way it confounds our expectations – thereby establishing the existence of a monster world as a given fact of the narrative – but also because it subverts conventional human emotions and attitudes towards monsters. It turns out that as well as *not* being 'naturally' scary (since they need to be trained to scare humans), monsters are in fact terrified of children and have to overcome their fear in order to be any use as 'scarers'. It further turns out that the reason they need to risk their safety to scare children is that children's screams are the primary energy source used for powering 'Monstropolis'.

The sequence I have described is what W. J. T. Mitchell (1994: 25), borrowing from Geoffrey Hartman, might call a 'recognition scene': a theatrical scenario of encounter which underpins, distils and concretizes a theory, enabling that theory to become amenable to reflexive knowledge (re-*cognizing* it) and making it visible not only within the particular text that presents it but as a point of reference and discussion for subsequent thinkers and texts. The recognition scenes discussed by Mitchell are enacted within theoretical or scholarly works: his key examples are Panofsky's encounter with a man raising his hat in his exposition of iconology (Panofsky 1972 [1939]: 3–5), and Althusser's 'theoretical theatre' (1984: 48) of a man being 'hailed' in the street in his account of the ideological interpellation of the subject (Plato's cave might be another recognition scene, albeit one that evocatively dramatizes human *mis*recognition). The Pixar sequence, in contrast, is the distillation of a theoretical premise conveyed by a work of popular fiction. The premise, in a nutshell, is that media are systems for the production and disclosure of worlds. Media are poetic infrastructures: they are generators and conduits of poesis as an existential power. The commonplace ideas that media create overtly fictional worlds, while at the same time constructing our sense of the real world, society, community and the body politic, are rooted in the poetic capacities of media.

Monsters, Inc., in fact, is a manifesto for media poetics. It is a 'manifesto' in a deeply poetic sense of the word, since one of the meanings of poetics – which I will outline in the introduction and variously explicate and demonstrate in subsequent chapters – is the making manifest of layers of representation, signification and existence, their palpable disclosure in the encounter with a particular message, text, artefact or device. *Monsters, Inc.* makes manifest fundamental media processes of world-production and world-disclosure.

What is it in particular that is made manifest in the scene that I have described, and how is it '*re*-cognized': made available again for reflection and rethinking? The first level of recognition is of the power of the imagination as a poetic force, and its generality across individual, social and species dimensions. The resonance of the scene for viewers is built upon the privacy of this experience of childhood fantasy and fear, its occurrence in childhood expressly when one is alone – in one's intimate solitariness on the darkened brink of sleep – as well as its familiar commonality, at the very least through fable and folklore, among most or all children in contemporary western societies and the adults they become. We recognize the visual 'existents' of the depicted world – the slant of the moonlight through the window in the darkened bedroom, the breeze catching the corner of the robe and momentarily making it resemble an arm – as exemplary expressions and projections which resemble our own memories, and through these projections we simultaneously enjoy the sharedness of our intimate recollections. What is recognized, then, is the imagination as a general poetic capacity that we all personally share.[3] Poetic = imagination

The second level of recognition concerns poesis and the unreal. Put simply, what the scene shows is that the child is not alone with his fears in his bedroom. The monster is real; or, at the very least, the monster has been imagined into existence. The same can be said of 'Monstropolis' and its inhabitants later in the film. Imagined beings and entities populate our world. They are connected to it, energized by it, present in it, disclosed as part of it. It is their habitat, and they cannot be confined to detached realms of fantasy and fable. They are even, some would argue, forces that drive our world's most fundamental psychological, social and political processes, among them religious worship and national sentiment.[4]

The third level of recognition concerns our relationship to the unknown: between ourselves, our familiar environments, and beings and worlds which are radically different or 'other' – so different that when they do appear as possibilities, they seem monstrous. The key moment of recognition is the reaction of the monster to the screaming child: the monster is depicted as a mirror-other, one whose response to the presence of humans – fear and panic – is an exact replica of our own feelings about monsters. There are in fact two intertwined moments of recognition in play at this level: the monster recognizes the human child as an 'other', as a member of a class of beings of extreme difference and great menace, whom it has previously regarded as monstrous and consequently learnt to fear. Monstrosity is therefore a product of imagination, and it turns out later in the film that the prejudicial perception of humans as monstrous is as widely disseminated and institutionally inculcated and legitimated

(2) the unreal

(3) the unknown

(including by state authorities and the police force) in monster
society as fear of monsters is in the human world. Yet the
film also 're-cognizes' this prejudicial perception and apprehension of the other as monstrous: since we viewers know
that *we* are not monstrous, by implication *our own* parallel
construal of monsters as frightening becomes reflexively
available for evaluation and critique. The very processes
whereby we perceive and envisage others — and develop categories of otherness (such as monstrosity) — are disclosed to
us for reflection and reformation. Absurd as it perhaps
sounds, given the great difference in genres and registers, this
recognition of the other as a similarly construed being to
ourselves echoes another recognition scene well known in
recent media studies. This is the opening to Roger Silverstone's *Media and Morality* (2007), where he recalls hearing
an Afghani blacksmith interviewed on BBC radio explain the
war going on in his country as a consequence of al-Qaeda
having killed many Americans and their donkeys and having
destroyed some of their castles in the 9/11 attacks. Silverstone
calls this man not simply an 'other' but also a 'double' of
ourselves, and the challenge he presents to our own poetic
capacities and routines is particularly powerful: 'But can we
imagine him imagining us? What will he have seen or heard
about the attack? And can we imagine ourselves to be his
strangers?' (2007: 2).

4   The fourth level of recognition foregrounds the power of
illusion, a key element of media's world-producing capability.
This is the recognition, dramatized by the film as a rupture
and demystification of the opening segment in the child's
bedroom, that the world we have been hitherto viewing,
have momentarily taken on trust, is a technologically manu-
factured fabrication: a simulation of a child's room, and
indeed of a child, which has successfully taken us in because
of its crafted verisimilitude, its correlation to our expectations about the look of reality and to our personal and collective childhood fantasies. In the startling revelation of a
training centre for monsters, the film takes viewers 'behind
the scenes' of technologies and corporations, the source of
organized illusions and deceptions, which humankind – still
apparently lingering unregenerately in Plato's cave (Sontag
1977: 3) – mistakes for the truth. The power of poetic world

creation so quickly established in the very opening sequence is transformed into the disclosure of a prior power, and a different world: the capacity of media technologies to create credible scenarios, however incredible and unreal we may know them to be.

Such media 'world-making', however, is more than simply a theme of *Monsters, Inc.*'s narrative, one among many topics of its discourse. It is a key activity of the film itself, the act that it performs in the experience of the viewer. Every scene and each character, every word of dialogue and soundtrack element, each pixel – from the most imposing visual features of the character's bodies to the most inconspicuous background components – is the result of intense and systematically organized work, the labour of creation by Pixar animators that brings the world of 'Monstropolis' into being, however fully-fledged and replete that world seems when it appears before viewers.[5] Moreover, for the duration of the film as seen by viewers (and possibly beyond), the self-sufficiency of its world is itself perpetually performed, accomplished in the ongoing interaction between the senses and faculties of viewers, the perceptual and symbolic structures of the film, and the technologies which enable it to be screened. The world of the film, like the film which creates it, is not an autonomous object or entity, but the result of an unfinished process of becoming, not least (though not only) because this particular technology – screened animation – depends upon technically enabled optical and psychological illusions which persuade us that there is a 'film' there in the first place, rather than a structured ensemble of rapidly shifting dots and lines flashing indiscernibly across a screen.

World-making activity is not of course restricted to this particular film, or to animation as an art form, though the etymological connection between animated film and 'animation' as the bestowal of life (the *anima* as soul, spirit or vital principle) should give us pause. Nor is the film by any means alone in extracting comedic profit from the reflexive depiction of the generic conventions which make its construction and comprehension possible: this has become something of a staple banality of 'postmodern' entertainment. Nevertheless, the power of Pixar's version of the scene of childhood imagining and the entire narrative of the film which follows go beyond both the performance of its key premises and its conspicuous and enjoyable pastiche.

For the film presents poesis not simply as a psychological faculty or as an aesthetic accomplishment but as a perpetually circulating social and existential *energy*. This is the central conceit of the narrative: that Monstropolis depends for its continued existence on the energy supplied by children's fear, and the conversion of their screams into power.[6] Later in the film, it is revealed that there is an even more efficient way of tapping into children's poetic energy: by making them laugh and capturing their laughter. Notwithstanding the change in the character and amplitude of the response and the power it generates, the idea here is clear: world-making and its associated emotions generate realities. Moreover, poetic energy can be elicited, captured, manipulated and redistributed. In other words, it can be subjected to processes of extraction, management and diffusion through the combined use of institutional practices (such as industrial routines) and technologies.

Within the story-world of the film, poetic energy is extracted and exploited by the physical and social interaction of animated beings – childish and monstrous – from two parallel and adjacent worlds, human and monster. The beings from these two worlds are brought together through a large institutional and technical apparatus: the power company Monsters Inc. Transferred to the level of discourse, however – the level of *Monsters, Inc.* the film rather than the fictional corporation – poetic energy is also produced and exploited through the interaction between beings from two interlinked worlds: in this case the world of the film and the world of its viewers. The encounter between these beings and their environments is also enabled and structured by a set of institutional and technological arrangements. Only here it is the industrial-aesthetic apparatuses of cinema and video that constitute the 'power company' extracting and managing poetic energy. Among the outputs of these encounters are the experiences and entertainment value generated for viewers, and the monetary value and reputation captured by producers, all of which can be further extracted, transferred, processed and circulated. Indeed, they were (though with less financial and critical success), twelve years after the release of the original film, in the sequel *Monsters University* (2013).

Finally, the film presents poetic processes in a way that allows us to 're-cognize' contemporary mediated experience. For the film depicts the relationship between the human world and the world of Monstropolis as one of interlinked adjacency: the worlds exist in parallel, permanently alongside and connected to one another. This relationship of conjoined adjacency, of connected side-by-sideness, is strikingly emphasized by the great symbolic and narrative weight that the film gives to doors. Doors are the entry points between the human and monster worlds: the doors, mainly opening into children's bedrooms, not only connect the physical spaces of the human world but also magically open onto the factory floor of the power company Monsters Inc. Doors are thus not only everyday mechanisms for entering or exiting through walls, as Bruno Latour (1992) describes them, but are metaphysical thresholds and portals linking disparate worlds. As Simmel says, 'life flows forth out of the door from the limitation of isolated separate existence into the limitlessness of all possible directions' (1997 [1909]: 173). They are 'communicating doors', symbolic of the communicative possibilities of being 'next door' – and of its terrors and joys. When the children on the human side of the door are felt to be potentially harmful, the door is labelled 'bad' and destroyed: one of the last acts of the film is the reconstitution of a 'bad' door that, the viewers know, is really good since it links the hero of the film, the monster Sully, to his human-child friend Boo. Even if he can't see Boo, the very existence of the door as a sign of her adjacent presence is a source of emotional and even existential security.[7]

How does this theme of connected adjacency, of parallel presence, illuminate contemporary experiences of mediation more generally? The very ubiquity of media in our everyday lives, increasingly conveyed by the metaphor of 'saturation', means that poetically generated worlds are not simply before us but are continually alongside us and with us: they keep us company. Such worlds and their entities need not be fictional (just as Sully and Boo are not fictional to one another): indeed, the chapters of this book explore media poetics through contemporary practices and objects that are not chiefly oriented to fiction, and that are in many cases routine and unremarkable, but that disclose the worlds we inhabit and their continual production. Furthermore, the company we keep with these worlds is often different from the direct relationship with imagined others constructed through dialogical, spectatorial or otherwise 'frontal' encounters with media texts, or from the organized technical and institutional imagination through which elevated observational viewpoints 'from above' are envisioned (and effaced). Adjacency translates into neither the intensity of spectatorship nor the instrumentality of observation but into the mediate and sociable relationship of companionship, of being-with. Little theorized or explored in communication studies, this adjacency of mediated entities to our lives is often conveyed as a peripheral and background intuition, an embodied registration of ambient co-habitation rather than a direct epiphany or passionate engagement with others.

Ultimately, then, *Monsters, Inc.* suggests that poesis needs to be taken seriously within media and communication studies as an intellectual project for understanding, explaining and potentially shaping our mediated lives. Media are generators for constructing and revealing worlds – including the 'actual' world that we imagine we live in and possible worlds that we propose as alternatives or refuges – and thus for their existence, maintenance and disclosure. It takes a world to make a world, as Nelson Goodman (1978) affirmed: the 'poetics of media' is an attempt to reflect upon how contemporary media perform this work as a matter of routine, and what the implications might be for our lives.

[Handwritten margin notes: "social media types?", "Parallel worlds"]

[Handwritten note at bottom:] ↑ I disagree with the idea of adjacency because the media world completes whilst also transcend and amends our is non-media world. The example of Google map: it defines strictly our interaction with material urban environment: it doesn't influence us, but it shapes our presence and activities in ways in which we carry on with our daily life.

1

Introduction

Media Poetics

Consider the following scenario. You wake up tomorrow morning in your still-dark bedroom, and before you open the curtains and look out of the window, you check for messages on your mobile phone. You notice that there is no reception; no sign of a cellular phone network whatsoever. You open your laptop computer and see that no matter what you do, you cannot connect to the internet. You turn on a portable radio and scan the spectrum in vain for a station, hearing only the sound of static. You turn on the television to be greeted by 'snow', the swirling dots of light and dark that reveal the absence of a signal. Finally, you rummage in the cupboard for an old landline telephone and plug the cord into the telephone socket: putting your ear to the speaker, you hear that there is no line. You still haven't opened the curtains and looked outside. How do you interpret this sudden isolation, an imposed solitude that has little to do with possible expectations about the particular media content you might receive and that has everything to do with the routine experience and expectation of connectivity made possible by your communication devices? What, in the most anxious recesses of your mind, do you imagine has happened? The answer is clear: it is the end of the world.[1]

Media are poetic forces. They perform poesis; they bring forth worlds into presence, producing and revealing them. As this 'disconnection scene' shows, media do this not just through representing worlds, imaginary or otherwise, but by connecting us to worlds beyond our immediate physical perception. The smooth functioning of media signals to us, in ways we usually take for granted and irrespective of the specific content they convey, that those worlds continue to exist even though we cannot directly perceive them. Though they are routinized to the point of invisibility, these signals of connectivity and perpetual world presencing, which we can call 'vital signs' since they are indicators of life elsewhere (see chapter 3), *do* become conspicuous precisely at the moment of their sudden cessation. It is in the *malfunctioning* or termination of what Jakobson (1960) calls the 'phatic function' of communication (the aspect of communication charged with opening and maintaining channels of connectivity, about which I shall have much more to say in the chapters that follow), that this world presencing and its importance for our sense of physical and social being in a shared world with others, frequently becomes overtly apparent.[2]

Of course, to say that media *produce* worlds is not a particularly controversial claim. It certainly appears pertinent to the development of rich and complex imaginary worlds that have accompanied the emergence of digital media technologies, thanks in part to the increasing significance of computer gaming as a cultural experience and the expansion of media franchising (*Star Trek*, *Marvel Comics*, etc.: see Johnson 2013) as a 'transmedial' mode of cultural production which fleshes out fictional universes (Wolf 2012).[3] The tenor of this book so far – with the prologue's attention to works of literature and narrative film, its invocation of middle-class childhood fantasies (and middle-class fantasies of childhood) – might misleadingly situate its concerns within a broadly 'fictive' intellectual school in media and communication studies, where genres of fiction, folklore and art serve as models for other, possibly more prosaic but politically more predominant, genres: the hardcore categories of journalism, news, opinion and documentary. More troubling still, it might also seem to endorse an approach to media that is removed from more phenomenological and ethnographic appreciations of how media intersect with everyday habits, experiences, interactions and lives.

Yet it would be a mistake to restrict media poetics to fictive artistry. The resulting exclusion of informational reporting or everyday communication would reiterate a widely challenged dichotomy, since the importance of narrative, metaphor, conjecture and world-making to journalism, the social and natural sciences and everyday discourse and experience has become a commonplace principle among many scholars in these fields.[4] Moreover, it would also threaten to confine our attention to the overt construction of worlds and to veil the fact that the poetics of media are crucial to world disclosure (Kompridis 1994, 2006) – to making present and revealing our being in a world *already experienced as given*. What can be called the 'fictive mode' of media poetics – usually intense imaginative engagements with conspicuously alternate worlds – is merely part of the story.

[margin annotations: very noticeable; worlds that are: 1) imaginative 2) unreal 3) unknown 4) illusory]

So, to repeat: media are poetic forces; they bring forth worlds into presence, producing and revealing them. Accompanying this more inclusive concept of media poetics are two key assumptions. The first is that our relations with media have a profoundly existential significance. This book is deeply sympathetic to recent writings foregrounding media, existence and 'the meaning of life' by such thinkers as Paddy Scannell (2014), Amanda Lagerkvist (2017) and John Durham Peters (2015); it also owes a debt to the prescience of Annette Markham who, in 2003, suggested that computer-mediated communication should be conceptualized as a 'way of being': 'a transparent state wherein the self, information technology, everyday life and other are *vitally* connected, co-existent' (2003: 10, my italics). Or as Peters puts it about media more generally: 'Media are our infrastructures of being, the habitats and materials through which we act and are' (2015: 15). Media are means for living, reflecting upon and defining our lives within shared human conditions and limitations. These conditions are several, and include natality (we are born), mortality (we die), dimensional existence (we inhabit dimensions of space and time), embodiment (we are physical bodies in physical settings; we grow, we decay), sociality (we are social), emotion (we can feel for ourselves and others), consciousness (we think, remember, imagine and are reflective), symbolization (we use symbol systems, primarily language) and – last but by no means least – technicity (we use and develop tools to survive and thrive and to aid in managing the other conditions of our existence). For all of the historical, social and cultural differences between individuals and groups that characterize human existence, this much – and it *is* much – we hold in common.

These human conditions of existence coalesce in experience through the formation of *worlds*. The principal world is that of our ongoing, everyday, shared sensate living and relationships: what phenomenological approaches have termed (with varying definitions) the 'lifeworld' – the world as already given, though dynamically so, to intersubjective experience and which pre-structures all systematic or deliberate attempts (scientific, philosophical, artistic) to analyse or explore aspects of existence.[5] Other worlds which overlap with the lifeworld, and can extend from and into it, include perceptual and symbolic worlds which are overtly imagined, such as fiction, and those which are beyond the possibilities of direct perception but which are presented or inferred as actual: e.g. the microscopic entities and environments, and macroscopic astrophysical systems, which science visualizes, as well as the cosmologies of mythic and religious cultures. Worlds are imbued with ontological density and complexity – they are understood to be populated by beings and objects but are not reducible to those beings and objects, which in turn are not reducible to the media or symbol systems by which they are perceived. Worlds possess a capaciousness that enables a sense of dwelling *within* them.

The various ways in which the lifeworld overlaps with or extends through these other worlds is, obviously, a crucial question. As the opening 'disconnection scene' suggests, media have become fundamental to encompassing and enlarging our lifeworld – the taken-for-granted ground of our lives – through the routine presencing *within* it of worlds beyond the horizon of immediate experience: both the worlds inhabited by actual others, which are seen as domains of a differentiated social reality (the 'small life-worlds' of social phenomenology: Luckmann 1978), and non-actual imagined worlds. These worlds become not merely 'accessible', as much possible-world theory would have it, but enfolded and incorporated into the lifeworld as existentially significant domains, as realms of life.

The second assumption accompanying the poetics of media is that our contemporary given world, the world 'we' – the inhabitants of the post-industrial Global North – experience as actual, as our primary habitat, is thoroughly technologized. While the poetic ability to create, shape and disclose worlds is a characteristic of technological media broadly conceived, across historical periods, the poetics of contemporary media are different in degree, if not also in kind, from the contexts that preceded them.[6] As Scannell says, 'The world that we (post-industrial people) inhabit is one in which we are totally dependent on the humanly created infrastructure that gives unceasingly, from moment to moment, hourly and daily, day in day out, the taken-for-granted conditions of our lives – in just about every conceivable way ... This world is without precedent' (2014: 11).

Communication technologies are a vital part of that unprecedented 'humanly created infrastructure'. The 'disconnection scene' with which I began makes this plain – we habitually depend on media for constant, unnoticed reassurance that the world 'out there' exists. This reassurance is provided both by the continual arrival of representations of the larger world and our habitual, unremarkable exposure to media's signs of their own smooth functioning as connective systems, such as the tiny symbols on our computer and smartphone interfaces indicating connection to wireless internet or cellular networks. Following Barthes, we might call these perceptually marginal, yet operationally perpetual, indications of smooth functioning the 'rustle' of media: the barely noticed background sound of 'happy machines'; the 'noise of what is working well' (1986: 76). More to the point, media construct and disclose worlds, much of whose 'content' is media themselves. Media observe themselves, make themselves the object of attention and discourse, as a culturally constructed 'second nature' imbricated within everyday existence. They are simultaneously *poetic infrastructures*, continually populating the extended lifeworld with scenarios, beings and objects – including themselves – to be encountered, and *poetic performances*, making the lifeworld available for apprehension, recognition and reflection. Given the ubiquity and visibility of media in our everyday lives, how could it be otherwise?

The idea that media have become ever more deeply embedded and intertwined with our lives in the world, to the point that they constitute a techno-cultural 'second nature' which is increasingly difficult to disentangle from a set of primary, putatively direct or unmediated, situations and interactions, is a key theme of debates in communications and media studies around the 'mediation of everything' (Livingstone 2009) and the concept of 'mediatization'. The latter term developed to highlight a threefold historical congruence: the separation and consolidation of 'the media' as a key social institution in the modern period, distinct from other social institutions; the adaptation and, in some accounts, subservience of other social institutions (politics, the economy, the judiciary, religion, the military) to the temporal, spatial and organizational 'logics' of the media; and third, the increasing mediation of everyday life – the ubiquity and even priority of technologically mediated communication in the experiences and behaviour of individuals (see, among others, Schulz 2004; Couldry 2008; Hjarvard 2008; Strömbäck 2008; Hepp 2013).[7] In their recent work on the mediated construction of social reality, Couldry and Hepp (2017) have significantly complicated and enriched thinking about these developments. They take as their starting point the idea that 'the social world is *fundamentally interwoven with media*' (2017: 16; original italics) since technologically mediated communication ('television, phones, platforms, apps, etc.') occurs in everyday social life alongside face-to-face communication and also interweaves with it (interrupts it, channels it, is referred to by it). Indeed, this interweaving means that in many respects face-to-face interaction is no longer unquestionably primary to social experience: for instance, face-to-face interaction becomes subject to coordination requirements – such as meeting times, mealtimes – achieved and sustained through interactions performed on and by networked mobile media (Couldry and Hepp 2017: 29).

It is important to note that Couldry and Hepp do not propose a simple dichotomy between societies or historical periods privileging face-to-face or technologically mediated interaction. They theorize a gradual, non-uniform, historical process of mediatization, occurring over six centuries of western modernity and divisible analytically into three overlapping 'waves' of communication development: mechanization (roughly, print); electrification (from the telegraph to broadcast media); and digitalization (computer, internet, mobile phone). This process produces what they call 'deep mediatization' in the contemporary era because it has led to the profound and intense embedding of media into the social world at increasingly small *and* large scales – from the intimate everyday lives of individuals to global communication infrastructures – that are themselves linked together in diverse, complex systems (2017: 3). The increased technical interconnectedness of digital media is accompanied by growing economic, social and cultural interconnectedness in their uses. Examples of this include the movement of production practices and texts across media (hence 'spreadable' content: Jenkins, Ford and Green 2013, and 'transmedia storytelling': Jenkins 2006) and the development of 'polymedia' (Madianou and Miller 2012) practices which highlight users' awareness of the range of media available for different purposes and the social ramifications of their use. Additionally, these increased interconnections across media can be seen through the creation of new forms of continual anticipation, action, feedback and counter-action at *diverse scales* of action and organization. These link institutions (such as media corporations), technologies (such as social network systems) and users through surveillance and profiling (Turow 2012), the 'datafication' on online behaviour (Van Dijck 2014), user-generated content and the varying compliance and non-compliance of users with social media algorithms (Bucher 2017).

Couldry and Hepp's analysis of these complex mediatized interconnections culminates in a very useful concept – first suggested though not developed in detail by Couldry (2012: 16) – which can also be appropriated for a poetics of media: the 'media manifold' (Couldry and Hepp 2017). Borrowed from topology, where it describes the adequate representation of a multidimensional space by a shape in a space of fewer dimensions, 'manifold' designates a 'two-level' structure of the contemporary media environment:

> The set of media and information possibilities on which a typical social actor, at least in rich countries, can now draw, is almost infinite, and organized on very many dimensions.

But it is in fact a reduced set of possibilities from which we choose every day: that reduced set is how, in practice, we actualize, for daily usage, that many-dimensional media universe ... The *relation* between this reduced set of daily options and the infinity of options in principle available is what is what we mean when we talk of our *relations with a 'media manifold'*. (Couldry and Hepp 2017: 56; italics in original)

This idea of the media manifold is significant for a poetics of media since it allows us to think about how media make worlds present within a (mediated) lifeworld. How does the experiential givenness of the lifeworld in and through media operate across these two levels of the media manifold? How is the vast multiplicity of potential mediations disclosed as *actualizable* within everyday experiences with media? How is the expansively mediated lifeworld given presence within the 'small worlds' of users which themselves are part of the imagined totality of media possibilities that the term 'manifold' includes? To use a slightly different terminology, how are contemporary media worlds implicated in relations of immanence (media devices, practices, objects, texts embedded *in* our everyday lifeworlds) and transcendence (our lifeworlds extended *beyond* their everyday horizons through media devices, practices, objects and texts)?

We can describe media's poetic relations as 'manifold' in two complementary ways. First, media do the poetic work of world presencing and world disclosure by *multiplying enfolding* worlds within other worlds: hence 'mani-fold'. They embed worlds within one another and populate our private and shared spaces with individuals and objects from other worlds, making them immanent to everyday experience, while at the same time enabling the extension and transcendence of experiential boundaries. This enfolding can strangely warp the relationship between macrocosm and microcosm, and between interior and exterior worlds. Take, for instance, a recent (and in some societies already historical) example: the traditional cathode ray tube (CRT) television set. A small and seemingly self-sufficient 'box', the television set nevertheless made present multitudes before its viewers on a global scale. Moreover, this gateway to vast worlds was itself usually enclosed within the domestic sphere, putting society on display as a spectacle for its own members through a form of radical miniaturization. It encompassed the external world, contracted it and re-expanded it within a shrunken space (recall Bachelard's idea of 'intimate immensity'), magically reproducing it inside one of its own subunits: the family home. Television thus shared the *multum in parvo* ('much in little') structure of earlier forms of miniature objects found in craft and art; it was 'monumental, transcending any limited context of origin and at the same time neatly containing a universe' (Stewart 1984: 53).

Such multiple enfoldings of worlds within worlds is a fundamental attribute of the everyday, largely overlooked work of media as poetic infrastructures. Hence the second poetic process associated with the manifold is to make *manifest* those enfolded worlds – and the very processes of embedding and populating that media routinely implement – through acts of disclosure and performances of unfolding. Broadly speaking, then, media operate in a double relation to the lifeworld and its multifarious extensions, enfoldings and incorporations: media shape their ongoing, largely taken-for-granted modes of being present by virtue of their connective, perceptual and symbolic attributes, and they make their modes of presence perceivable, available for recognition and reflexive exploration, in (occasionally extreme) moments of overt disclosure and recognition, such as the scenario of disconnection imagined above. Media are thus involved in constructing the experiential 'givenness' of existentially intertwined worlds and enabling their revelation through representation and tangibility. The 'given world' is given *through media*.

Poetics As Creative Production

The term 'poetics' echoes this double relation of media to the lifeworld, to world production and world disclosure, and draws on the tangled origins and semantic development of a cluster of words: 'poetic', 'poetics' and 'poiesis/poesis'.[8] The *Oxford English Dictionary* (OED Online 2018) entry for 'poetic' provides seven definitions of the adjective. The first and oldest, with cited examples from 1490 and 1509, reads 'Of, belonging to, or characteristic of poets or poetry; appropriate to a poet. Formerly also: †fictitious, imaginary (obs.).' All but one of the remaining six definitions echo the link to poetry and poets: the exception (definition number 6) offers a broader meaning that reinforces the emphasis on production: 'Making, creative, formative; relating to artistic creation or composition. Cf. poesis n., poiesis n. Obs. Rare.' The entry for 'poiesis' itself defines it as 'Creative production, esp. of a work of art; an instance of this', with the etymology given as 'ancient Greek ποίησις creation, production < ποιεῖν to make, create, produce (see poet n.)'. These definitions trace the use and understanding of 'poetic' in relation to concepts of creating and imagining, with poetry as a privileged exemplar.

The noun 'poetics' underscores a similar relationship between creative processes and poetry as a literary form. The *OED* gives two main definitions: the first casts poetics as 'the aspect of literary criticism that deals with poetry; the branch of knowledge that deals with the techniques of poetry. Also: a treatise on poetic art, spec. that written by Aristotle,' while the second again emphasizes creative production beyond poetry: 'The creative principles informing any literary, social or cultural construction, or the theoretical study of these; a theory of form.' Poetics, then, in this conceptual and semantic configuration, clearly marks out both the practice and theory of creative production epitomized by poetry but also extending well beyond it. 'Media poetics' thus emphasizes the world-creating capacities of media.

However, there are two complications to this use of the term which will be central to my own understanding of 'media poetics'. The first harks back to Aristotle's *Poetics* as an exemplar in the *OED* definition above, where 'poetics' is used at a meta-theoretical level to designate the area of knowledge and inquiry defined as the study of 'verbal artistry' (Bauman and Briggs 1990: 79), as 'an understanding of the devices, conventions and strategies of literature, of the means by which literary works create their effects' (Culler 2002: vii). This use particularly characterized literary theory influenced by Russian formalism, where 'poetics' came to designate the systematic attempt to delineate the distinctive yet shared 'literariness' of literary works through reference to their internal textual construction and operations, rather than through seeming externalities, such as their authors' intentions or psychological states, or the experiences and responses produced in readers (Erlich 1973; Todorov 1981). This literary focus of poetics has been expanded across media, most obviously to film studies (Bordwell 2008) but also to television (Mittell 2015).[9] As Bordwell puts it:

> *Poetics* derives from the Greek word *poiesis*, or active making. The poetics of any artistic medium studies the finished work as the result of a process of construction ... Any inquiry into the fundamental principles by which artifacts in any representational medium are constructed, and the effects that flow from those principles, can fall within the domain of poetics. (2008: 12; italics in original)[10]

The expansion of poetics as a field of inquiry across a range of media has not, however, necessarily extended its application to a wide variety of textual classes, genres or contexts of use. Although Bordwell connects poetics to any 'representational medium', the formalist conceptual lineage associating the term with literary distinction, and the philosophical and cultural connection with poetry, mitigate against such gestures (as does Bordwell's own use of the term 'artistic medium' earlier in the cited paragraph). Poetics seems to be concerned with heightened, if not high-born, texts, works and artefacts. One can detect the residual hierarchies at work in the category if one thinks of possible binary opposites to the word 'poetic': 'ordinary', perhaps, but also 'prosaic'. What would a poetics of the prosaic look like?[11]

One answer to this emerges from the discussion of the communicative functions of language among the Prague Structuralists. Probably the best-known formulation is Jakobson's (1960) concept of the poetic function of a linguistic utterance, which coexists alongside other communicative functions that refer to different aspects of a communicative interaction (respectively: contextual reality, speaker, addressee, the channel of communication or connection and the code used). The poetic function draws attention to the particular sonic, somatic or other formal and material qualities of the signs used in the message itself and can characterize utterances and texts across genres. As Jakobson notes:

Any attempt to reduce the sphere of poetic function to poetry or to confine poetry to poetic function would be a delusive oversimplification. Poetic function is not the sole function of verbal art, but only its dominant, determining function, whereas in all other verbal activities it acts as a subsidiary, accessory constituent. This function, by promoting the palpability of signs, deepens the fundamental dichotomy of signs and objects. (Jakobson 1960: 356)[12]

The *palpability* of signs. The glass frosts, and the window-pane of language becomes opaque. Poetics changes the figure–ground relation between meaning and form, signified and signifier, inflating the latter in a gestalt shift that brings to prominence the physical substance of signs, as distinct from their 'object' or referential meaning. In Jakobson's own text, such sensuousness is poetically performed by the very word 'palpability' as it is propelled into sound by pursing lips and flexing tongue. If the world is constructed through imaginative representation – the generation of relationships of substitution and equivalence that make us perceive one thing (letter, sound, image) as another – then poetics emerges through revelatory moments of sensuous literalization. Such moments allow us to reverse-engineer not only distinctive artworks, but the world-generating power of everyday media as a poetic infrastructure.

Jakobson's 'poetic function' foregrounds *attention* as central to media poetics: the message draws attention to its own palpable materiality. This idea of poetics as a gestalt shift which makes present to consciousness new layers of signification and existence, that reverses the relations between figure and ground, suggests that the modulation of attention enables new encounters with the worlds produced and disclosed by media: poetics as refocusing. Certainly, too, the connection of poetics with moments of shock and crisis, where one's profound involvement with media is revealed as existentially critical, potentially jarring to the self and its orientation in the lifeworld, is also premised on a sudden jolt that shifts attention.

Attention is a complicated and much disputed term in philosophy and psychology (Mole 2011). In relation to media, it is closely tied to overtly marked and powerful experiences, such as 'immersion in' or 'transportation to' represented worlds, as well as to the 'public attention' (Webster 2011) produced by media through exposure of specific topics or texts to large populations.[13] In the first sense, attention is a fundamental precondition for the creation of intense aesthetic and representational experiences through media technologies and symbolic forms. For instance, the apparatus and norms of cinema as a medium of public display in western societies (darkened, soundproof projection space, large screen, theatrical pew-style seating, relative immobility and the silence of spectators) have evolved to encourage heightened forms of perceptual, emotional and cognitive attention to the films being shown – despite the fact that the economics of multiplex cinemas are also fed by potentially distractive accompaniments to the viewing experience, such as the consumption of popcorn. Attention is therefore important to the way particular media organize our sensuous, cognitive and emotional capacities for certain kinds of world disclosure.

Indeed, so deep is the association between attention and sensuous, intensely felt mediated experiences that its centrality is often taken for granted in accounts of audience responsiveness to artworks and other cultural products. This has led to what I call, in chapter 2, the 'attentive fallacy' underpinning much thinking about how cultural forms are encountered and media technologies engaged with: the assumption that the significance of representations is generated through an intense, focused interchange between an attentive addressee and a formally distinct, unified text. A concomitant of the attentive fallacy is either neglect or suspicion of inattentive and distracted modes of reception. Distraction is seen as the handmaiden of hegemony, either because it is thought to encourage superficial and therefore uncritical (or, in another version, insufficiently ecstatic) sensuous and imaginative encounters, or because it makes commodified forms of consumption and 'pre-digested' pleasure the default available means for dealing with the sheer quantity of representations crying out for our attention.

Exceptions to this bias are rare but immediately enriching, such as Ben Highmore's formulation of 'absent-minded media' (2011). Highmore, drawing deeply on Kracauer and Benjamin, pays attention to 'reception in distraction' as an everyday cultural accomplishment, arguing that, given how successfully and commonly we achieve it, 'it might be better, then, to see distraction as a form of promiscuous absorption, of attention flitting from one thing to another, and multiplying its objects' (2011: 134). Even Highmore, however, concludes by validating such egalitarian, undiscriminating absorption through the idea of a 'breach' or 'rupture' (2011: 132) – terms he borrows from Rancière – in its disinterested promiscuity, which suddenly produces moments of rapture and recognition that portend the new (Highmore's main example is music). Highmore's is a beautiful account of conspicuous world disclosure as epiphanic intensity, but it does somewhat leave the habitual and inattentive absorption of absent-minded media as only retroactively justified by the intensities it can give rise to. What might be lost, in this rapture of rupture, is the possibility that inattention can be a way of generously populating mediated worlds with the manifold voices and bodies of others, making possible non-intense relationships of cohabitation with (and within) those populations, all in the unremarkable background of everyday life. As I will argue in chapter 2, mediated inattention, in certain conditions, makes available *indifference* as a potentially moral force in the given, pre-reflective world – and indifference is a powerful, if much maligned, potential salve against hostility and conflict. In contrast, the final chapter, on the aesthetics and moral affordances of the graphic user interface, foregrounds attention as a zone of connective and operative interactions with the figures of (suffering) strangers that make possible but also impose new kinds of ethical responsibility on minute, habitually performed, movements of the eye and hand.

Poetics As World Disclosure

Is the study of moments of sign-palpability in Jakobson's 'poetic function' an investigation of world *construction* or world *disclosure*? Of the creation of worlds or the revelation of worlds? Jakobson's description tends to evade traditional differentiations between imaginary and real, fiction and fact.[14]

It does, however, emphasize the bringing into presence of (sensuous, material) aspects of signs which are not usually noticed, *producing* them to consciousness not as an act of original creation but as one 'produces' an item as 'evidence' before a courtroom, making it present as an entity on display.[15] It therefore moves us towards the second complication in the history of 'poetics' which influences my thought, one which further troubles the privileging of overtly fictive acts of world construction in media poetics.

Bordwell, quoted above, claims that '*Poetics* derives from the Greek word *poiesis*, or active making' (2008: 12; original italics). Agamben offers a different interpretation in *The Man Without Content* (1999). He argues that the Ancient Greeks 'made a clear distinction between *poiesis* (*poiein*, "to pro-duce" in the sense of bringing into being) and *praxis* (*prattein*, "to do" in the sense of acting)' (1999: 69; original italics):

> As we shall see, central to praxis was the idea of the will that finds its immediate expression in an act, while, by contrast, central to poiesis was the experience of pro-duction into presence, the fact that something passed from nonbeing to being, from concealment into the full light of the work. The essential character of poiesis was not its aspect as a practical and voluntary process but its being a mode of truth understood as unveiling. (Agamben 1999: 69)

For Agamben, this distinction becomes increasingly blurred and almost lost in western philosophical and artistic traditions, with – in summary, since the history he traces is complex – poetic production as bringing forth into presence becoming largely subsumed under the idea of art as willed creative action, as the deliberate labour of making and construction.

This shift of emphasis in the understanding of poetics – and its connection with Jakobson's 'poetic function' of language – is the source of my opening statement that media are poetic forces because 'they bring forth worlds into presence, producing and revealing them'. 'World disclosure' is the summary term I have used so far for this process. Nikolas Kompridis (1994, 2006) defines 'world disclosure' across two levels: 'first-order' and 'second-order' (1994: 29), which he later renames 'pre-reflective' and 'reflective' disclosure respectively (2006: 34). Pre-reflective disclosure concerns 'the background structures or conditions of intelligibility necessary to any world- or self-understanding', while reflective disclosure designates 'the ways in which these background structures of intelligibility are reopened and transformed through novel interpretations and cultural practices' (Kompridis 2006: 34). While, the 'deliberate ambiguity' (1994: 29) of the overall term 'world disclosure' derives from the extreme difficulty in making a clear and consistent distinction between these two levels, Kompridis nevertheless conceptualizes them in terms of a dynamic, unceasing relation of feedback and opposition. The world is perpetually disclosed and re-disclosed to us *pre*-reflectively, as the already interpreted, given world in which we find ourselves and that is intersubjectively intelligible to us; this perpetual process can reinforce the contours and substance of the disclosed world's givenness, but it can also enable new, secondary, interpretive possibilities (reflective disclosure). Additionally, reflective disclosure can itself be subdivided according to whether 'the effect it produces *decenters* or *refocuses* a prior understanding of the world', the former enabling radically dissonant reinterpretations of taken-for-granted structures, the latter increasing awareness of previously unnoticed interconnections and enabling their articulation, repair and reintegration. 'Whether disclosure is of a decentring or a refocusing kind, and sometimes it is not easy to distinguish the one from the other, it always arises from a critical impulse, from consciousness of disturbance, breakdown, crisis' (Kompridis 2006: 35–6; original italics).

Kompridis's formulation has great clarity. One can see how it might inform contemporary conceptualizations of media (including the 'media manifold'): media are multiply enfolded within the lifeworld, their ongoing activity extends, produces and continually discloses the lifeworld as pre-reflectively structured across multiple dimensions, and media make available both dissonant and refocusing reflective interpretations of the disclosed world. Furthermore, attention seems similarly implicated in the movement from pre-reflective to reflective world disclosure since 'to reflect upon' something involves taking that something as one's object of interest and thought, usually in preference to some other thing. How can one reflect upon the disclosed world without attending to it? This means, of course, that attention is the concomitant of media poetics as a *deliberate analytical project* – in fact, the kind of project undertaken in this book. At the same time, the importance of the lifeworld as a given, pre-structured domain, and the kinds of generous, promiscuous receptivity that Highmore values so greatly in its (absent-minded) media, signals a central role for forms of existence and experience that are 'inattentive' and unattended to. Media poetics is therefore implicated in the effective endorsement of attention as its own mode of 'reflective' practice, while at the same time retaining an openness to the various possibilities for mediated experience across a range of pre-reflective cognitive and affective relations, including the habitual and the distracted.

However, while Kompridis's schema certainly informs my understanding of media poetics – and the analyses in the chapters to follow of how particular media objects and practices are world structuring and world disclosing – it is limited in two particular ways. Kompridis's initial insights regarding the pre-structured ontological capaciousness of disclosed worlds are compromised, certainly in the cited passages, by his overt privileging of the 'critical impulse', by which I mean that both decentring and refocusing modes of disclosure are made necessarily dependent on the consciousness of disturbance and crisis, and an implicit suspicion of the worlds disclosed.[16] While poesis, as bringing into presence, *can* be experienced as crisis – the key examples in this book are in chapter 3 (on the screenshot) and in chapter 4 (on being tagged) – it certainly need not be. More to the point, there are arrangements of the given, mediated world which, in their disclosure, can be reflectively understood as benign and even beneficial, this being the topic of chapter 2 on the composite image, and to a degree chapters 5 and 6 (on the selfie and the graphical user interface). In other words, disclosure becomes implicitly incorporated, almost against the better intentions of Kompridis himself, into a discourse of critical unveiling that tends, as a reflex response of thought, to treat what is hidden from view as suspect.

Paddy Scannell is probably the most important critic of this reflex of critical thought in media studies. In *Television and the Meaning of Live* (2014), Scannell contrasts interpretations of the given lifeworld that result from a 'hermeneutics of suspicion' with those that emerge from a 'hermeneutics of trust'.[17] The former, epitomized by ideological critique and characteristic of critical approaches usually inspired by Marxism, 'regards what is hidden in things as the deceptions of power which it is its critical duty to unmask' (2014: 17). The latter, derived from a reading of Heidegger's phenomenology, 'proceeds from a wholly different standpoint from that of the hermeneutics of suspicion – one that is struck by and seeks to account for the goodness of things and the wonder of the ordinary everyday world' (2014: 17).[18] For Scannell, the 'goodness of things', which is no less hidden by their proper functioning than exploitation is hidden by ideology in the 'critical paradigm', is described by what he calls their 'care structure'. This is 'nothing more or less than the human thought, effort and intention that has gone into producing the thing *as* that which it is. This care, of course, disappears into the thing, is subsumed by the thing, which stands independent of all the creative labour that produced it' (2014: 14). Scannell deliberately sets out to promote this hiddenness of the care structure of things in general, and media technologies in particular (his chosen medium here is television, though he has written similarly about radio [1996]), as a crucial virtue of the lifeworld:

> The gift of things is that they allow us to take them for granted. I wish to make a strong claim for the goodness of the world as immanent in the things of the world, a goodness that can be determined exactly by the measure of unthinking and unconditional trust that we are able (or not) to invest in it. The natural attitude towards the everyday world is one of faith and hope in its ordinary unremarkable workability. (2014: 12)

Scannell is pointing to the kinds of 'pre-reflective' world disclosure (in Kompridis's terms) that habitually, routinely occurs in the lifeworld as we encounter and use media that 'work' – media that, time and again, connect us beyond our immediate physical environments without us thinking about them or making particular effort. This is *pre*-reflective disclosure since the tacit knowledge that identifies the hand-sized oblong thing before me – which has a flat shiny screen and which responds to touch – as a mobile communications device, is a world-dependent understanding based on my previous experiences and my expectations regarding the (relatively) stable structures of the world, and it does not need to stand out in my consciousness independently of my practical relationship to my iPhone. Indeed, my continued use of this device further discloses and reinforces my implicit sense of its workability, and the stability of the world in which it works, contributing to the extension of my expectations about it in the future.

Such undemonstrative (though continually demonstrated) virtuous workability of the world becomes – again translating Scannell into Kompridis's terminology – available for *reflective* disclosure only in certain situations. One of those situations is when the workable ceases to work, precipitating the 'consciousness of disturbance, breakdown, crisis' (Kompridis 2006: 36). This is the poetics of 'the glitch' as an '(actual and/or simulated) break from an expected or conventional flow of information or meaning within (digital) communication systems that results in a perceived accident or error' (Menkman 2011: 10).[19] It is also the poetics of catastrophe or the mediated 'limit situation' (Lagerkvist 2017, borrowing from Jaspers), imagined in the 'disconnection scenario' at the beginning of this chapter, which brings into presence the conditions of existence in the lifeworld by making palpable, through the shock of dysfunction, the profound everyday intertwining of media and life.[20] Another is what we might call the poetics of epiphany, which is the sudden making-present, in heightened intensity, of the formal attributes of media's entanglement with the lifeworld and which is often associated with aesthetic experience (Gumbrecht 2003). Finally, there is poetics as a deliberate intellectual project of making present to thought and reflecting upon the givenness of media in a given world.

The second limitation of Kompridis's account of world disclosure is that his terminology shifts too easily and too quickly from worlds as ontological frameworks – as grounds of being – to worlds as hermeneutic constructs, to talk of 'meaning' and 'interpretation'. In a sense, this is hardly surprising since the traditions he engages with, and the medium – writing – through which both he and they engage others, foreground the world-producing significance of verbal language. Moreover, questions of meaning, a word which can associate (and elide) existentially oriented ideas such as significance, purpose and destiny, along with concepts of semantic sense and reference, are by no means irrelevant to the lifeworld. However, this hermeneutic framing of the lifeworld is *insufficient* to a poetics of media, for several interconnected reasons. Poetics emphasizes processes of bringing into presence as much as it does processes of interpretation; in the case of media, this requires a sensitivity not simply to the presence of constructed symbolic or perceptual representations created through the media (texts, images, etc.) but also to the making present of media as technologies and objects with which we interact. Additionally, the modes by which worlds are brought into presence – and the intertwining of media in them – are not simply verbal or textual but also pictorial, audial and tactile; world presencing is multi-modal. And finally, our own presence in worlds and our relations with the media that are in them and that produce them are more than cognitive and semantic; they are multi-sensuous and embodied. Our embodied relations with media are numerous and protean, yet patterned, and arguably have altered dramatically with changes in media technologies and with the introduction of digital devices and interactive interfaces.

All of these reasons for the insufficiency of the interpretive framing of world disclosure associate media poetics with what Gumbrecht (2003) calls 'presence culture'. Based on an ideal-typical contrast with modern 'meaning culture', 'presence culture', which historically Gumbrecht identifies with medieval European societies, privileges – among other things – the body rather than the mind, the mutual embeddedness of bodies and things rather than a subject-centred worldview, knowledge revealed through 'events of unconcealment' rather than through acts of interpretation initiated by the subject, and an understanding of the event as repetition and regularity rather than innovation and surprise (78–86).[21] Gumbrecht's argument is intricate and bold, is (perhaps predictably) indebted to Heidegger, and also involves an avowed evacuation of morality from aesthetics – something which should perhaps trouble a Heideggerian more than it seems to (see note 18 this chapter). Crucially, however, for the purposes of media poetics, 'presence effects' and 'meaning' are not mutually exclusive: indeed, they always appear together (and, in distinctively aesthetic experiences, in overt tension): 'For us, presence phenomena always come as "presence effects" because they are necessarily surrounded by, wrapped into, and perhaps even mediated by clouds and cushions of meaning. It is extremely difficult – if not impossible – for us *not* to "read", not to try and attribute meaning' (Gumbrecht 2003: 106; original italics). One of the most obvious tensions in media poetics is that it is concerned both with the disclosure of presence effects of media and with the meaning of those effects. It describes media's presence in the world and their poetic making-present of worlds, while, as an intellectual practice, offering interpretations of that poetic work.

A Poetics of Plural Media?

An important question arises: how might diverse media and cultural forms shape world disclosure in distinctive ways? So far, 'media' have been mentioned in the plural: their involvement with our lives is said to be manifold, their presence multiple and the 'disconnection scenario' imagined at the outset projected the cumulative effects of dysfunction across almost all contemporary connective media. Nevertheless, the question remains: what kind of difference does it make to the elicitation and production of worlds – and to the phenomenological experience of those to whom they are disclosed – *which* medium or media are in use?

There is, of course, the immediate issue of what we mean by a 'medium'. Definitions of the term abound. Some of these are well known and much cited, lauded or derided: perhaps the most famous is McLuhan's phrase that media are 'extensions' of ourselves, technological prostheses that enhance particular human sensory, affective, cognitive and communicative capacities, while usually constraining others (McLuhan 1994). Other definitions are less familiar and more obviously intended to synthesize ostensibly unresolvable quarrels between champions of technological agency and guardians of social construction.[22] The unresolvable character of these quarrels may be 'built into the concept of media as such', as Mitchell observes (2005: 205): 'The problem arises when we try to determine the boundaries of the medium ... If media are middles, they are ever-elastic middles that expand to include what look at first like their outer boundaries. The medium does not lie *between* sender and receiver; it includes and constitutes them' (Mitchell 2005: 205).

John Durham Peters provides a minimal definition that, I think, does meet these elasticity requirements. 'Media', he says, are 'symbolic connectors consisting of three interrelated dimensions: message, means and agents. Every medium has a "what", a "how" and a "by/to whom"' (2010: 266). This minimal definition of media benefits not only from concision but also, thanks to its generality, from a large degree of historical and contextual agnosticism about how each of the three dimensions – 'sign-content, delivery device, and authors and audiences' – will be configured in any given period or society.[23]

Peters's definition has an additional virtue, one that is self-evident and unremarkable for most people: that media are defined as *something*. Calling this a virtue seems perverse, if not actually tautological. There would be little point in offering a definition of a medium if one did not already believe that such a thing existed, or that it is or should be thinkable as a delineable entity. However, the seemingly radical technical instability of media in an era of technological change – where all media appear to be 'in transition' (Thorburn and Jenkins 2003), or where, if we are to accept the prognosis of Friedrich Kittler, 'the general digitization of channels and information erases the differences among individual media' (1999: 1) – has markedly increased uncertainty, both historical and philosophical, about what a medium is. This uncertainty has been coupled with approaches that favour processes of flux and becoming rather than potentially essentialist ontologies of objects and being, leading to a philosophical revaluation (and even devaluation) of the concept of medium in some quarters. To speak of a medium is to transform processes of mediation, or historically shifting, complex arrangements of hybrid entities, actors and actions, into a thing. As Carolyn Marvin has observed, 'media are not fixed natural objects; they have no natural edges. They are constructed complexes of habits, beliefs and procedures embedded in elaborate cultural codes of communication' (1988: 8).

Kember and Zylinska (2012) have recently made a distinctive and radical contribution to rethinking relations between media and mediation. They do not decry the objectification of 'media'. Rather, they reverse the poles of much media and communications theory, conceptualizing media as instantiations of a fundamental (and vital) process of mediation, rather than mediation as the localized effect of media. They describe media as part of the work of mediation itself: 'media need to be perceived as particular enactments of *tekne*, or as temporary "fixings" of technological and other forms of becoming. This is why it is impossible to speak about media in isolation without considering the process of mediation that enables such "fixings"' (2012: 21).[24]

Though constructed, however, such 'fixings' may become no less solid than natural entities.[25] Media do, at given social and historical junctures, acquire institutional solidity and experiential coherence as habitually encountered, unremarkable and workable things which can be distinguished from other things. These things exist in the lifeworld and make it perceivable, and the range of their technical and social operations become clarified and, to a degree, calcified: this is what Callon (1991) might call 'punctualization', or the formation of an object – in this case, a medium – as a 'black box' whose heterogeneous workings and origins are no longer visible and which becomes a 'single point or node in another network' (1991: 153). This *contingent* solidity allows us to analyse the 'communicative affordances' (Hutchby 2001) of a particular medium – the readily understood range of its materially enabled applications and meanings – without insisting that these are naturally given, extrinsic to social forces or impervious to change.[26] Such affordances make it more probable that distinct kinds of interpretation, experience and interaction will emerge in our lifeworlds as we use or are addressed by different media and genres. Hence the literary novel has become, for those familiar with it as a cultural form, strongly associated with modes of narrative imagination and experiences of intense immersion that are not usually associated with holiday snapshots, television weather reports and email messages from the office.

Having said this, it is both possible and important to move beyond the specific world-disclosing inclinations of phenomenally distinct media to give an account of mediated world disclosure in other conditions of variability, not just across different media but through and among *similar* or intersecting media. The variability of media as both agents of world disclosure and distinctive presences within the lifeworld fluctuate historically: there can be periods of more explicit medium specificity, and others of more overt media similarity, since the perception of distinctiveness and resemblance between media is itself a phenomenal product of the lifeworld, produced by fluctuating relations between media (as 'fixings') and their discursive and material construction in use. Much of the recent work on multi-modality, intermedial and transmedial relations, mediation as a process, remediation, the computer as a meta-medium, convergence and mediatization is an attempt to grapple with the contemporary conditions under which previously self-evident forms of medium specificity (that is, institutionally powerful and experientially commonplace categorizations of media) have shifted, apparently in some cases to the point of collapse. In these conditions, it is useful to think not just about the particular character of distinctive media as poetic agents and entities, but more broadly about new transmedia configurations for world disclosure.

In the chapters of the book that follow, this movement between medium specificity and transmedia configurations is crystallized through my overt interest in photography. Photography is discussed in all but chapter 6 (on the interface), first in relation to the composite image, then the screenshot, then tagging in social media, and of course in the chapter on selfies. Though photography is often deliberately decentred in these discussions and shares the stage with another medium or practice (respectively: television, the document, the name, the gesture), it undoubtedly remains my own preferred test case, the object medium that I find 'good to think with', as Sherry Turkle (1997) once put it, about medium-specific and transmedia poetics. In part, this is due to the poetic character of much theorizing *about* photography; the assessment of the medium as a privileged vehicle of world disclosure, from Daguerre's declaration that his new invention gave nature the 'power to reproduce herself' (1980 [1839]: 13), to Barthes's description of photography as an 'emanation of *past reality*: a *magic*, not an art' (2000: 88; original italics), to Kaja Silverman's claim that photography is 'the world's primary way of revealing itself to us – of demonstrating that it exists, and that it will forever exceed us' (2015: 10–11). In the striking language of Hariman and Lucaites, 'photography's peculiar combination of mimesis and abstraction allows the plenitude, energy and interdependence of the cosmos to emerge within the spectrum of human visibility' (2016: 253). Yet my continual return to photography as a point of reference for media poetics also derives from its resilience, popularity and creative fecundity as an ordinary and extraordinary technique for making present, reflecting upon and communicating the lifeworld – a mode of world disclosure that, for all its frequent conventionality (indeed, because of its conventionality), appears to have become genuinely accessible and appealing across individuals and groups, almost irrespective of who and where they are.

Close Reading As a Poetic Method

As 'an inquiry into the fundamental principles by which artifacts in any representational medium are constructed' (Bordwell 2008: 12), poetics has been performed through the systematic investigation of representational forms (especially genres), definitions, analysis of parts, rules of construction and the like, with Aristotle's *Poetics* as the classical authority for the character of such investigations. An inquiry into poesis as world disclosure, however – of the multifarious existential intersections, entanglements and layerings of media as infrastructures, performances and representational forces in the lifeworld – invites a different approach: theoretically informed close reading. Partly inspired by a tradition of literary pedagogy formalized mainly in early twentieth-century England rather than in ancient Greece, the chapters of this book treat particular media objects, practices and technologies as things to be read intensively and attentively (as attentively as one reads poems), perhaps fastidiously, and through such reading as paths to discovering and uncovering how media disclose worlds.[27]

This deliberate attempt to grasp the poetic 'manifold' of media by unfolding specific manifestations – rather than, for instance, first outlining general principles or building arguments from overall categories – superficially echoes the phenomenological injunction to examine the structure of experience through the 'appearance' of things. There are, however, two important caveats. The first is that the analysis of the objects and practices I have chosen invokes rather than brackets out their historical, anthropological and philosophical resonances. The chapters present empirically anchored encounters that move back and forth (one is tempted to say dialectically, though there is no necessary moment of sublation or synthesis) between the objects themselves and theoretical and historical points of reference, especially those connected to other media and cultural practices. This kind of reading procedure does not sit easily with conventional understandings of phenomenological method and constitutes my attempt to put into practice a phrase attributed to Nietzsche which has long captured my imagination: to rub the abstract against the concrete in the hope of producing sparks.

The second reservation regarding the pseudo-phenomenological character of my approach is that the 'things' attended to here – media – are expected and intended to make *other* things (symbols, texts, images, sounds, entities, beings, worlds) appear to us 'in', 'through' and 'on' them, often making themselves disappear as media when they do so (see note 2, this chapter). As Wendy Chun emphasizes, *'our media matter most when they seem not to matter at all, that is, when they have moved from the new to the habitual'* (2016: 2; original italics). In line with this sense that media disappear into the lifeworld while making other things appear (disclosing them), my inclination has been to select objects and practices, or aspects of them, which have garnered *relatively* little attention among scholars of media and culture. I have also tended to choose objects and practices – such as screenshots and tagging – which trouble generalizations that have become either commonplace for media scholars or seem self-evident, among them the prima facie distinction between non-digital and digital media. This doesn't mean that I reject claims that media have changed (and that changes in media are implicated in changes in life); rather, it is that close readings of particular digital media objects and practices can reveal that their differences from older media configurations – when they are clearly identifiable – are not always what we suspected they might be.

The Structure of the Book

In the chapters that follow, I attempt to produce a poetics of media, and to investigate how media are already poetic, in the following ways. Chapter 2 begins chronologically in the pre-digital era, taking as its object *inattention* as a profoundly significant and moral feature of our experience of two 'old' media, photography and television. My exploration and comparison between these two media privileges, against the grain of most previous scholarship, the non-reciprocal, semi-generic, ambient and transient characteristics of their modes of connecting us and of displaying representations. By virtue of these characteristics, I argue, they populate our intimate spaces with images of strangers, cultivating 'indifferent' and therefore non-hostile habituation to their perpetually mediated presence. This presence of multiple unthreatening others is conceptualized as an aggregate, but fluid, 'composite image' of 'the human' which continually attends and accompanies us in the lifeworld.

The subsequent chapters shift to overtly digital media. Chapter 3 argues that the *screenshot* is not only among the most commonplace and overlooked of digital objects, but that it confounds prevalent theories of digital media – and digital images – as performances in perpetual flux. Investigating the screenshot as a vehicle of communicative stability and fixity in digital times, it explores its semiotics and functions as a kind of document and as a remediated photograph, delineating the epistemological and ontological assumptions that underpin its ubiquity. The chapter then examines the screenshot as a mode of witnessing, which in turn implicates its displayed 'content' – especially the interfaces of social media systems which we see and save on our screens – as witnessable worlds in their own right, persisting in intimate adjacency to the physical world. Ultimately, the screenshot discloses that social media and mobile devices have become so intimately intertwined with our existence that they are far more than new systems for circulating messages or managing social relationships. They are domains in which life and death are performed, experienced, witnessed and laid bare.

The condition of *being tagged* in photographs uploaded to social networking platforms such as Facebook is the subject of chapter 4. It argues that social tagging is deeply indebted to long-standing procedures for establishing and maintaining our being: the naming of persons and the figural incarnation of bodies. However, tagging in social media doesn't only connect names to bodies in images (over and over again). It is a semi-public operative and generative procedure: when you tag someone your contacts and their contacts are notified, and the tagged image is frequently replicated in these contacts' various feeds. Tagging, therefore, while a technological accomplishment, is also a kind of magical incantation, where uttering the name instantly reproduces and circulates body images of the named. It is a way of performing sociability through the 'selving' of others – by virtue of their named body images – frequently without their prior permission. Finally, tagging materializes the social network platform itself as a social body that is populated through the named body images of its own constituent members. It thus produces a powerful poetic effect: the palpability of the apparatus as a sensuously inhabited world.

From being tagged by others in photographs to disclosing oneself in photographs – over the past few years the selfie has risen to prominence as an everyday cultural practice and photographic genre of extraordinary popularity, accompanied, perhaps inevitably, by public controversy and hostility. At the same time, the selfie has also become an object of burgeoning scholarly interest. Surprisingly, however, relatively little scholarship has drawn systematically on the intellectual resource most closely associated with the aesthetics of the selfie's host medium: photography theory. Chapter 5 addresses this lacuna by reconfiguring three concepts from traditional photography theory – indexicality, composition and reflection. It argues that the selfie is a 'gestural image' that reveals everyday photographic representation to be an instrument of mediated, embodied sociability. Selfies conspicuously integrate photographs into a circuit of sociable connectivity: this circuit binds together the bodies of those taking selfies, their tracked mobility through actual places, and the micro-bodily hand-and-eye movements we use to operate the interfaces of our digital devices. At the same time, selfies can be employed poetically to disclose the power asymmetries that structure, and limit, sociability as a fundamental human activity.

Chapter 6 returns to questions of our moral engagement with others encountered through media that were raised earlier, especially in chapter 2 on photography and television, and reconsiders attention in relation to characteristics of digital interfaces. It asks whether the introduction of user interfaces and changes in the sensuous, aesthetic and material conditions of engagement with media potentially shift the ground of interaction with others who are made present to us as co-inhabitants of our lifeworld – especially in conditions of suffering and vulnerability. Focusing on the mainstream graphical user interface (GUI), the chapter proposes a phenomenology of user experience centred on the moral obligations of attending to, engaging with and acting upon digitized Holocaust survivor testimonies. The GUI, it argues, produces a regimen of eye–hand–screen relations that oscillates between 'operative' and 'hermeneutic' modes of embodied attention, creating a default condition of bodily restlessness that threatens prolonged, empathetic encounters with depicted others. Nevertheless, attributes of real-time screen interaction, haptic sensuousness and user indexicality enable moral engagement with the witness-survivor, while translating information – sharing into the moral action of co-witnessing and networked world disclosure. These attributes facilitate the conversion of sensorimotor responsiveness into moral responsibility. Digital interfaces have established a historically novel situation, I argue, where our exposure to, and disclosure of, distant suffering depends on the smallest movements of our fingers and eyes.

Each of these chapters can be read separately as a stand-alone exploration of a particular object or practice. However, each also contributes to, and helps to develop, core themes of media poetics that recur throughout the book: (in)attention; phatic connectivity; embodiment; witnessing; and moral relations with others. Reading the chapters together should therefore produce conceptual and analytical reverberations, and an aggregated amplification of argument, that may be missed by readers who dip into single chapters. The first two thematic dimensions have already been discussed in this introduction in relation to poetics, but a few words are in order regarding the others.

Embodiment is developed in two related but different ways. Media are physical, and our engagements with all media, throughout history, have been performed and experienced through the body. A leitmotif of theory and research about digital technologies has been that they realign relations between our bodies and our communications media, from late twentieth-century visions of cyborg hybridity and virtual disembodiment (or re-embodiment) to more contemporary explorations of digital technologies and embodied space, wearable technologies, the mediation of presence and digital affect.[28] My own take on embodiment borrows eclectically from these sources and others in order to keep in mind the following: that no account of how media produce and disclose worlds can ignore the character of our physical and sensory contact with the technologies we use, and of its routinization as a set of acquired bodily skills with disciplinary and expressive propensities (important caveat: discipline and expressivity are not opposites, as I note in my discussion of the selfie). In addition, while advanced technologies such as virtual reality laboratories have often served as fertile exploratory arenas for thinking about digital media and the body, as have digital artworks (Hansen 2006), my attention will remain focused on the digital media devices which fill our lifeworlds most extensively, such as computers and smartphones. Hence there will be, in most of the chapters to follow, not a few prosaic references to the patently obvious things we all know about and do much of the time (and which I am doing as I type this text): hand gestures, finger swipes, cursor movements and mouse clicks, among other seeming banalities. Occasionally, these references will be made at the height of otherwise abstruse theoretical discussions, just to keep the poetics of media grounded in everyday embodiment.

They become increasingly central as the chapters progress, culminating in the conceptualization of the selfie as a 'gestural image' which performs 'kinaesthetic sociability', and in the idea that graphical user interfaces have created a new form of minutely embodied moral potentiality, an 'ethics of kinaesthetics'.

The other sense of embodiment which I pursue builds on the idea of poetic palpability, extending it in several directions. These include the multi-sensory tangibility of remediating practices, which I analyse in the case of the screenshot, but they also take on a broader – quasi-metaphorical – character. This is particularly evident in my discussion of the photographic incarnation of the self in social media tagging, where accumulated images of our bodies, and their 'magical' reproduction through incantatory acts of naming, gives palpability to the social network itself as a living environment. Gesturing towards historically resonant analogies between individual bodies and the collective body – the 'social organism', the 'body politic' – I suggest that new digital platforms technologically 'flesh out' such analogies in ways that imbue these platforms with the poetic capaciousness (and ideological power structures) of populated worlds.

Witnessing, the next core dimension of media poetics, is obviously central to mediated world disclosure, particularly in its 'reflexive' aspect. At base, witnessing involves the representation of aspects of our world that we have beheld or experienced to others who have not. It is a deliberate communicative practice, rooted in notions of representational adequacy to the real (testimony cannot be fictional: discovered to be such it becomes, at best, 'false witness') and is designed to produce a part of the world before others, to bring it into their presence and share it through disclosure.

Witnessing, of course, is by no means a new phenomenon; it occupies a central position in legal, religious, scientific and philosophical traditions of thought that long predate both mass and digital media. Yet the advent and expansion of these media do seem to have transformed it. As Walter Lippmann (1922) noted nearly a century ago, we are all – almost whether we like it or not, as a condition of our participation in modern public life – the recipients of reports by others about the events they have experienced. The extension of media systems over the last few centuries, using new technologies of representation and telecommunication to connect different parts of the globe at increasingly fast speeds, has forced us to assess and digest with ever greater frequency reports of far-flung and often horrifying events, related by people whom we do not know personally. This unremitting exposure to the discourse of strangers about their lives has become a defining characteristic of what it means to be modern (Thompson 1995). Mass and now digital media have multiplied the number of witnessed events reported to distant others and multiplied greatly the number of those distant others. Most significantly, perhaps, these media have altered the relationship between witnesses and their address-ees through the intervention of complex organizational and technical apparatuses. It is no accident, therefore, that 'wit-nessing' has become a key word in the practice and study of journalism (Zelizer 2007), as well as an organizing idea and operational mechanism among globally oriented human rights organizations (Hopgood 2006; Ristovska 2016).

I have written elsewhere (Frosh 2006) of the necessary routinization of witnessing as an everyday mediated practice that makes others sufficiently (through never totally) compre-hensible, maintaining a ground of civil equivalence between strangers which I understand as a morally empowering cul-tural achievement, for all its precariousness and risks. In chapter 2 of this book, I develop these thoughts through an exploration of the impersonal structures of photography and television as 'world-witnessing' media, as commonplace mechanisms for making strangers present and transforming them into tolerable companions. I even propose that this continual habituation to multiple images of strangers under-pins our notion of the 'human' as a composite category of minimal solidarity and care.

In subsequent chapters, however, I suggest that something has changed with the advent of digital media: a radical inten-sification and extension of the possibilities for witnessing that reflect the existential conditions of contemporary mediation. It is not simply that digital media perform witnessing through novel everyday objects and practices, like the screenshot and the interface, which generate epistemic stability and moral engagement with strangers. It is that these media witness at new, often minute, scales of bodily action which implicate us more than ever in the companionship of strangers. And, perhaps above all, digital media also reveal *themselves* as witnessable worlds that are constantly immanent in our lives, as continually fluctuating domains of being with others; as the poetically produced, and poetically encountered, second nature in which we find and make our meaning.

2
Composite

The Morality of Inattention in Pre-digital Media

The lives of most individuals in affluent western societies, and many others beyond, are lived with, through and in media more than ever before. Thanks to the proliferation of interactive mobile digital communication devices and their infrastructures, media penetrate our everyday lives, saturate our physical and symbolic environments, occupy our fantasies and dreams, put us to sleep, wake us up, locate us, remind us, record us, promote us, entertain us, inform us, excite us and distract us. Media have become omnipresent – if not omniscient: we meet them, and are greeted by them, at every turn. The complex material, semiotic and communicative layering of this environmental profusion of digital technologies, its significance for our sense of being in relation to others and the world, is at the centre of media poetics as exemplified in the main chapters of this book. These chapters, as I briefly outlined in the introduction, address the poetic operations of some key contemporary digital media objects (screenshots, tags, selfies, interfaces) that construct our embodied and semantic worlds of reference, sociality and existence, and also examine how those worlds are disclosed to us – occasionally in disturbing moments of sudden revelation – in their full, palpable reality.

In this chapter, however, I set out a somewhat different exploration of the nature and consequences of media ubiquity, by outlining an argument in favour of a much maligned (though also somewhat overlooked) characteristic of pre-digital media culture: the centrality of inattention and composite representational forms, specifically in the realm of visual media and mass-disseminated images. For the idea of media saturation is neither new nor unique to our digital times: it is a powerful cultural motif of modernity as an increasingly dynamic historical process which transforms the scale of social organization and human experience through techniques – including communication technologies – of mass production, replication, coordination and dissemination. As in the contemporary digital era (McCullough 2013; Pettman 2016), so in the nineteenth and especially twentieth centuries, a concomitant of increasing media saturation was concern over *attention* to particular messages, tasks, or others, where the deepening presence and rising demands of mass media seemed inimical to individuals' efficient information processing, task performance, emotional involvement and – the focus of this chapter – moral concern for the fate of strangers. This anxiety over the loss of attention ignored, however, important kinds of world constitution that so-called 'inattentive' communicative structures enabled in the past, in particular the poetic population of worlds with ever more mediated presences; these extended our routine horizons of experience and habituation to include the non-threatening presence, in our personal spaces, of multiple images of strangers.

To pursue this argument, I first discuss the role of attention – or assumptions regarding attention – in conceptualizations of visual culture, before briefly reframing the idea of inattention as a material communicative practice performed in relation to media technologies. I then take up the question of visual inattention in the case of two different pre-digital media, revisiting a fictional dramatization of photographic viewing, and then developing my analysis to consider pre-digital television. Through these two cases, I will offer a somewhat counter-intuitive account of the morally enabling role of routinized, mediated inattention in producing 'the care structure' (Scannell 2014) of modern societies, especially our moral concern for the well-being and welfare of distant strangers. This account will in turn serve as a background – and, especially in the case of the final chapter, as a possible contrast – to some of the forms of world disclosure performed by digital media which the rest of the book explores.

The Attentive Fallacy

The majority of visual images circulating in contemporary media-saturated societies are experienced, it is probably safe to say, as fleeting and unremarkable ephemera. Vast numbers are daily encountered as objects of routine inattention and distraction. Barely registered consciously, our engagements with these images are 'unstoryable' in Paddy Scannell's sense (1996), so mundane that they are unworthy of notice or particular comment and are hard to recall with any specificity.

Worryingly for those who create these images, our everyday disregard of them bears no obvious or direct correlation to the quantity of professional care and resources that have been lavished on their production. Research on media production – from news journalism to commercial advertising images – uncovers the commonplace fact that the images, texts and narratives which we habitually treat inattentively as a kind of unremarkable wallpaper are nevertheless the products of highly concentrated institutionalized forms of attention, routinely practised by journalists, photographers, designers, editors and other cultural professionals (Frosh 2003; Dayan 2009).

Indeed, there appears to be something morally unseemly, or at least profoundly unsettling, in this lack of correlation. It may seem a blessing to be able to ignore the mass of unwanted appeals from 'intrusive' images, particularly advertisements and marketing messages. But what of images of others' suffering? Surely our moral connection to unfamiliar others depends upon a willingness to engage attentively the particular depictions of their personal distress? Doesn't the visual elicitation of moral responsiveness to distant sufferers, including by means of the kinds of 'impartial' and even 'theatrical' spectatorship proposed by Adam Smith and elaborated more recently by Boltanski (1999) and Chouliaraki (2006, 2013), require forms of imaginative engagement – and concomitant modes of aesthetic representation – that are inimical to the uncommitted and indifferent routines of a culture of distraction (Moeller 1999; Slovic 2007)?

To be interested in our relations – particularly our moral relations – to images in conditions of inattentiveness invokes an obvious methodological paradox, one already intimated in the previous chapter's discussion of attention as a central methodological condition for 'reflective' world disclosure. Put succinctly, how should one pay attention to inattention? Analysis requires specifying and focusing on images as distinct objects of interest and inquiry. But in so doing it threatens to treat them in a way that makes it difficult to account for our indifference towards them, as well as for their potential and actual indifference towards us – except perhaps in terms of a 'bad object' of inquiry, in which conceptual and phenomenological slipperiness appears to compound the charge of moral dubiousness.

Such a methodological paradox sits uneasily with the main assumptions of many of the disciplines that traditionally take visual media as their central concern. For instance, in the case of art history – long the paradigmatic intellectual context for the analysis of images – Michael Ann Holly has argued that there is 'a productive correspondence of rhetorical ideologies between image and text. Representational practices encoded in works of art continue to be encoded within their commentaries' (1995: 385). Offered as a critique of scholarly postures of objectivity, this claim nevertheless operates within the framework of a discipline where the identity and boundaries of the discrete individual works can often seem self-evident and straightforward, and where the corresponding issues of spectatorial and analytical attention – as that which the work demands prior to its particular 'commentary' – do not pose any difficulties and go largely unnoticed. The idea that attention – curatorial, scholarly and intellectual (not to mention economic) – may be foundational to the special status enjoyed by art objects, art history and art criticism is simultaneously underscored and concealed by the deceptively commonsensical observation that, to quote Holly, 'paintings are, after all, meant to be looked at' (Holly 1995: 373). This assumption of an *intentionality* of attention – that something is looked at because it is intended to be looked at – allows Holly to develop a critique of how spectatorship implicates observers in the rhetorical tropes of the works they view. At the same time, it precludes a critique of the framing of art itself as a privileged regime of visual attentiveness.

What, however, of those entities, images and practices whose intentionality as objects of the attentive gaze is in doubt, or – even if they are meant to be looked at – are more often than not overlooked? How is one to seize this inattentiveness and to transform it into something stable enough for us to comprehend? How is one to capture and arrest the dynamism and mobility of that which eludes or resists our focused concentration, 'the rapid crowding of changing images, the sharp discontinuity in the grasp of a single glance' (1997 [1903]: 175) as Simmel puts it, to enable elucidation, analysis, critique? Metaphors of violent immobilization are almost invariably evoked here (as I have evoked them) – seizure, capture, holding, grasping, arresting – as though the very attempt to bring critical attention to bear on these phenomena involves a kind of visual subjugation. Moreover, these procedures are suggested by the terms 'critique' and 'analysis' themselves, the former associated, through the meaning of its Greek root *krinein*, with separation, distinction and judgement ('crisis' shares the same root), the latter referring to the dissection or breaking down of a phenomenon into constitutive components: both terms are implicated in the distinction of a body from its surroundings.[1] Such a distinction accompanies the primary act of attentiveness upon which the 'ground of the image' may be constituted (according to Nancy 2005), separating the object from temporal and spatial dynamics of flux and inchoateness and detaining it in front of the viewer. It is this attentiveness that creates a mutually productive affinity between the scholarly-critical gaze and the discrete images that are its object. It results in the attentive fallacy that informs many theoretical approaches and methodologies that engage with images: the seemingly self-evident idea that the significance of images – and the path to understanding them – is generated through a distinct, focused encounter between a visually immobilized viewer and a discrete and equally stationary image.

The 'attentive fallacy' has not gone unnoticed or unchallenged. In *Vision and Painting* (1983), Norman Bryson charted the historical development of western art history in terms of the opposition between an immobilizing and attentive Gaze and its suppressed other, the Glance, 'a furtive or sideways look whose attention is always elsewhere, which shifts to conceal its own existence' (1983: 94). Beyond the field of art history, others have also been concerned with issues of visual mobility and attentiveness in relation to media products. In film studies, Anne Friedberg (1993), developing Benjamin's (1992 [1936]) comments on the relation between contemplation and distraction, has discussed cinema in the context of modern technologies that achieve a perceptually immersive visual mobility through the physical immobilization of spectators' bodies and their attentive fixity within the cinematic apparatus. In media studies, John Ellis (1982) and John Caldwell (1995) have engaged in a minor disagreement over whether television is viewed in less or more attentive modes (a debate to which I shall return later on). And perhaps more than anyone else, Jonathan Crary (1992, 2002) has promoted the critical historicization of the theme of attention, and the socio-historical dialectic of visual mobility and immobilization in modern spectatorship. Central to his theses is that the 'subjectivization' of vision in the nineteenth century – the perception that vision had become unstable and unpredictable because of its intimate dependence on the psyche and the body – also gave rise to corresponding strategies for controlling and managing the individual observer, chief among which was 'a disciplinary regime of attentiveness' (Crary 1992: 24).

Last but by no means least, one could argue that the very theorization of the postmodern as an aesthetic of surface play, opposed to modernist depth and penetrating insight (Jameson 1991), depends at least in part on the implied opposition between modes of distraction and attention. This opposition was quickly transposed to investigations of digital media, such as Turkle's (1997) account of the shift from the MS-DOS command line to the graphical user interface of the early Macintosh computer, which she presented as a contrast between a modernist 'depth' aesthetic and epistemology and a postmodern emphasis on surface mobility and play. It is perhaps hardly surprising, then, that the question of attention continues to be raised in scholarly and public debates about contemporary digital media, a topic I will touch upon in my discussion of the aesthetics of the interface in chapter 6.

Inattention and Materiality

Given the significance of the attentive fallacy as a normative model that has pervaded much traditional and critical scholarly analysis of visual media, how are we to conceive of 'inattention' in a fashion that suspends its negative connotations? To begin with, I use 'inattention' to cover a *spectrum* of receptive modes, all of which have in common brief duration and low cognitive and emotional intensity. It is tempting to subsume these modes under the rubric of 'affect' as it is currently being employed in the humanities and some of the social sciences: 'autonomic' bodily responses that exceed and precede conscious states of perception, cognition and emotion, pointing to a fluid, dynamic and trans-subjective 'visceral perception' that embodies potentiality and indeterminacy (Massumi 2002; Clough 2008). Conceiving of inattention as affect, however, risks losing much of the routinized, semi-conscious and determinate nature of the modes I will be exploring. Rather, I treat visual inattention as a category of social-material practice.

I mean two things by this. First, visual inattention is clearly an *embodied* routine, organized by practical knowledge that – while rarely experienced as a cognitively conspicuous event and only infrequently rendered into discourse – is nevertheless amenable to conscious reflection and articulation. As Reckwitz notes, 'A social practice is a regular bodily activity held together by a socially standardized way of understanding and knowing' (Reckwitz 2002: 211). We – our bodies, eyes, hands, minds – 'know' how to watch television, just as we 'know' how to scan images as we flip through magazines and newspapers or scroll through smartphone apps. The first kind of materiality with which inattention is imbued is therefore that of the body's routine practical activity.

At the same time, however, inattention is a practice that is materialized in predictable and habitual situations of contact with artefacts. These artefacts are not just the 'objects' of a practice, the functional surfaces upon which it is performed or the instruments through which it is realized: they are co-agents of its social constitution and production in particular forms under 'known' conditions: 'The things handled in a social practice must be treated as necessary components for a practice to be "practiced" ... When human agents have developed certain forms of know-how concerning certain things, these things "materialize" or "incorporate" this knowledge within the practice ... Things are "materialized understanding"' (Reckwitz 2002: 212). In the discussion below, the 'things' that act as 'materialized understandings' of a social practice (in interaction with our bodies) are media technologies (photographs and photographic albums; television images and television screens). And the practices they materialize and routinely co-constitute – among others – are modes of visual inattention.

This double significance of 'materiality' – the practical materiality of the body in routine intersection with artefacts – also suggests a double negation. The first negation is that materiality itself is often defined in the humanistic disciplines most concerned with representation as the exterior of meaning: the non-representational substrate, the physical or functional residue that remains once a sign has been 'de-semanticized' and stripped of its semiotic kernel. The material, in this hermeneutic schema, is the body-vehicle that carries meaning but is external and supplementary to it: it is the result of the evacuation of representation.[2]

Gumbrecht, in an article that anticipates his more extensive conceptualization of 'presence effects' (2003), challenges this negation – and the matter–spirit dualism on which it is ultimately based – by defining 'materialities of communication' as 'the totality of phenomena contributing to the constitution of meaning without being meaning themselves' (1994: 398). Yet this attempt, laudable as it is within the hermeneutic parameters of the humanities, risks simply inverting the matter–spirit dualism in a manner all too familiar to social scientists, privileging the extra-hermeneutic category of 'material conditions' (including variables associated not just with the economic 'base' but with 'social structure' more broadly) as 'underlying' *determinants* of meaning (Brown

2010). So the humanistic negation of materiality needs to be met not with its own inversion (a negation of the negation) but with a continual questioning and crossing of the matter–meaning distinction itself: no matter without meaning, and no meaning without matter.[3]

Visual inattention offers a particularly rich field for such questioning and crossing. On the one hand, it is a socio-material practice that integrates and emerges from a network of interacting forces: bodies in action, spatial and temporal frameworks, technological artefacts and forms of representation. On the other hand, since these forces repeatedly construct it, 'inattention' needs to be conceived of in terms that resist its own designation as *in*-attention: as the mere absence of a positive value, as the negation of the very connective conditions (focus, concentration) thought to enable the meaning-carrying unit – the image-sign – to signify in the first place. Visual inattention, I hope to show, is a significant material practice not because it precedes, negates or is entirely external to representation, but because it participates in the routine modulation of alternate forms of connectivity; these in turn are productive of ways of making-present, of pre-reflexive world disclosure, that are not reducible to the discrete, attentively viewed image. It is these alternate energies that, I go on to argue, underpin our everyday moral concerns for distant others.

The Indifference of Photography

Wayne Wang's 1995 film *Smoke* contains a beautiful and extremely illuminating cinematic construction of pre-digital photographic viewing. In a scene near the beginning of the film, Auggie shows Paul his photograph albums. Each page of these indexed and dated volumes contains six white-framed black-and-white images; each image was taken on a different day, at precisely 8 o'clock in the morning, from exactly the same spot (the corner of Third Street and Seventh Avenue in New York), at the same angle and of the same view (the street corner in front of Auggie's tobacco shop), every day of the year. Auggie explains that he can never take a holiday because he has to be on 'his spot' every morning to take a picture, in all weathers, 'Sort of like the postman'.

As he flicks through these albums, Paul is amazed by the sheer excess of identical photographs (more than four thousand of them), and the self-defeating futility of Auggie's enterprise. 'They're all the same!' Paul observes. Auggie responds:

> They're all the same, but each one is different from every other one. You've got your bright mornings and your dark mornings. You've got your summer light and your autumn light. You've got your weekdays and your weekends ... The earth revolves around the sun, and every day the light from the sun hits the earth at a different angle.

Paul needs to slow down, Auggie suggests: 'You're going too fast. You're hardly even looking at the pictures.' He needs to contemplate every image separately if he is to see that in fact each image – and the momentary reality it depicts – is unique. Though initially sceptical, Paul begins to follow this advice, focusing his attention on individual photographs, which are made to fill the screen in a cinematic re-presentation of his activity. Finally, he comes across an image of his dead wife Ellen, and he cries. The scene then suddenly shifts to a shot of Auggie standing behind his camera in his 'spot' opposite his store in the morning: he looks at his watch, presses the button on his camera to take a picture, then looks through the camera's viewfinder and makes a note in his notebook.

There are many things one could say about this sequence and in particular about the habits of looking that it exhibits and performs. Most obviously, perhaps, it suggests that there is a connection between photographic resemblance and the material (bodily) mode and context of viewing, specifically the duration, mobility and concentration of the look, as well as the material (artefactual) method of displaying the photographs. I use the term 'photographic resemblance' in a double sense here. On the one hand, it designates the production of iconic similarity between photographic images, the creation of a typological identity that allows one to say of a group of photographs 'They're all the same'. On the other hand, it refers to the indexical singularity of each and every photograph: the photograph's semiotic status as 'an imprint or transfer off the real' (Krauss 1986: 110), as what Barthes calls the 'absolute Particular, the sovereign Contingency' (2000: 4), a unique material trace of its referent at an unrepeatable moment in time.

Mobility, duration, intensity, mode of presentation; this scene demonstrates that these factors can radically alter our sense of the sameness or dissimilarity of images. As the iconic similarity between photographs is made more conspicuous, so their fidelity to particular referents is diminished; as the indexical singularity of each image is emphasized, so their correspondence to one another decreases and it becomes erroneous to say that they are 'all the same'. Paul's original inattentiveness takes its cue in part from Auggie's decision to display the photographs in albums: he is merely performing the everyday visual-tactile practice of image scanning and page-flicking by which we work our way through newspapers, magazines and, indeed, family photo albums (especially other people's). Auggie actively has to intervene in order to overcome this embodied-technical routine of glancing, urging Paul to slow down and pay attention. In the process, he not only raises the act of looking to the level of consciousness, de-routinizing and disclosing vision itself; he also reconstitutes it around an altogether different set of bodily practices and technical instruments, the exhibition spaces (museum, gallery) and prolonged gaze appropriate to the proper reception of art.

By associating immobilization with the 'truth' of photography, as against the viewer's roving, scanning, distracted glance, this scene shows how the problem of visual movement becomes particularly aggravated in the case of photography.[4] For thanks to the almost infinite reproducibility of photographic images, the multitude of contexts in which they can be seen and the variety of material vehicles on which they can be displayed, as well as their consequent proliferation across social and cultural realms, photographs seem to be integrated – more seamlessly perhaps than other representations – into a total, fluctuating environment in which the individual image loses its singular claims on the viewer's attentive gaze. As Victor Burgin has observed: 'It is therefore not an arbitrary fact that photographs are deployed so that we need not look at them for long, and so that, almost invariably, another photograph is always already in position to receive the displaced look' (1982: 143).

Ultimately, Auggie's need to intervene in order to alter the way Paul looks at his photographs raises the suspicion that viewers are indifferent to the photographs that they see. This indifference is not one of boredom, ennui or alienation, but is a habitual material practice: a routinization of embodied and perceptual connective energies, both tactile and visual, that produces sameness from movement in a context characterized by the *abundance* of representations and perceptual stimuli. In other words, against the hierarchal privileging of singularity and visual attentiveness as key characteristics of photographic significance, it is actually the qualities of indifference, sameness and visual displacement that routinely serve as the ground for experiencing photography's way of showing the world.

The indifference of the viewer is strikingly paralleled in this scene by the indifference of the image producer to the detailed representational construction of his own images. One of the most perplexing things about Auggie's albums in *Smoke* is that they represent an oeuvre based almost entirely on a mechanized and automated indexical process. Once Auggie has set the parameters for all the photographs (time, place, field of view), his presence at the scene becomes irrelevant to the actual production of the pictures; the same results could be obtained from a computer-operated camera. Each photograph in Auggie's albums is the result of an arbitrary, uniform and inexorable predetermination (to take a picture at exactly the same time of exactly the same scene, day after day) that, once set in motion, prevents meaningful, context-sensitive human intervention. He is so removed from influencing the content of his images that we see him check the camera's viewfinder only *after* he has actually taken the picture. In a manner that fully echoes Fox Talbot's (1844–6) famous description of photography as the 'pencil of nature', reality seems to reproduce its own image through the agency of light and a mechanical device. As Baker notes, 'in any photograph, the object depicted has impressed itself through the agency of light and chemicals alone, inscribing a referential excess beyond the control of the creator of any given image' (1996: 75). Auggie simply takes this breach between image and author to its extreme, voluntarily maintaining his indifference to the particular content of any particular image.

This referential excess of the photograph – what Berger calls its 'weak intentionality' (1982: 90) – is closely related to the indifference of viewers. No longer asked to reproduce the primary perception of an artist, the viewer's eyes are confronted by a reality which appears routinely to recreate itself as a matter of course.[5] Rather than a series of singular images attracting and returning the gaze of the viewer, photographs aggregate into a fluctuating ambient backdrop which is 'taken in' rather than intensively viewed, producing the seemingly unmotivated autopoetic unfolding of a disclosed world.

So if photography enjoys indifferent relations both with the world it discloses and the viewers who behold it, how might these possess anything resembling moral significance? Much of the answer to this will be developed in the discussion of television and in my concluding remarks, but for the moment a few intermediate points are required.

First, photographic indexicality – by virtue of its weak intentionality – is radically inclusive (this is, of course, another central meaning of the word 'indifferent'): it registers both the principal subject and the extraneous detail, this being a key condition of Barthes's *punctum*. John Ellis makes this one of the main themes of his claim that mass media have created a new generalized mode of relating to the world, a new form of witnessing – though Ellis uses the word 'witness' – and what is true for photography is even more apposite for cinema and television:

> The most astonishing thing [about the experience of early cinema] was that everything in the picture moved, 'even the leaves on the trees' as one observer put it … It was the sudden ability to witness the incidentals of life just as they were that produced the effect of witness. … Photography had the ability to capture everything that lay in front of the lens. The film camera was able to give it all motion. Together they introduced the audiences of a century ago to a new potential to witness events and phenomena in the world around them. (2000: 19–20)

Auggie of course takes this to its extreme; by surrendering virtually all control of detail, he makes the accidental and the incidental decisive elements in the production of each image. In this, he is representative of the witnessing effect of audio-visual mass media more broadly, generalizing witnessing from this specified event and that particular experience to the perpetual disclosure of worlds. Indeed, we can call this new testimonial form 'world-witnessing' (see chapter 3).

Second, while the photograph is the result of a mechanical process, it is nevertheless 'programmed'. There is always a *generic* intentionality in operation behind it – cameras, even automated ones, do not appear of their own accord – and this intentionality can be interpreted by viewers. Auggie's generic intention is documentary as well as proprietary: to report on his 'spot', his little corner of the world. He claims that in order to 'get' his project, one needs to slow down and appreciate the particularity and singularity of each image and the uniqueness of each individual represented. But this only makes sense within the framework of an overall project of indifferent world-witnessing, whereby one 'inattentively' judges these photographs to be 'all the same' in the sense that they indifferently record *the same world* – an actual world of contingency shared by the viewer – and the individuals appear simply by virtue of the fact that they have wandered into it at that moment. It is the intentional ground of homogeneity and identity ('this spot') that acts as the fundamental frame-work within which specific encounters with particular images and particular individuals then become possible (Ellen, says Auggie, just happened to be passing on her way to work).

This allows photographic indifference to be revolutionary in another sense in that it gives a central role to *indexical anonymity*: you can be reproduced through a causal and physical process in an image in exquisite detail, in an exis-tentially unrepeatable field of space and time – it is defini-tively you, there, then – and yet remain unknown to your photographer and to your viewers: this occurs most conspicu-ously in particular 'iconic' images (Hariman and Lucaites 2007) where anonymous individuals – such as Dorothea Lange's 'Migrant Mother' – can come to stand in for larger collectivities and events which are not depicted. Moreover, photography potentially extends this gift to anyone, however irrelevant to the putative central topic of the image, simply by virtue of their entering the camera's field of view at the moment the photograph is taken. It therefore speaks *simultaneously* to social generality – you appear as an unidentified anyone – and to unique individuality – it is you, a particular someone, and no other, in that place and at that time. Ellen is singled out by Paul and by Auggie, but she is in fact no different to all those other 'anyones' who populate Auggie's images and who are also always potentially someone in particular to a viewer somewhere.

Finally, what Auggie's project demonstrates in microcosm is photographic indifference as a relentless, routinized, bureaucratic system of same-world disclosure. It is no accident that Auggie cannot take a holiday, that he has to be on his spot at 8 am every morning, rain or shine, or that he compares himself to the postman, thereby invoking the first modern mass communication bureaucracy. And, like mass media, Auggie's project is also relentlessly bureaucratic and archival: at one point in the scene described earlier, Paul chuckles incredulously on being presented with the next in a long line of carefully labelled and dated photograph albums. Auggie's photographic indifference is perpetual and regulated, mundane and everyday. It happens irrespective of whether or not there is a particular individual or event judged a priori as worth attending to because it does not convey specific information or experience but presents us with an inclusive chronotope, an unfolding world.

The Non-Reciprocity of Television

So far, I have linked the inattentive character of much habitual viewing of photographs – dramatized in the scene from *Smoke* – with the inclusiveness, contingency and indifference of photographic indexicality and the rise of world-witnessing: this is an example of the way material practices are bound up with the poetic making-present of worlds. The iconic similarity attributed inattentively to photographs as a routinely encountered visual environment complements the same-world disclosure that emerges, paradoxically perhaps, from their indexical character. Television is, of course, a different medium, materially and socially constructed with different affordances, expressive constraints and possibilities, and contexts of engagement with viewers. Inattention, in the case of television, is chiefly associated with what later came to be called 'glance theory': the thesis that viewers' engagement with the medium is largely characterized by a lack of visual concentration. John Ellis made probably the best-known and most persuasive case for this idea in *Visible Fictions* (1982): the relatively small size of the traditional cathode-ray tube television screen, coupled with the distracting domestic circumstances of viewing, meant that 'TV is not usually the only thing going on, sometimes it is not even the principal thing. TV is treated casually rather than concentratedly' (1982: 128). 'Glance theory' has been challenged over the years, most comprehensively and engagingly by John Caldwell, who criticized the generality of the claims made for casual viewing and Ellis's neglect of the hard material and stylistic labour invested by programmers in attracting viewer attention as a matter of narrative and commercial necessity. 'The viewer is not always, nor inherently, distracted', Caldwell concluded. 'Theorists should not jump to theoretical conclusions just because there is an ironing board in the room' (1995: 27). One might update this observation with the advice that we contemporary theorists should also not jump to conclusions because there are second (and third) screens in the room.

In Ellis's defence, his argument was published some thirteen years prior to Caldwell's critique and with reference to British rather than US television (Caldwell acknowledges as much: 1995: 365, note 57) – though it was also controversial when first published (Winston 1984). Ellis also works from a phenomenology of the viewing experience, whereas Caldwell focuses on the logics, technologies and practices of television production, which are concerned with attracting and maintaining viewer attention in the context of multi-channel competition and a relatively weak apparatus of attentiveness (compared to cinema). Both, of course, are partly justified in their claims: Ellis in arguing that being distracted is more likely and acceptable, even a horizon of expectation, when watching television at home than when going to the cinema;

Caldwell in insisting that television systematically employs numerous visual techniques – many of them decidedly cinematic – for attracting and holding attention.

However, the terms of this disagreement are largely conditioned by an emphasis on television as a representational device: a machine for making images. Since, however, visual inattention primarily describes forms of connective energy, it makes sense to explore it as a socio-material practice – along with its moral potentialities – in relation to another well-documented feature of television: its character as a medium of connectivity between viewers and the social whole, in particular through conventions of temporal simultaneity and 'para-social' interaction (Horton and Wohl 1956).

In making this shift from representation to connectivity, it is helpful to recall Jakobson's discussion of the phatic function of language, mentioned in the introductory chapter. This serves 'to establish, to prolong, or to discontinue communication, to check whether the channel works (Hello, do you hear me?), to attract the attention of the interlocutor or to confirm his continued attention' (Jakobson 1960: 355). Jakobson's definition is in fact an instrumentalized version of Malinowski's earlier and sociologically richer notion of 'phatic communion', defined as 'a type of speech in which ties of union are created by a mere exchange of words' (Malinowski 1923: 315), irrespective of those words' informational content, and against a background where 'the breaking of silence, the communion of words is the first act to establish links of fellowship, which is consummated only by the breaking of bread and the communion of food' (1923: 314). What for Jakobson is a technical linguistic resource for channel maintenance between a communicating pair, addresser and addressee, is for Malinowski an expression of fundamental human sociability among multiple others that fulfils 'the mere need of companionship'. It is a performance of connectedness between individuals and their social whole that is 'one of the bedrock aspects of man's nature in society' (Malinowski 1923: 314). Significantly, phatic utterances and exchanges are performed without the conscious attention or intention of their speakers, or the attentive engagement of their recipients: 'they are neither the result of intellectual reflection, nor do they necessarily arouse reflection in the listener ... language does not

function here as a means of transmission of thought'
(Malinowski 1923: 315).

Phatic communion is not limited to linguistic performance.
It is a communicative dimension of modern media systems,
including television. Our experience of television is informed
not only by our exposure to particular transmissions, which
we view – as Caldwell rightly observes – with varying degrees
of concentration and involvement, but also by our habitual
recognition of the potential for transmissibility that the television enables and symbolizes (Meyrovitz 1986). Even when,
in their early history, television programmes would come to
an end late at night, transmission certainly didn't: behind any
and every programme is the signal itself, given memorable
and uncanny life for many older viewers by standard test
patterns broadcast during non-programming hours. As Silverstone observed in his account of television as a transitional
object (1994), even when there are no programmes being
transmitted, no representations to attend to – indeed, even
when the set is off – the television signifies our connection
with an outside that is separate from us, as well as the perpetual availability of that connection. Hence the constant
technical performance of connectivity, irrespective of informational content, is a dimension of modern media that
underpins routine audience experiences, expectations and
relations to the world beyond their immediate perception.[6]

The idea of phatic communion as a fundamental yet largely
tacit feature of audience experience involves a shift in our
thinking about audience engagement. It suggests that something important is still going on when audience members are
not paying much attention to the representational particulari-
ties of media texts. Audience inattention needs to be taken
seriously, then, not as a moral or political deficiency in reception, nor as a defence mechanism against the presumed
psychic perils of over-stimulation, nor even as the anarchic
antithesis to disciplinary regimes of attentiveness, but as an
ecological achievement of mediated sociality: one can disengage from media texts *without* relinquishing connectivity –
without severing the links to others and to 'the social' that
television routinely enables and symbolizes.[7] In this context,
the word 'inattention' may in fact be inappropriate since it
operates with reference to media as representational devices.

But it is not the paying of particular attention to specific programmes that constitutes the ground of audiences' experience of mediation but the presence of media perpetually *in attendance* in our lives and intimate spaces, available when needed.

Television also introduces, however, a socially novel form of *visual* connectivity: non-reciprocal face-to-face communication. Television allows one to be 'face-to-face' with another person and *not* pay them any attention. The appearance of another's face on the screen, even when accompanied by direct verbal address, the illusion of physical proximity and temporal simultaneity (live transmission), is an indication of their non-presence at the location of viewing. One can maintain an attitude of utter indifference, even when apparently being directly spoken to, ignoring both their faces and words. Crucially, this non-reciprocity is itself mutual, a result of the systemic organization of technologies of 'mediated quasi-interaction' (Thompson 1995). The actor, the anchor in the studio, the politician speaking to camera – all are impervious to our efforts at interruption and are entirely ignorant of any lack of attention on our part.

Though the rhetorics of direct address, combined with the logics of mediated non-presence, have long been analysed in a variety of ways (see Horton and Wohl 1956; Scannell 1996; Tolson 1996), the fundamental moral significance of this mutual indifference should not be underestimated. Saying so may raise some eyebrows, however. What positive moral relations could possibly be produced by the ability to *ignore* others? Non-reciprocal face-to-face interaction seems to resemble the kinds of indifferent visual encounters that characterize actual physical proximity and co-presence in modern public spaces – such as Simmel's 'blasé' attitude (1997 [1903]) and Goffman's 'civil inattention' (1963; see also Koch 1995). To its potential discredit (though I will argue otherwise), television appears to introduce such mechanisms for ignoring others into the home.[8] This domestication of inattentive relations with strangers invites a severe critique: surely it is an extension of alienated public interaction norms into the private sphere, de-ethicalizing others by turning them into mere background figures (Bauman 1990)? Critiques similar to this are common in media studies. The non-reciprocity of media is transformed into a figure of moral distance between viewer and viewed: the lack of congruence between those depicted and the local 'relevance structures' of 'direct experience' in the lives of viewers hinders the nurturing of care and responsive action (Tomlinson 1999). Audiovisual media technologies create non-reciprocal non-encounters between viewers and viewed and are perceived to insulate the viewer from ethical responsibility to those represented on the screen: the screen functions as a window but also as a barrier, allowing us 'to maintain a considerable distance from what we see and thus to acquire an anaesthetised form of knowledge' (Morley 2000: 184).

There is, however, an alternative assessment: that non-reciprocal face-to-face communication allows the faces of strangers to appear in the sphere of intimacy without creating alarm or triggering a defensively hostile response (because these faces can be safely ignored). Like the critique of de-ethicalization, this more optimistic view also sees televisual non-reciprocity as an extension, domestication and enhancement of 'civil inattention' in public contexts, but reaches an entirely different conclusion concerning its moral potentialities. It assumes that encounters with multiple strangers in public are potentially a recipe not for dialogue but for the defensive expression of hostility and aggression, and that encounters with the uninvited faces of strangers in the private sphere – on one's own personal territory – are potentially even more explosive. In this context, civil inattention, epitomized by the way individuals briefly glance across the eyes and faces of physically proximate others in a public space, is 'perhaps the slightest of interpersonal rituals, yet one that constantly regulates the social intercourse of persons in our society' (Goffman 1963: 84). Its great moral importance is invested in the equal connection that it accords to anonymous others, recognizing their co-presence as non-threatening, and therefore as unworthy of particular attention or interest: 'By according civil inattention, the individual implies that he has no reason to suspect the intentions of the others present and no reason to fear the others, be hostile to them, or wish to avoid them' (1963: 84). What one would wish to avoid, in other words, is uncivil attention, the kind of attention lavished upon strangers in public places by children who have yet to learn that it is rude to stare or point at those who look different, or by security forces in the days following terrorist attacks, when the non-hostility of strangers is a matter of deadly uncertainty (Frosh 2007).[9]

Television's performance of non-reciprocal face-to-face communication is therefore morally significant as a domesticator of civil inattention. It allows the faces and voices of strangers to populate the sphere of intimacy without their very appearance in the home creating alarm or triggering a defensively hostile response. The multiplicity of ignorable faces on the television screen makes a diverse range of strangers constantly quasi-available, often unattended to but always in attendance, like the medium itself, potentially connected to viewers who can choose to engage with them or not, and who need not feel threatened by them. By neutralizing the potential threat of the stranger, televisual indifference ensures that vast numbers of unknown others can cohabitate with us over the long term, becoming livable with in our homes and personal lives, perpetually disclosed to us, pre-reflectively, in our intimate lifeworlds.

The Aggregate Image and the Face of Humanity

The unthreatening habituation to multiple strangers made possible by televisual non-reciprocity nevertheless seems to command a high price: responsiveness to the particularity of an individual other. The lack of attention paid to the faces of others, apparently looking at and speaking directly to us, reduces the intensity of our encounter, but it also potentially undermines the perception of their singularity. More to the point, the lack of attention built into the very structure of televisual non-reciprocity is reinforced by another feature at odds with the immobilizing assumptions of the attentive fallacy: the ephemerality of most strangers on television.

Ordinary individuals on television are transient. They appear for a few seconds before being replaced by other images, other faces and bodies. Indeed, it is their very transience on screen that helps to mark them as 'ordinary people' who hail from the shared 'real life' reference world beyond television, as opposed to the corporeal familiarity of celebrities, journalists, actors and presenters whose repeated appearance on television situates them within 'the media' as a seemingly autonomous realm (Couldry 2000). Unlike the case of characters in novels, or fictional characters in television serials and soap operas, we do not have time to 'get to know them' and to develop feelings of intimacy with their personalities or to form imaginary emotional attachments to them. They are somewhat similar to strangers encountered in public places: we tend to overlook them rather than look at them, and can rarely recall them in any detail as unique individuals.

Forgettable and largely unknowable as specific individuals, these transients usually undergo a process of generalization. There are two intertwined mechanisms shaping this process. The first is the particular semiotic combination of indexical, iconic and symbolic dimensions of modern visual and audio-visual media already discussed in the case of photography and the scene from *Smoke*, which makes possible the indexical anonymity of individuals. Yet, as with photography, with television there seems to be a price to pay for turning the individual into a metonymic emblem of broader, undepicted populations and events: the erasure of the individual as a singular being, a memorable, unique person who can form the basis for a concrete appeal to moral action among audiences. The move from index to emblem can appear to obliterate the former.

Unlike photographs, however, television images do not stand still: or rather, their circulation and mobility is technically automated rather than a product of visual, bodily and material practices performed upon still pictures. Hence the second mechanism shaping the generalization of depicted strangers on television has to do with the incessant temporal flow of images, sounds and texts that is a default technical characteristic of the medium's mode of display. It is not only the viewer's gaze or attention that wanders: the medium is based on the succession of images. Though there is certainly an economy of attentiveness and familiarity created by the repetitive cycles of television programming (daily, weekly and seasonal schedules; reruns: Ellis 2000; Kompare 2005), as well as a less predictable recycling and circulation of particular images, the individuality of strange faces and bodies is affected by both the viewer's movement across stimuli and by a key temporal dimension of the medium itself. In this context, images of individuals can be generalized as *units of aggregation* across texts and genres, overlaid with multiple others judged to be similar in an incessantly accumulating image stream.

The relationship between the generalized image and the singular individual, then, is as much a matter of expansion and accumulation as it is of erasure. It is the erasure of the *boundaries* of the particular individual, not the annihilation of the individual per se, that is accomplished. If most ordinary individual strangers on television are viewed indifferently and transiently, in routine, unremarkable, non-hostile encounters, then their constant and cumulative presence within the home is a significant historical accomplishment. It makes present for viewers in their intimate spaces a serial aggregate of the human figure as a shared 'condition', an instrument of similarity and interconnection, an interminably fluctuating and ever-present *composite image*: perhaps even the 'face' of humanity itself. It is only in so far as they are recognizable constituents of this serial aggregate (to which they are in turn added) that the ethical appeal of particular images and stories of specified individuals can be produced.

The term 'composite image' has a troubling history. Its association with social Darwinism and the racist and eugenicist missions of nineteenth-century practitioners such as Francis Galton behooves us to treat it with a degree of caution (Sekula 1989). But it is also important to recall Carlo Ginzburg's (2004) description of the composite image as a kind of 'family resemblance', which in aggregating a multitude of individual faces produces not uniformity and homogeneity but a porous, overlapping and fluid identity that is in excess of the disciplinary frameworks in which it was developed (indeed, in Sekula's well-known account this – largely indexical – excess underpinned the failure of the composite image as a useful tool of social engineering). To be com/posite is to be situated with, alongside, in company with (an idea that I also pursue in chapter 5 in connection to the selfie). The non-threatening serial aggregate of televised strangers produces a visual figure for the composition of multiple selves and others, for our constitutive superimposition and intermingling as *both* singular *and* similar beings, for our ever-emerging and changeable 'human' commonality. To go out on a limb here, it is a figure of what Nancy (2000) would call our singular-plural 'compearance', our foundational situation of 'being-with'.

Of course, the status of 'the human' as such and as the product of a putatively inclusive visual 'language' has been the subject of much criticism. Especially well-known is Barthes's essay 'The Great Family of Man' in *Mythologies* (1993 [1972]) in which he attacks both the universality of the photographic medium and the universality of 'man' as myths whose effects are to dehistoricize and naturalize the current social order. Against this critique, I would argue that the production of an unthreatening, perpetually aggregating composite image of strangers nevertheless socially institutionalizes a space in which each individual's extended and abstract relations of similarity with distant, unfamiliar others become definable under the category of 'the human'. This space is *moral* rather than ethical in the sense that it guides our 'thin relations', our behaviour 'toward those to whom we are related just by virtue of their being fellow human beings' (Margalit 2002: 37), rather than our 'thick relations', our behaviour towards those with whom we enjoy strong social bonds (family, friends, etc.). Inattentive and indifferent relations to a fluctuating serial figure of 'the human' act as an unexciting but central routinizing procedure for the moralizing of strangers as human: they establish 'proper distance' (Silverstone 2007) with others not as an intermediate position on a scale between poles of closeness and detachment but as a framework for the maintenance of *distance itself* in ways that are moral. Based on a logic of superficial iconic similarity – of sufficient substitutability between individuals (they're all the same!) that nevertheless preserves their singularity – televisual indifference, along with the indifferent same-world unfolding of photography, means that 'others' are always already other *people*. As Nancy observes: '"People" clearly states that we are all precisely *people*, that is, indistinctly persons, humans, all of a common "kind" ... This existence can only be grasped in the paradoxical simultaneity of togetherness (anonymous, confused and indeed massive) and disseminated singularity (these or those "people(s)", or "a guy", "a girl", "a kid"' (2000: 7).

The Composite As Human Totem

Photography and television are two distinct media, and although my account of their inattentive and indifferent relations to their viewers highlights commonalities between them, it is to a degree an abstraction concerned with typifications of viewer behaviour (glancing, non-reciprocal connectivity) and technical affordances (modes of display, image transience), rather than an analysis of how inattention is performed and embedded in the lives of empirical viewers. While I have described visual inattention as an embodied and technically realized socio-material practice, it is nevertheless a 'genus', a taxonomic category distinct from the specificities of viewers' lifeworlds. In its generality and distance from 'actual' data, my discussion has constituted a second-order materialism, one level of the multiple 'orders of materiality' that, according to Brown, comprise an (unrealizable) 'ideal materialism' (2010: 59).

There is, then, a formal affinity between the aggregative consequences of inattention that I have teased out and the aggregative method of analysis that I have employed. At worst, my discussion is the product of an insufficiently attentive approach, one insensitive to the myriad practices, affects, structures and relations that terms like 'indifference' both designate and conflate. I would venture, however, to suggest that my analysis also proceeds 'totemically', basing my claim on the revitalization of the concept of the totem by W. J. T. Mitchell (2005). It is totemic in at least one obvious sense: it has detailed the routine production and performance of a totemic being – the composite image of 'the human' – 'where the species-being of the individual is "crystallized", as it were, and rendered as a kind of concrete universal' (Mitchell 2005: 178, note 22). This totemic being is unusual in terms of traditional anthropological understandings of the concept since its form is not that of an animal or natural object, but rather that of the human face and figure. Or rather, perhaps, this difference bespeaks the givenness of an immediate perceptible universe populated more by images of distant human individuals and multitudes from whom we take our measure than by facets of the non-human 'natural' world. The culture of media and image saturation has become, ultimately, 'second nature' to the extent that 'humanity' has become auto-totemic: it is its own lived clan-symbol.[10]

The composite image produced by inattentive viewing, image mobility and media ubiquity is, like the totem, *animated*. It is fluid, unfixed, constantly modulated not only by the individual and social materialities of viewing, but by the additive and cumulative dynamics of contemporary media themselves. This means that the composite image of the human is constituted through incessant transformations. The sameness it produces by accumulation and aggregation are 'repetitions' that enable recognition of multiple others *as such*, as definable figures against the flux, and as always prior to and beyond singularity: 'See statis, see station, as a special case of movement (a special case of reiterative movement: that allowing recognition)' (Massumi 2002: 66). Having said this, there are undoubtedly political and economic structures to this accumulation: certain populations enjoy considerable representation (in both political and semiotic senses of the word) and recognition, while others remain undepicted and abject – unrecognized as subjects of discourse (Butler 1993). Hence the moral productivity of inattentive viewing also needs to be considered relationally, in connection to forms of institutionalized media attention that are usually highly centralized (notwithstanding the development of digital technologies and networked media).

This sense of the composite image as a human totem remains entirely susceptible to Barthes's ideological critique of the myth of the 'Family of Man' mentioned earlier, as a naturalization of the particular social and historical conditions that produce it. But to make this critique is – again in Mitchell's terms (2005: 189) – to reduce the totem to an idol, an image of (false) veneration and power that invites iconoclastic deconstruction.[11] However, in tracing the correspondence between aggregations and frameworks of viewer inattention, as well as the ubiquity, mobility and indifference of images in modern media, another feature of the totem has been engaged: that the totem embodies, symbolizes and performs relationality.

By this, I mean not only that the totem explicitly expresses and performs social bonds (whereas idols and fetishes tend to disguise or replace them), though it is of more than mere passing interest that 'totem' literally means 'relative of mine' in the Ojibway language from which it was originally taken (Mitchell 2005: 98). Rather, it is that it operates in the cumulative and connective tenor of 'both and', rather than the analytical binary of 'either/or'. The inattentive mode of viewing photographs is connective rather than discriminating; non-reciprocal face-to-face communication on television enables a plurality of weak ties with ever increasing numbers of unfamiliar strangers rather than exclusive commitment to particular, identifiable individuals. The composite image itself is *both* indexical *and* emblematic, singular and general, someone and anyone, change and repetition, concrete particular and abstract universal. It links the habitual operations of inattentive and indifferent modes of viewing, performed by individuals in their everyday spaces and lives, to the cohabitation of extended worlds with many anonymous others. In the process, it produces 'humanity' as both a background figure in perpetual attendance – a stranger-companion – and as the ultimate social aggregation.

The Companionship of Media

In *The Community of Those Who Have Nothing in Common* (1994), Alphonso Lingis describes a limit case of communication: being called to the deathbed of a parent. As with Malinowski's concept of phatic communion (1923), this case exemplifies the primacy of the saying over the said: 'You have to be there, and you have to say something. You have never been more clear about anything. ...What is imperative is that you be there and speak; what you say, in the end, hardly matters' (108). 'This situation', Lingis continues, 'is not only the end of language – the last moment when all we have to say to one another ends in the silence and death for the one to whom it has to be said and in the speechlessness and sobs of the one who has come to say something. It is also the beginning, the beginning of communication' (113–14).

I have described media, specifically photography and television, as world-producing and world-disclosing devices of composite representation and connectivity that are in attendance in our lives. They are in attendance in the way one is in attendance at a bedside: one is adjacent to, beside; one keeps company; it is important simply that one is there. Media studies tends to model communication on dialogue or dissemination (Peters 1999): these are not to be dismissed lightly, as Lingis does not dismiss the 'common rational discourse' of the said. Yet media studies has less to say about the moral consequences of media as constant companions rather than as interlocutors or transmitters, about the perpetual, habitual, reliable rustle of media in our lives as poetic tokens of an expansive world of others, of 'the human' itself as the ultimate aggregation. Rather than the ethical dyad of the viewer and a specified other, the morality of traditional mass media rests primarily on this companionship, in our intimate spheres, of multiple transient strangers, and in the overlapping of our com/posite worlds. For is not the extension of companionship a proper and primary purpose of communication – to continually disclose to us that we are not alone?

3
Screenshot

The 'Photographic' Witnessing of Digital Worlds

The screenshot is the unglamorous drudge of digital culture. Unlike selfies – the topic of chapter 5 – screenshots are largely neglected in public debate and scholarly research, despite the fact that they are everywhere put to work. Utterly ubiquitous as a method of quoting from digital media, usually *within* digital media, the screenshot continually escapes our attention as a distinctive cultural practice, a representational form that draws upon and promotes a particular set of epistemological and ontological assumptions. These assumptions concern not just the status of the screenshot itself and its claims, but also the character of the reference world – most particularly social network platforms – that the screenshot discloses. The extent of our innocence about the screenshot, and of our unreflective habituation to its utility, simply does not bear comparison to the scepticism and even cynicism (or, alternatively, the awe and admiration) that we have learned to display, as badges of honour, with respect to other cultural forms. To date, it is almost impossible to bring to mind a single case of either public or scholarly controversy over the fidelity or truthfulness of a screenshot, even though, in many key respects, screenshots are no less malleable, and no less ideological, than digital photographs. To use Richard Lanham's (1993) terms, we almost exclusively 'look *through*' screenshots to focus on what they depict, and almost never 'look *at*' them to foreground how they operate.[1]

Though significant enough to have become an object of discourse (after all, the screenshot has acquired a name), in its routine use it is among the most transparent of digital phenomena.

Take, for instance, a well-known example from 2017 (Figure 3.1). This tweet appeared in President Donald Trump's Twitter feed just after midnight on 31 May 2017; it was deleted just before 6 am on the same day. Since Trump had at that time around 31 million Twitter 'followers', many will have seen the tweet 'natively' on the Twitter app, either from Trump himself or through (frequently mocking) retweets. Many more, however, will have heard about it from other sources since it was widely reported, discussed and derided in online news outlets, blogs, social networking platforms, as well as by traditional broadcasting and print media. These outlets, however, did not by and large simply *report on* Trump's tweet, its verbal content, its utter weirdness and its strangely delayed removal. They almost invariably reproduced the tweet itself (often along with others commenting on it) by means of screenshots. For instance, Figure 3.2 shows part of an article from the news section of *The Guardian* website on the same day (and which was still available when I made a screenshot of it many months later).

Donald J. Trump ✔
@realDonaldTrump

2. Follow

Despite the constant negative press covfefe

RETWEETS LIKES
11,029   13,430

12:06 AM - 31 May 2017

↩ 7.8K   🔁 11K   ♥ 13K   ✉

Figure 3.1: Screenshot of US President Donald Trump's Twitter tweet, 31.5.2017.

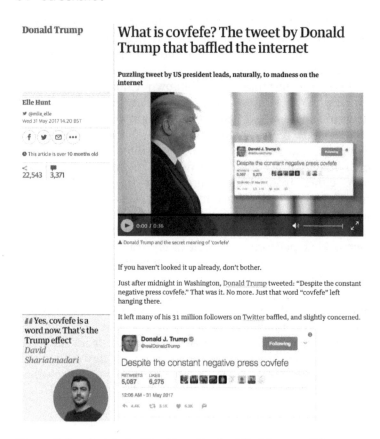

Donald Trump

What is covfefe? The tweet by Donald Trump that baffled the internet

Puzzling tweet by US president leads, naturally, to madness on the internet

Elle Hunt
🐦 @mlle_elle
Wed 31 May 2017 14.20 BST

f 🐦 ✉ •••

🕐 This article is over 10 months old

< 🏳
22,543 3,371

▲ Donald Trump and the secret meaning of 'covfefe'

If you haven't looked it up already, don't bother.

Just after midnight in Washington, Donald Trump tweeted: "Despite the constant negative press covfefe." That was it. No more. Just that word "covfefe" left hanging there.

It left many of his 31 million followers on Twitter baffled, and slightly concerned.

❝❝ Yes, covfefe is a word now. That's the Trump effect
David Shariatmadari

Figure 3.2: Article in *The Guardian* by Elle Hunt on US President Donald Trump's 'covfefe' tweet, 31.5.2017. (Courtesy of Guardian News & Media Ltd.)

In one sense, the screenshot is superfluous since the verbal content of the tweet is cited, word for word, in quotation marks in the second paragraph of the article. Note, moreover, that the screenshot is not captioned or marked in any way: it simply appears (twice in fact, once in the opening shot of the video, once in the written article), its provenance unexplained, its presence apparently warranted as the primal stuff of the reported event, a chunk of elemental news matter extruding into the text.[2] Absent are any indications that the screenshot is a mediation or a representation – an image – of the depicted tweet.

To be more precise: the reflexive indicators of *self-mediation* are absent – signs which draw attention to the screenshot itself as a media object. In contrast, the screenshot is brimming with signs belonging to its 'content' or reference medium. For the screenshot doesn't just reproduce the verbal text of the 'covfefe' tweet, it displays it along with all the additional indicators and information that appear on the Twitter interface, such as the name of Trump, his photograph, the time and date of the tweet, the number of retweets and likes at the time of the screenshot. This is important for two reasons, which I will elaborate later on: first, because it establishes the screenshot as a seemingly unmediated act of capturing the tweet in its putative raw form, and, second, because it establishes the Twitter interface itself as the site of ongoing activity, as a domain of action that exists in so-called 'real time'.

So what is a screenshot, and from what do its transparency and mimetic potency derive? More to the point: where do they lead? Technically, a screenshot is created by extracting the information from a computer or mobile device's 'frame buffer', a section of memory which stores the visual information displayed on the screen at a given moment, along with instructions to the device to interpret this information as an image file format like JPEG. Communicatively, however, the screenshot is something else entirely; several things in fact: the screenshot is a kind of document, a remediated photograph, and a mode of witnessing and poetic world disclosure.

From Performance to Document

Lev Manovich claims that contemporary 'software culture' is characterized by a shift from the static 'document', as the basic 'atom' of modern twentieth-century cultural practice, to dynamic performances:

> I use the word 'performance' because what we are experiencing is constructed by software in real time. So whether we

are exploring a dynamic website, playing a video game, or using an app on a mobile phone to locate particular places or friends nearby, we are engaging not with pre-defined static documents but with the dynamic outputs of a real-time computation happening on our device and/or the server. (2013: 33–4)

This argument makes the screenshot a somewhat paradoxical object. For while it is – as Manovich would rightly point out – created, stored, shared and displayed on our devices through real-time computational 'performances', it appears to us, definitively, *as* a static form. Screenshots, like printouts, appear to bring fixity, stability and stillness to the fluid and shifting stream of performances that constitute digital media. If there is indeed a historical path leading from static textual objects to dynamic performance in contemporary media culture, the screenshot seems to indicate a counter-trajectory.

One can of course take historical issue with the dichotomy Manovich evokes. The kinds of fluidity and continual transformation he describes are by no means novel or unique to contemporary culture or digital media. Variability and perpetual transformation are key themes of nineteenth- and twentieth-century modernity as such (see Berman 1983 and Kern 1983 for classic treatments, and the later works of Bauman [2000] on the increasingly 'liquid' character of modern social life), while television broadcasts, for instance, were long ago conceptualized by Raymond Williams (1990 [1975]) as forms of 'flow', rather than discrete encounters with static-media texts (the same term could be applied to radio). Documents themselves – as the complex bibliographic and editorial histories of both manuscripts and printed texts continually aver – have never simply been fixed 'atoms'; Manovich's language tends to naturalize their deeply historical and performative character, and the dichotomy between analogue fixity and digital fluidity confuses technological infrastructure with communicative function.[3] Tellingly, documentation is central to both the history of computation and to contemporary digital practices: think of the near standard 'My Documents' folder in personal computers, as well as the popularity and rhetoric of Adobe's PDF document format

(Gitelman 2014). The continued ubiquity of documents in the era of digital media is hardly surprising since they help to produce the 'communicative stability' that enables the construction, maintenance and coordination of social institutions and everyday life. 'What the death-of-fixity arguments miss is the significance of communicative stability. The ability to keep talk fixed, to guarantee its repeatability, is a basic building block of human culture. ... It would be strange indeed if, in making talking things out of new materials, we were somehow to omit this crucial ingredient' (Levy 2001: 37).

Yet in challenging Manovich's dichotomy between documents and digital performances, we need to re-contextualize his definition of what a document is: 'some content stored in a physical form, that is delivered to consumers via physical copies (books, films, audio records) or electronic transmission (television)' (2013: 33). As Levy mentions (and he is not alone), stasis and physical form are not exclusively properties of documents: other things in the world are thus perceived which we would not call documents. A document is a particular kind of *thing*, including, according to some scholars of documentation, software or algorithms (Buckland 1998).[4] What, then, makes the screenshot a document, and what follows from calling it one?

Although scholarship on documents and documentation emphasizes the variability of the term across historical periods and academic disciplines (Francke 2005; Lund 2010), Buckland (2014) identifies three major approaches. The 'material view' – the most traditional – defines documents as 'graphic records, usually of textual form, inscribed or displayed on a flat surface (clay, tablet, paper, microfilm, computer screen) that are material, local, and, generally transportable' (2014: 180). Noteworthy is that this definition provides a generous understanding of materiality: the 'graphic record' does not require a discrete physical form as its vehicle, as shown by the inclusion of the computer screen as possible surface material catalogued alongside clay and paper. The second view he calls 'instrumental': 'on this view almost anything can be made to serve as a document, to signify something, to be held up as constituting evidence of some sort' (2014: 180). This approach is exemplified by the assertion of Suzanne Briet

(2006), in a widely cited 'manifesto' originally published in 1951 on the nature of documentation, that while an antelope in the wild would not be a document, an antelope captured as a specimen, kept in a zoo, turned into an object of study, catalogued, recorded on audio tape, filmed and (after its death) stuffed and exhibited in a museum would be a document – and the films, recordings, scientific articles and so on would be 'secondary' documents.[5] Less exotically, perhaps, a pebble in a river would not be a document, but the same stone exhibited in a museum of minerology would be. Documents are objects – not only graphic records – that have been intentionally made into documents and treated as such through (mainly institutional) framing processes (Buckland 1998). This severing of the category of document from the seemingly inherent qualities of particular artefacts (principally textual forms) effectively prioritizes contextual practices of *documentation* rather than documents as the focus of inquiry since these practices precede and structure the objects they produce. Such a procedure de-essentializes documents as being quasi-natural entities that are 'pre-defined' as cultural 'atoms', as Manovich puts it, based on their character as physical storage. Finally, Buckland argues, a third 'semiotic' approach further broadens the definition to include 'anything that could be *considered as* a document if it is regarded as evidence of something regardless of what its creator (if any) intended (if anything)' (2014: 192).

This last characterization reiterates the epistemic core underpinning these increasingly inclusive definitions: the idea of the document as evidence. Without this core, the definitions threaten to make 'the document' coextensive with virtually all signifying objects, while at the same time de-historicizing its development as an object of knowledge and practice and as a force for knowledge production.[6] Noting that 'the word "document" descends from the Latin root *docer*, to teach or show', Lisa Gitelman specifies this core as follows: 'documents help define and are mutually defined by the know-show function, since documenting is an epistemic practice: the kind of knowing that is all wrapped up with showing, and showing wrapped with knowing' (2014: 1).[7]

The dominance of the know-show function is manifest in the example of the screenshot in *The Guardian* report on Trump's 'covfefe' tweet (shown above in Figure 3.2). The screenshot is not redundant since it acts as evidence of the tweet (it contains it and displays it), something a mere quotation of the words cannot do: its evidentiary purpose is so clearly communicated in its own appearance within the article that it achieves total, replete *self*-evidence and does not require a caption to clarify its status as a representation (or an image) of something else. Indeed, when compared to the text of the report in which it appears, the screenshot constitutes the 'show' binary in a familiar aesthetic opposition between 'showing' and 'telling' as modes of representation: while the verbal text can only recount the tweet within a narrated diegesis, the screenshot replicates it mimetically, bringing it immediately and seemingly straightforwardly into perception, producing a kind of 'direct witnessing' (Chatman 1978: 147) of the tweet as a communicative act.[8]

In part, then, the rhetorical sleekness of the screenshot, its evidentiary potency and self-evidentiary transparency, derive from conventions of the document as a genre. 'Genre', for Gitelman, 'is a mode of recognition instantiated in discourse' (2014: 2): a genre refers not only to a class of texts with some shared formal or referential attributes but to categorizing schemas and practices that form 'specific systems of hypothesis and expectation' (Neale 1990: 49) among addressers and addressees concerning the purpose and character of a particular text (or collection of texts) in relation to others. Hence those making, encountering and interpreting documents treat them generically (and often unreflexively) as units in which instructive knowledge is contained and exhibited, which in turn reaffirms and reproduces the self-evidence of the know-show function such artefacts perform.[9] Manovich's assertion that a document is 'content stored in a physical form' is not *entirely* wrong then. It just takes at face value what needs to be accounted for: the production of the very idea that a particular material or symbolic object can be a stable communicative container, a vehicle for the secure storage and verisimilar display of 'content'. And in the case of the screenshot, this can happen very quickly, with little epistemological fuss about veracity, truth-value and other matters, in a putative age of digital fluidity.

Framing the Screenshot

To achieve this stability as a communicative container, the screenshot employs a crucial graphical convention, one that is all too easily overlooked or mistakenly deemed trivial: a rectangular shape with explicitly marked borders. Screenshots are almost always rectangular, and they invariably appear on a background within rectangular frame lines (either the frame lines associated with an open window in a graphical user interface or graphically reproduced frame lines). For some devices, such as smartphones and tablets, this rectangular shape signifies that the screenshot is coextensive with the whole of the device's screen: the native camera app does not allow one to make a screenshot of only part of the screen.[10] In contrast, screenshots of desktop and laptop computers can cover part as well as all of the screen, though again, rectangular shapes are predominant in the screenshot functions that are native to the main operating systems.

Rectangular frame lines associate the screenshot with a double lineage of framing: the lineage of western pictorial display, especially oil painting and photography; and that of the document as an autonomous material object, predominantly associated with the sheet or leaf of paper mounted on a background. Notwithstanding the important differences and historical variations of these two lineages, they combine to produce powerful ontological and epistemological effects – effects on our implicit understandings of what a screenshot is and how it constructs and displays knowledge.

These effects can be subdivided across two interlinked procedures: the construction of images as representational spaces; and the attribution of object properties. To begin with, the screenshot's frame lines perform the 'basic graphical principle' of '*rationalizing a surface*' (Drucker 2014), 'setting an area or space apart so that it can sustain signification' (71).[11] The frame lines further create compositional connections and distinctions between graphic elements (both textual and pictorial), so that those elements situated within the frame lines are interpreted as significantly similar and continuous with one another, and discontinuous with those outside the lines (Kress and Van Leeuwen 2004: 214–18).

This semiotic effect occurs even when the material of the internal 'document' enclosed within the frame lines and the external 'background' of the entire surface is exactly the same (this applies of course when frame lines are printed on paper surfaces, as well as when they appear on screens). Yet the repercussions of frame lines for the screenshot extend further. For frames are fundamental enabling structures for the performance and intelligibility of *images* as representational constructs.[12] Perhaps the best way to illustrate the power of this operation is through a well-known example: the importance of the frame to the perceptual conversion of two dimensions into three achieved by linear perspective. Alberti's famous treatise *De Pictura* (published in Latin in 1435) describes fairly blithely this extraordinary transformative power of the frame: 'Let me tell you what I do when I am painting. First of all, on the surface on which I am going to paint, I draw a rectangle of whatever size I want, which I regard as an open window through which the subject to be painted is seen' (1991 [1435]: 54).[13]

In this account, the (window) frame precedes the picture, is its condition of intelligibility as a type of representation. It not only marks the boundary between spaces – inside and outside the rectangle – but between the perceptual modes which construct those spaces: between the perception of a singular surface outside the frame and the perception of a distinctive world – in this case, a world in depth – within and 'through' it. A concomitant of this shift in perceptual modes is that, inside the frame lines, the physical surface of the picture – and its existence and effectivity *as* a representation – become transparent or 'disappear'. As we observed at the beginning of this chapter, the screenshot, despite its pervasiveness, is rarely noticed *as* a screenshot, even when it is in front of our eyes: we look 'through' it rather than 'at' it. The theorization and usage of the graphic frame, on so simple a level as a drawn rectangle, already imbricates perceptual-cognitive and semiotic attributes: without this co-activation, the frame does not work as a frame (it remains a rectangle).[14]

This pictorial lineage of the screenshot's frame lines is reinforced by the second procedure underpinning their ontological and epistemological force: the attribution of object status. Frame lines are often graphical echoes of the physical boundaries of material objects that are traditionally used as surfaces for texts and images: sheets of paper and card, writing boards, picture canvases, photographic prints and so on. They also perform in visual form the idea of material enclosure, autonomy and self-sufficiency that is associated with physical objects. In the case of the screenshot, this object status is augmented by its quasi-physical properties as an interactive object that (like some other digital entities) can be moved and re-sized across a computer desktop, and detached, transferred and repositioned across a variety of textual, graphical and image editing programmes on digital devices. The screenshot can be *handled*, responding to our own hand gestures on the mouse, trackpad or touch screen as if it were a spatially distinct and solid artefact, with the frame lines acting as the object's outer edges – the stable horizons, as it were, of the screenshot's opacity as an object located 'on' the screen surface (and blocking our view of the other surfaces or objects it appears to move 'over').[15]

The formal integrity and quasi-solidity of the screenshot as a discrete bordered object is ultimately reinforced by its seeming autonomy as a separate computer file. The similarity with paper documents (and their historical association with bureaucratic practices) is functional as well as metaphorical: the screenshot cannot only be handled and moved between locations of display, it can also be saved and filed away.[16] As Gitelman says of the document more generally, 'Closely related to the know-show function of documents is the work of no show, since sometimes documents are documents merely by dint of their potential to show: they are flagged and filed away for the future, just in case' (2014: 2).

The screenshot's movable, saveable and retrievable attributes as an enframed and self-sufficient object go against the grain, as we have seen, of claims for the primacy of fluidity in digital media. Indeed, they appear to give form to an ideological characteristic of information in the contemporary era: information as what Nunberg calls an 'intentional substance present in the world' (1996: 110), seemingly autonomous of the particular cultural practices and technical infrastructures which produce it. As 'stuff' that is abstract yet real, information is implicitly endowed with an imagined material structure. This structure is amenable to 'morselization': 'Unlike knowledge, which we often regard holistically, information is essentially corpuscular, like sand or succotash. It consists of little atoms of content – propositions, sentences, bits, infons, *morceaux* – each independently detachable, manipulable and tabulable ... we can break off pieces of information and ship them around while at the same time preserving their value' (Nunberg 1996: 117; original italics).

The screenshot, then, is an agent and manifestation of informational morselization: its very existence seems to confirm the qualities ascribed to information according to Nunberg. In fact, Nunberg's critique of the dominant concept of information within digital culture is astonishingly resonant (*avant la lettre*) of the 'atomic' language used by Manovich to describe documents as part of a previous, *pre-digital* media regime. Undeterred by the latter's assertion that documents are giving way to fluid digital performances, the screenshot emerges as a stable symbolic form which routinely incarnates the idea of information as divisible into fixed units.[17]

There is, however, another aspect to the screenshot's performance of informational stability which moves us away from a primarily spatial and semiotic consideration of the screenshot as a document, and towards a temporal and more poetic apprehension of the screenshot as a mode of witnessing and of world disclosure. Documents, says Daniel Levy, are 'talking things. They are bits of the material world – clay, stone, animal skin, plant fiber, sand – that we've imbued with the ability to speak' (2001: 23). This act of ventriloquism is not a one-time affair: documents produce *relative* communicative fixity over time, preventing an utterance or communicative event from changing or vanishing (classically, through writing – though not exclusively, as we know from Briet's antelope), removing it from the flux of immediate time into less turbulent, decelerated temporalities of repetition, history and the archive. The screenshot thus talks to us of something that is constantly altering: the very need for its fixity *implicates* (implicitly connotes) its reference world as one of movement and mutability. In the case of Trump's 'covfefe' tweet, this evidentiary implication of a world in flux was reinforced by the original tweet's *removal* from Trump's Twitter feed several hours after it appeared. The mutability of the reference world is also the satisfyingly ironic implication of the widespread use of screenshots to circumvent the deliberate evanescence of images on applications like Snapchat, where photographs and videos sent using the app are designed to disappear from recipients' screens within ten seconds. We might even say that the screenshot is the avenging angel of traditional photography, undermining Snapchat's radical project of severing photography from its conventional mnemonic and evidentiary uses.[18]

A Remediated Photograph

If the screenshot is a talking thing, in what particular form does it speak? It should be obvious by now that the screenshot is not just any kind of digital document (of which there are indeed many). As its name suggests, the screenshot is a powerful 'remediation' of photography, a reconfiguration of aspects of one medium in another medium (Bolter and Grusin 1999), reproducing particular photographic conventions of nomenclature, production, imagery and viewing.[19] This remediation is not only implied by the allusion to the vernacular photographic term 'snapshot' but is usually amplified by the clicking sound of a mechanical shutter opening and closing as the screenshot is created; the same sound is made when we take a regular digital photograph with smartphones, even though no such shutter mechanism is being operated in *either* case. Hence an experiential equivalence between digital photographs and screenshots is created through the remediated sound of a *pre-digital* optical device: the analogue camera. This equivalence at the moment of production is reinforced at the point of consumption: also by default, my screenshots, like my photographs, are accessed via the same native iPhone app – which just happens to be called 'Photos'. Though technically produced in ways that are very different to digital photographs, screenshots are thus performed as photographs in the way we describe them, are sonically experienced as photographs at the moment we produce them and are classified as photographs by the software that archives them. Screenshots aspire, so to speak, to the photographic condition – linguistically, sensuously and taxonomically.

What does such a photographic condition entail? The first characteristic – connected to the 'know-show' function of documents more generally – is that the screenshot benefits from the evidentiary power and transparency that have long been ascribed to photography. 'Photography furnishes evidence', says Sontag. 'Something we hear about, but doubt, seems proven when we're shown a photograph of it ... A photograph passes for incontrovertible proof that a given thing happened' (1977: 5). As with documents, however, the evidentiary power of photography is a techno-cultural, ideological and institutional construct, as generations of thinkers and researchers on the topic have repeatedly averred.[20] Indeed, the existence of the sub-category called 'documentary photography', defined not only in relation to a tradition of unembellished depiction of social realities directed at social change (Rosler 1989; Price 1997) but also in contrast to other – presumably less 'documentary' – categories of photography (advertising photography, art photography, domestic photography), indicates that the evidentiary power of photography is not evenly distributed across photographic practices, genres or images. Claims as to the quality of verisimilitude in photographs, or their mechanical impersonality and objectivity, or their indexical relation to what they depict (the three 'realisms' of photography as analysed in Slater [1995]: representational, mechanical and ontological), have never been sufficiently robust to resist arguments demonstrating how each of these features can make photographs unreliable as conveyers of knowledge.[21] The converse of this is that, since photographic evidentiary power is discursively constructed rather than technologically inherent, it can also be transferred to technologies and images which do not exactly share photography's technical or semiotic character, but are – like the screenshot – repeatedly treated and connoted as kinds of photographs.

In fact, the screenshot may have supplanted photography as the object of what Finnegan, writing in the rhetorical tradition, has called the 'naturalistic enthymeme'. The rhetorical force of the (pre-digital) photograph depended, according to Finnegan, on viewers applying culturally specific and largely hidden assumptions about its character as a kind of visual argumentation: namely, 'we assume photographs to be "true" or "real" until we are given reason to doubt them' (2001:

135).[22] More recently, Pfister and Woods have proposed a radical inversion of this position, arguing that contemporary digital visual culture is characterized by an '*un*naturalistic enthymeme' – an implicit and widely shared suspicion that photographs are *not* true or real because they are likely to have been digitally manipulated. 'Enhanced skepticism about the representative veracity of images increasingly prevails in public conversation' (2016: 250).

The screenshot, however, seems to undermine this argument. This is not to deny that there have been shifts in public attitudes towards the truth status of photographs, though one should be wary of generalizing across different photographic practices and genres. Rather, it is to make the following observations: that contemporary attitudes to digital images remain diverse and include the *persistence* of the 'naturalistic enthymeme' in many contexts; that – as mentioned in the opening to this chapter – unquestioned assumptions about evidence and realism are applied with extraordinary ease and effectiveness to a type of image that is *digitally native*, the screenshot; and that these assumptions are produced and reinforced through intersecting practices of remediation which still derive their authority from photography (in an age in which photography is supposed by Pfister and Woods to be widely suspect).

Evidentiary power is only one facet of the screenshot's photographic condition. The second is its stillness, and the understanding of that stillness in relation to the spatial, and especially the temporal, movement of the world. 'One might say that there are no still photographs ... by not being in motion, it [the photograph] provides a better basis for communicating some facets of motion, such as a sense of potential energy' (Hariman and Lucaites 2016: 253–4). Photography theory tends to conceptualize the static nature of the photographic image less as a semiotic and technical construction produced by marks on a particular kind of surface (as one might comprehend the still character of a drawing or painting) but as the preservation and appropriation of 'frozen' slices of time. The photograph, says Bazin, 'embalms time, rescuing it simply from its proper corruption' (1980: 242).

The remediation of stillness as a 'photographic' quality of the screenshot is, yet again, evident in discourse.[23] As with photographs, we say that we 'take' screenshots, which in turn 'capture' tweets, Snapchat images, indeed anything we have momentarily made visible on our screens and wish to preserve as a picture before it changes. Remediation delegates to the screenshot tacit beliefs regarding the metaphysical powers and ontological distinctiveness of photographic 'capture': in part, the screenshot seems still *by virtue* of its capacity to snatch and preserve a fleeting instance. What is interesting is that the terminology shows that remediation is not only a semiotic activity but is also a discursive and performative means for delegating perceived states, expectations and practices from one medium to another: just as photography is defined in much photography theory and everyday language as being about time, so this 'being' is imparted to the screenshot.[24]

The importance of 'capturing' or 'taking' becomes even clearer if we recall two alternate names for the screenshot. One is the 'screencap', short for 'screen capture', which also boasts a verb form (hence the activity of 'screencapping').[25] Another, though slightly less common, is the 'screen grab'. Photographic capture here feeds into the aesthetics (and haptics) of fragmentation, appropriation and circulation that Terri Senft (2008) has connected to the webcam, and more recently to the selfie (2015), and which she calls 'the grab': 'social media viewers produce, consume and circulate visual material not by gazing (as one would at a traditional film shown in a cinema), nor by glancing (as one might do with a television turned on in a room), but in a segmented and tactile manner I have come to think of as grabbing' (2015: 9). Just as the screenshot grabs an instant of time, it itself – as noted earlier in the discussion of its object properties – is designed to be grabbed.

From what does the screenshot grab? Here the comparison to photography becomes even more important. A chief characteristic of photographs is that they depict a pre-photographic visual field (including when this field, a conjunction of objects in space and time, is arranged or 'staged' especially in order to be photographed). In regular photography, whether analogue or digital, the pre-photographic visual field is *something other* than the camera or photographic device being used. In contrast, in the case of the screenshot, what is reproduced is the displayed content of the device itself. The photograph 'captures' an image of the world; the screenshot 'captures' an image of the device.[26]

This second clause requires clarification. The screenshot is obviously not an image of the internal computational or physical state of the computer or smartphone from which it is taken. What the screenshot 'grabs' is the visual data displayed on the screen at a particular moment: interface elements, desktop/home-screen background, open tabs, windows and apps (and their content), occasionally the position of a cursor. The screenshot momentarily and deliberately intercepts the ever-changing fluctuations of contemporary screens as 'transit hubs for the images that circulate in our social space' (Casetti 2013: 17). Moreover, the screenshot is an image of the state of the device *as it presents itself for viewing and interaction with a user*, as subject to human intentionality and temporality. It preserves an instant of what we could call the 'screenscape': the dynamic, contingent, humanly oriented 'face' of the device as it appears on the screen.[27] To stretch an analogy somewhat, the screenshot is the selfie of the device.

Yet might not the screenshot also capture an image of the world, or at least of '*a* world', by virtue of and through the device? There are two reasons why I would argue that it can and does: the first has to do with screenshot's remediation of another photographic attribute, namely 'the cut', and how this attribute implicates a world beyond the frame while introducing ethical agency into the screenshot's work as a form of mediation; the second concerns the screenshot's activity as a mode of witnessing a particular kind of content – social media – and the condition of the latter as a *witnessable world*.

The Photographic Cut and the Hardness of the Screenshot

The screenshot, as discussed earlier, remediates the stillness of the photographic image. This remediation is expressed conceptually and performed discursively through the language of 'capture' and of 'the grab'. However, the concept of the 'cut' and 'cutting', along with a semantic clan of associated terms such as cropping, incision, excision (and ultimately, as we shall see, piercing), add important temporal, spatial and existential dimensions to the screenshot's remediation of the photograph.

In classic photography theory, the cut designates a force field of relations between the image and what is outside the frame: the cut/crop separates the photograph from the world and also signifies the existence of an excluded world outside the image, *by* the image. In spatial terms, the cut builds on the performance of representational distinctions produced by frame lines which I discussed earlier; however, the cut also invokes the idea of cutting into, and out of, the flow of time. Stanley Cavell, in *The World Viewed* (1979), argues for the photograph's ontological continuity with the world it shows and with that world's implicit spatio-temporal extension beyond it: 'The camera, being finite, crops a portion from an indefinitely large field ... When a photograph is cropped, the rest of the world is cut out. The implied presence of the rest of the world, and its explicit rejection, are as essential in the experience of a photograph as what it explicitly presents' (1979: 24). Metz also stresses the excluded 'off-frame' (that which is spatially exterior and temporally prior and subsequent to the image) as an absence that is implicitly included within the photographic frame.[28] But for him this operation is violent, and the cut is deadly: 'like death', the photographic snapshot 'is an instantaneous abduction of the object out of the world into another world ... Photography is a cut inside the referent, it cuts off a piece of it, a fragment, a part object, for a long immobile travel of no return' (Metz 1985: 84). Where Cavell presents photography as a form of world disclosure through implication, Metz understands it as a terminal act of seizure ('abduction'), an incision into the spatio-temporal flesh of the world that results in an excision of the referent. The cut creates a stasis defined against, *and wrested from*, plenitude, movement and animation, the ongoing flux of life.[29]

Similar conceptualizations of the photograph as a cut into the spatio-temporal continuum of the world have been taken up more recently by theorists of digital media, and

the discussion has significant implications for our understanding of the screenshot since it echoes and significantly
expands arguments about digital fixity and fluidity raised
earlier. Hoelzl and Marie (2015), for instance, observe that
'it is precisely the cut that constitutes the endlessness beyond
the frame (photographic *off*) as the imaginary counterpart
of the object confined within the frame (photographic *of*). ...
The photograph is a partial object constantly pointing to its
absent other' (2015: 40). They contrast this traditional photographic cut to 'expanded photography', the contemporary
image practices 'that make use of digital montage, collage,
animation and loop as a means of transcending the spatial
and temporal confinement of photography' and that are moti-
vated by a 'desire for endlessness' – for including the endlessness of space and time within the photographic frame (2015:
40). By incorporating both movement and digitally stitched
and looped spaces into the frame, contemporary expanded
photography deprives the photograph of 'its *obscenity*, its
pointing to what is "off scene"' (2015: 40; original italics).

Interestingly, the tone of this analysis implies a critique of
contemporary digital image practices: the authors subsequently declare that 'expanded photography' results from a
'limited understanding of photography' (2015: 40) – in comparison to the world-connoting power of traditional photography. This is a surprising concession in a work which – like
Manovich – embraces the 'death-of-fixity' rhetoric based on
technological shifts away from what they call the 'photographic paradigm': 'The image as the termination (fixation)
of meaning gives way to the image as a network terminal
(screen). It is no longer a stable representation of the world,
but a programmable view of a database that is updated in
real-time' (2015: 3–4).

In short, insist Hoelzl and Marie, 'what was supposed to
be a solid representation of a solid world based on the sound
principle of geometric projection (our operational mode for
centuries), a *hard image* as it were, is revealed to be something totally different, ubiquitous, infinitely adaptable and
adaptive, and something intrinsically merged with software:
a *softimage*' (2015: 132).

One could counter, of course, that the 'hard image' of the
photograph was never all that hard, as the variability of

prints from the same negative demonstrates. Additionally, the photograph as 'hard image' has by no means disappeared within digital culture. In fact, notwithstanding persistent concerns over image manipulability and image transience (again, these have venerable historical precedents in the case of traditional photographs), the treatment and production of hard photographic images (most obviously, printouts) from 'soft' computational performances remain prominent material photographic practices (Hand 2012). Indeed, digital culture itself has produced a new 'hard image' of a quintessential 'softimage': for what is the screenshot if not a definitive *hardening* of that ultimate and primary 'softimage', the still image produced by our digital screens that is (technically) not still at all but an optical illusion created by a continuously moving electronic signal. The very ubiquity and inconspicuousness of the screenshot, this sharp-edged, self-sufficient vehicle of remediated photographic fixity, shows just how much hardness is required of images in 'the society of the screen' (Manovich 2001: 94). As Wendy Chun notes, 'An image does not flash up only once. The pressing questions are, Why and how is it that the ephemeral endures?' (2008: 171).

In contrast to the dichotomy between fixity and flux, hard photographs and soft images, that informs Hoelzl and Marie's discussion of the cut, Kember and Zylinska (2012) propose an attitude they call 'differential cutting', or 'cutting well'. First, they offer an alternative perspective on the flux/fixity dichotomy by defining mediation within philosophical traditions (principally Bergson and Deleuze and, to a degree, Heidegger) that emphasize human–technical relations as vital processes of becoming, bringing-forth and creation: 'mediation is the originary process of media emergence, with media being seen as (ongoing) stabilizations of the media flow ... media need to be perceived as particular enactments of *tekhne*, or as temporary "fixings" of technological and other forms of becoming' (2012: 21). The fixity/fluidity distinction is thus falsely conceptualized if it is isomorphically overlaid onto dichotomies between specific media (photography/ moving images), media technologies (analogue/digital) or media eras (old/new): there is mediation, and there are historically, technically and culturally varying instantiations of it *as* particular media, genres, artefacts. Second, these 'fixings' accompany inevitable irregularities and interruptions in processes of mediation which they conceptualize as 'cutting' or the 'cut'. While cutting is common to *all* mediation practices (since these transform matter and regulate temporality), Kember and Zylinska do suggest that photography provides a particularly clear exemplification of it. The cut is not something, then, that is inherent to a particular medium or socio-historical practice (hence digital 'softimages' will also cut, since they organize matter and time, though in ways that may be different to photographs). More to the point, cutting has both ontological and ethical dimensions because it divides the flux of the world into entities, but 'it is also an act of decision with regard to the boundaries of those entities' (Kember and Zylinska 2012: 82).

> *It is precisely in the gap between photographs as media objects, and photography as a practice of mediation that aims and fails to capture the passage of time, that an ethical imperative presents itself.* This imperative entails a call to make cuts where necessary, while not forgetting the duration of things. Rather than being reduced to a technique for providing false renderings of the world which is ultimately unstable and moving, photography can be said to lend us a helping hand in managing this duration of the world. (Kember and Zylinska 2012: 81; original italics)

This is, of course, a less deterministic understanding of the photographic cut, and of mediation and media more generally, than Hoelzl and Marie's argument for a wholesale technological transformation. Moreover, unlike Metz's association of the photographic cut with death, with violent excision from a temporality perceived only in terms of flux, Kember and Zylinska's more stratified conceptualizations of becoming and time place photographic cutting within processes of life, as an ethical and poetic bringing-forth that enables us to 'manage' the world's duration.

Thinking about the screenshot as a practice of cutting in Kember and Zylinska's sense requires, of course, that we say a little more about the 'world' that such cutting instantiates and implicates, and how the screenshot can help us to 'manage' its duration – not just technically, as in 'organize', but experientially and existentially, as in 'cope with'. We need to understand how the screenshot renders what it depicts and implies as world-like, and in particular how it constructs and reveals that world as witnessable.

Social Media as Witnessable Worlds

The screenshot, we have said, captures an image of the device at a particular moment: not the internal state of the device but the screenscape – its zone of representation and interaction with a human user, human intentionality and temporality. Here we encounter an important caveat. The screenshot *can* be world disclosing in various ways, depending on what is on the screen and what that implies about the existence, perception, intentions and desires of those taking the image. But not every screenshot cuts in quite the same way or discloses the same kind of world. Recall the screenshot of Trump's tweet with which this chapter began. This was a cut not only in the fluctuating screenscape of one person's device but in the temporal flow of Twitter as a system of data streams linking many devices and many people to one another. Hence the screenshot does more than preserve one moment in one particular feed on one device, and more than connote the *private* 'world' of a specific user which can be inferred from the preserved content of their screen at a particular instant.[30] Rather, the screenshot implicates Twitter itself as a shared, populated domain that changes as it extends and connects. By capturing the tweet, the screenshot simultaneously entails the ontological commonality of Twitter as a witnessable world and transforms the tweet into an event in and of that world.

A world can be witnessed if it fits the 'two faces' of the testimonial condition as described by John Durham Peters (2001): the transformation of *experience* into *discourse* for others who were not present either in space or time at an event. Thus it is the possibility of absolute *absence* from an event within a given world which makes witnessing both possible and necessary: 'testimony is another's discourse whose universe of reference diverges from one's own' (2001: 710). However, the spatio-temporal framework of such a reference world must make *impossible* both the literal reversibility of time (as opposed to its representational preservation or reversal through recording technologies, rituals or imagination) and the simultaneous cohabitation of totally identical points in space. If the world we inhabit allows me precisely and coextensively to occupy your exact location in time and space, witnessing becomes redundant. Witnessing, then, makes *non-identity* an ontological constant of the witnessed world, a fundamental structure of being shared and potentially recognized by all who inhabit that world. Such witnessable worlds thereby resemble the temporal and spatial structures of physical existence. It is because of this non-identity that witnessing works as a communicative practice linking, imperfectly and partially, diverse positions within it.

Social networking systems are witnessable worlds because they share these dimensions of communication across nonidentical locations. Take, for instance, the temporal configuration of social media that Carr and Hayes (2015) call 'channel disentrainment'. This refers to the facilitation of asynchronous participation and interaction as and when it is wanted by a particular participant: 'Asynchronous tools do not require simultaneous attention from interaction partners, [and] make temporal commitments discretionary' (2015: 50). However, the crucial point about disentrainment in social media is that it is performed on *persistent channels*. It is not simply that the channel becomes available whenever a user wants it; rather it continues to operate even when an individual user is not online or active. Channel persistence, moreover, is rendered explicit in social media by phatic indicators of presence 'in' the network, constantly making visible our real-time connectivity. We experience the persistence of the channel through markers of online presence *and* absence – you can see when I am online (and hence also offline) on Facebook and when I was 'last seen' *and* currently online on WhatsApp – as well as by chronological metadata: you can see when the various posts were written and when responses were made.[31] Channel persistence is the technical and ontological *ground* of these 'disentrained' absences, presences and synchronizations.

The persistence of social media platforms enables shared temporal experience (including simultaneous existence in time) and the differentiation of temporal domains associated with linear chronology and the division into core tenses of past, present and future. These characteristics parallel – though they do not entirely simulate – temporal structures of the 'offline' world. They also approximate to *one* of the traditional senses of broadcast 'liveness': social media are live in that they endure and change in parallel to the duration and chronology of 'real time'. However, the temporal framework of social media also differs in important respects from the liveness of mass broadcast media like radio and television. It is not associated with the collective experience of centrally produced and authorized texts that virtually everyone in a whole society can and occasionally does receive together (e.g. media events) but a *socially* differentiated experience of common time attuned to the characteristics of one's personal network and its algorithmic manifestations. This 'group liveness' (Couldry 2004: 357) is largely dependent on semi-coordinated individual practices of posting, uploading, forwarding and responding, and on dissemination through technologically mediated interpersonal connections which register both the presence and absence of members on the system. It is these ongoing practices – like Trump's 'covfefe' tweet – that constitute the *events* of social media. And such events can be witnessed by the screenshot because I can be absent from them, because I can *miss them*, because I happen not to be 'on' Twitter or Facebook – or connected to the particular person who posts them – at the moment they occur.

In addition to their temporal configuration as persistent, continuous witnessable worlds, social media provide shared experiential frameworks which act as virtual proxies for the sense of commonality in physical space. Like physical space, we can share the space of social media, but we cannot occupy identical points of that space at the same time. You are a solid object, and I cannot stand precisely where you are standing unless I make you move. Similarly, because of the variance of social networks and the idiosyncrasies of user histories, different users share Facebook as a common framework but cannot be located in its system in exactly the same place. Space is differentiated: there are (ever so many) places on the social network where I will not be as things are posted. Again, this creates the possibility for acts of witnessing, for using objects like the screenshot to recount for others events on social networks at which they were not 'present'.

These temporal and spatial characteristics of social networking systems make them witnessable worlds: ongoing, shared experiential frameworks in which one can be present and absent in time and space. What, then, is the core act of witnessing in social media systems, and why is the screenshot so significant in its understanding? The core act of witnessing in social media systems is registering as 'an event' something that appears on the screen of my device at a particular moment and that can be, needs to be, conveyed to the screens of others. Whether it is something that I post, or something that I see in my feed, its occurrence – the 'when and where' of it as an event in time and space – 'happens' on my screen.

This idea of screen-based eventfulness both draws upon and complicates an important distinction that is much employed in discussions of witnessing as a cultural practice: the distinction between an observation-based witnessing aimed at imparting detailed and accurate accounts to others 'objectively', and a sensibility-based witnessing which emphasizes the emotional and sensory intensity of subjective experience and the ultimate impossibility of rendering it adequately as discourse. Harari (2009), in an important discussion of the emergence of these forms of witnessing in the context of modern warfare, names the first by the conventional expression 'eye-witnessing' (I was there, this is what I saw, now you know), and applies to the second the term 'flesh-witnessing' (I was there, this is what I felt, you can never truly know). While both of these modes of witnessing can be expressed through screenshots, depending on what is on the screen at the time, the screenshots of social media also present us with a third kind of witnessing. This third kind emerged with the rise of modern visual and audiovisual media: in the previous chapter, I called it 'world-witnessing', drawing on Ellis's (2000) analysis of the radically inclusive character of mass media 'witness'. By world-witnessing, I mean that contemporary media do not just witness through conveying 'objective' information or 'subjective' experiences but by routinely presenting actual worlds – or at least worlds *generically interpreted* by viewers as being actual. The screenshot presents the social network as an actual, witnessable world linked existentially and not just informationally to the physical world; the screenshot presents itself as a mimetic trace of that world as it unfolds and takes form as a screenscape. Like the photographic world-witnessing described earlier, the screenshot is 'indifferent' to what appears within its frame, mimicking the 'referential excess' or 'weak intentionality' of the analogue photograph discussed in chapter 1 (recall that it shows not just the text of Trump's 'covfefe' tweet but also the world-implicating, extraneous details of the Twitter interface); at the same time it also presents a particular viewpoint on that world: what appears on my screen – and my Twitter or Facebook feeds – is not absolutely identical to what appears on your screen and in your feeds. Hence the screenshot, as an agent of world-witnessing, is not simply a technique of undifferentiated recording. It is a document that speaks to us of a judgement that one's own screenscape, one's device-specific interaction with social media as a populated world, requires preserving and circulating on others' screens. The screenshot is a procedure for ethical 'differential cutting' – for 'cutting well' (or cutting badly) – into a world of existence, in action and in flux, and that calls for a response.

Speak to Me, My Life

The profound ethical and ontological stakes of both the screenshot as an agent of world disclosure, and social media as actual and witnessable worlds intimately and routinely intertwined with physical existence in space and time, are most acutely foregrounded at moments of extreme crisis or 'limit situations': those potentially life-defining occasions where our circumstances of digital existence are 'principally felt, and our security is shaken' (Lagerkvist 2017: 98) and where the fragility of life is made unbearably tangible.

Figure 3.3 shows the front page of the printed edition of *Yedioth Ahronoth*, one of Israel's most popular daily Hebrew newspapers, from Monday, 9 January 2017. The main story concerns an event which happened the previous day. A Palestinian driver had driven his truck into a group of soldiers

Figure 3.3: Front page of print edition of *Yedioth Ahronoth*, 9.1.2017. (Courtesy of *Yedioth Ahronoth*.)

disembarking from a bus on a popular promenade in Jerusalem, killing four of them. Instead of a standard headline, the entire upper half of the page is dominated by a screenshot from the smartphone of the mother of one of the dead soldiers, Shir Hajaj. The screenshot shows her WhatsApp instant messaging application and – as described by a caption – 'The last message sent by Shir's mother to her daughter'. The lines of text in the screenshot begin with the name of the person with whom contact is being attempted, including the name 'Shiri', her WhatsApp profile image, and the formula – familiar to anyone who uses the app – 'Last seen today at 12.39'.[32] Then there are these two messages which make up the main headline:

Shiri speak to me urgently 13:47
My darling [literally, 'My life'] speak to me 16:46

Both of these lines are followed by two beige ticks.

This screenshot is nothing less than an 'about to die' image (Zelizer 2010), a genre traditionally associated with photography, and which operates through the intense oscillation between the photograph as evidence – the 'as is' – and the photograph as a subjunctive temporal cut – the 'as if' of what *could* have transpired, but which we know did not. It evokes a poetic sensibility of world disclosure that is extraordinarily powerful. The screenshot is poetic in Jakobson's (1960) sense, in that it accentuates the material palpability of signs, but also in Agamben's (1999) sense of poesis as revelation and disclosure, bringing forth into being, unexpectedly (and violently) producing a heightened encounter with the conditions of existence. Part of the poetic power of this screenshot has to do with the tragic irony of a conventional figure of speech no longer being figural. 'My life', a common term of endearment in Hebrew among certain social groups, especially between parents and children, is made shockingly literal, becoming the question: you are my life, but are you alive? However, much of the poetic power has to do with inclusion of the commonplace indicators of social media connectivity reproduced by the screenshot, and their sudden transformation in this moment of interruption. The phrase 'last seen' that we know so well, the deictic term 'today' – rather than the simple calendar date – evoking shared simultaneity in time only to cast it into the existential abyss of the irrecoverable past.[33]

Above all, the presence of the two ✓ and their telltale beige colour, shows that the message has been sent but – since the ticks aren't blue – that it has *not* been read on the app by the intended recipient because the intended is no longer either live or alive, and this letter will never reach its destination.[34] Abducted by the cut of the screenshot from the flux of the WhatsApp interface, these ordinary phatic signs of routine system functioning suddenly become poetically palpable as something far more serious. Extraneous details, accidental marginalia accompanying the main text of the mother's message and the wrongly coloured ✓, are an existential glitch in the otherwise noiseless functioning of the communication channel (Menkman 2011: 12), as well as the site of a wound in the witnessed world, cutting with and through the interface into the social network as a domain of life and death, cutting back into this viewer with the force of a blade. These ticks are the accidental element 'which rises from the scene, shoots out of it like an arrow, and pierces me' (Barthes 2000: 26): they are the *punctum* of the screenshot.[35] In more than one sense, the screenshot is a 'hard' image indeed. It is hard because 'it bruises me, is poignant to me' (Barthes 2000: 27). It is hard because it not only grabs and immobilizes the perpetual flux of 'soft' digital performances, it reveals the termination of connection within and beyond the mediated world it displays; it discloses the 'grand interruption' of death (Lagerkvist and Andersson 2017). It is hard because, by bringing into presence that mediated world, it also reveals whole worlds destroyed: Shir's; and her mother's.[36]

No doubt there are biographical and contextual factors explaining the particular emotional resonance of these ticks and this screenshot for this viewer, this writer: cultural proximity to those killed, a pervasive (though far from unique) Israeli discourse which frames soldiers as 'our children', a resemblance in parental position to Shir's mother (one child, so far, conscripted into the Israeli army) and other connections to this incident. Others less personally invested, or on the other side of the Israeli–Palestinian conflict, may feel differently. However, while the affective intensity of this particular screenshot is not universalizable, the screenshot's ubiquity and functioning as a kind of document, and as a remediated photograph, grant it this world-disclosing – and world-destroying – power. The pervasiveness of digital networks and devices, our habituation to their live permeation and registration of everyday interactions and bodily movements, mean that symbols such as ✓ are no longer simply remediated tokens of message delivery or task accomplishment: they have been delegated with existential powers as *indicators of life*, or to borrow an appropriate medical expression – *vital signs*.

W. J. T. Mitchell uses this term to argue for a consideration of the 'varieties of animation or vitality that are attributed to images … that make pictures into "vital signs," by which I mean not merely signs *for* living things but signs *as* living things' (2005: 6). However, the ticks in this screenshot are vital in two additional and overlapping senses. They are signs *of life itself* as a (fragile, finite) state of being, signifying life through technical infrastructures of connection and cultural conventions of imputed presence. And they are vital as some of our organs are vital: urgent, crucial, *critical* to the being of an organism. Moreover, the ticks stand in for a more general category of vital signs which include all multi-sensory indicators of connectivity conveyed through our devices.[37] We carry these devices around; they are close to our bodies, frequently in direct, sensuously experienced contact with clothing or skin. Imagine Shir's mother not only seeing the ticks but also waiting for her smartphone to vibrate or emit a sound signalling an incoming message from her daughter. Imagine her responding with agitation, hope, frustration, mounting panic, utter despair, to other messages – both from the device itself (reminders, etc.) and from other people (some perhaps sharing her mounting anxiety) that capture her attention instead, as she waits for Shir's reply. Imagine, perhaps, her experiencing 'phantom vibration syndrome' – the commonly felt false sensation of non-existent vibrations – in the increasingly prolonged, and ultimately endless, postponement of the one sign that is truly vital for *her*: the response from Shir.[38] Vital signs routinely perform and reveal the intense embodied *presencing* of others through our digital devices as near-perpetual companions in life, perhaps as never before. Tragically, the vitality of these signs is principally foregrounded, as it is here, when disclosed in a state of critical disconnection. Capturing and witnessing that state, the screenshot shows us that social media and mobile communication technologies have become so intimately intertwined with our existence that they are far more than new infrastructures for circulating messages or managing social relationships. They are domains in which life and death are performed, experienced, witnessed and laid bare. For if, as Mark Deuze (2011) argues, we now live 'in' media and not just with them, then we obviously also die in media. We log in astride of a grave, the screen gleams an instant, then it's night once more.[39]

4
Tag

Naming Bodies and Incarnating Selves in Social Media

You have been tagged.

The first time I received this message, from Facebook – alerting me to the fact that I had been identified by name in an uploaded photograph – it was not, in fact, the first time I had been tagged. I had probably been tagged as a newborn baby in a maternity ward, and I definitely recall being tagged with a plastic bracelet on several other occasions in hospitals. More memorably, I had been tagged during military service: one metal dog tag hung on a chain around my neck, another was inserted into a special opening in my boot – a redundancy designed to offset the difficulties that bodily dismemberment or severe trauma might cause in identifying me following a battle.[1] Surprisingly, however, none of these existentially significant instances of tagging, enforced by powerful social institutions (medical, military) tasked with managing the life, disease and potentially violent disintegration of my body or mind, caused nearly as much anxiety as the message from Facebook. This anxiety had nothing to do with the nature of the uploaded image, an unremarkable old photograph (which I had never seen before) of me, aged fifteen or so, sitting next to a friend at school. What disturbed me was the mere fact of being tagged: by whom, for what purpose and in view of whom was not immediately certain. All I knew was that somewhere out there, in the uncircumscribed vastness of 'the

Web', a photograph was passing before unknown eyes; and it had my name on it.

Being tagged in uploaded photographs has today become a commonplace feature of digital culture, and this intense initial experience of ontological insecurity – the acute perception of exposure and disturbance to my sense of self-possession – has declined, though it has not vanished entirely. Indeed, the aftershocks of being tagged seem to persist as an ongoing yet manageable condition of mild unease. That the condition is both unsettling and manageable emerges from Martin Hand's brief but illuminating discussion of tagging as part of his research on students' photo-sharing practices. Hand observes that while tagging has become ubiquitous, many are highly selective about how – and of whom – they use it, remaining wary of the practice because it gives unauthorized (and not entirely predictable) access to others' profiles and images, and because it is frequently interpreted as an assertion of ownership over an image of someone else (2012: 179).[2]

Admittedly, such wariness seems inconsequential when weighed against the existential gravity of non-digital forms of tagging in securing the integrity of the self at moments of supreme vulnerability. Being tagged in a Facebook photograph occurs in a lighter, more frivolous, sphere of the lifeworld than being issued dog tags to wear in battle. Nevertheless, in this chapter I will embrace Amanda Lagerkvist's contention 'that the mundane and the extraordinary co-found (while often remaining separate fields of experience in secular cultures) the existential terrains of connectivity' (2017: 97). Tagging on social network platforms, I will argue, is deeply indebted to seemingly weightier practices for establishing and maintaining our being in the world, and the experience of being tagged provides a catalyst for reflecting on some of the existential and poetic characteristics of digital media.

Two important practices which precede and inform being tagged will be at the centre of my discussion: the assigning of names to persons and the incarnation of bodies through photographs. These practices – each of which enjoys a venerable and diverse history – qualify as humanly significant: while their particular forms and execution may vary widely between cultures and periods, there appears to be no human society that does not give names to persons or make figural images (or, at the very least, institute a taboo against making such images). Naming and figuration are also strongly connected to the life of the *self*, its presentation and extension in space and time, its entry into symbolic and imaginary psychic registers, and – as my opening comments on medical and military tagging suggest – to 'limit situations' of being such as birth and death. Naming and figuration combine to construct and extend the self through objects which instantiate, replicate and disseminate the individual subject discursively, visually and materially.

Digital tagging, moreover, reinforces and transforms practices of naming and figuration by virtue of an additional property. The digital tag is an operative sign whose use alerts those connected to the tagger and the named person to the latter's appearance in a photograph. This operative dimension not only means that social network systems such as Facebook repeatedly employ the powers of naming and figural incarnation but that these powers are exercised as technological feats of magic – incantatory in the case of names, and sympathetic in the case of images – that animate the digital social network.[3] By alerting our contacts to the fact of our being tagged every time it happens, by making being tagged a recurrent cultural rite of naming and incarnation that invites confirmation and assent (likes, comments), these systems flesh out the exchanges among contacts into the reflex responses of a social 'body' that is more than merely informational. The everyday existential condition that results reveals digital media as sensuously and symbolically entwined worlds, domains of individual and collective life that should not be reduced, in either thought or nomenclature, to abstract schemas of computation, information or networking.

Tagging, in short, is a profoundly poetic procedure for populating and disclosing worlds. It contributes to the creative construction of social media as epistemic and symbolic worlds through the naming and renaming of beings within it; it gives bodies to named entities, revealing them as palpable figures who alter with the passage of time; and it overtly discloses the conditions and consequences of acts of naming and incarnation by continually assembling multiple others in the confirmation of one's existence as a body, all within the larger body that is the social network system.

The Incantation of the Name

With the rise of online social network services (SNS) like Facebook as key mechanisms for storing and displaying photographic images, new techniques for identifying, classifying and circulating images have become important. Tagging is perhaps the most prevalent of these techniques, though it is not restricted to photographs: 'Web-based *tagging systems*', Marlow and colleagues observe, 'allow participants to annotate a particular *resource*, such as a web page, a blog post, an image, a physical location, or just about any imaginable object with a freely chosen set of keywords ("tags")' (Marlow et al. 2006: 31; original italics).[4] While tags can be algorithmically generated, for instance by using the metadata automatically embedded within an image file (e.g. geotags based on the camera's location), they are widely produced by users creating their own verbal associations and annotations, and especially through identifying others in images.

Social network services such as Facebook actively encourage the tagging of people since it helps to maintain and intensify connective activities via their platforms, to amass data about users and their social behaviour and to develop automated face-recognition algorithms (Norval and Prasopoulou 2017).[5] The utility of tagging, both for social network platforms and for users, is not simply due to its role as a 'folksonomy' (Beaudoin 2007) – a bottom-up taxonomic procedure for creating new associations between images and labels – but, in the case of proper-name tags, because tagging actively circulates photographs among the contacts of both those doing the tagging and those being tagged. For example, when you tag someone in an image on Facebook, it is seen by many of your own Facebook 'friends', but it is also likely to be seen by 'friends' of the tagged – irrespective of whether they are also your 'friends'. Following the overall imperative to 'share' in social media (John 2016), this circulatory function is structured asymmetrically in the interests of platform connectivity rather than personal privacy. The default setting on Facebook, for example, is that you can be tagged without giving prior permission, though you can change this setting (and review all tags before they appear), and you can also remove tags of yourself *post facto*; you cannot, however, remove the image from Facebook itself without the cooperation of the person who uploaded it.

While tagging refers to the more or less unconstrained attachment of keywords to a range of digital resources, the experience of *being tagged* in uploaded photographs presents us with a special case: the allocation of one's name to the visual image of an identifiable body.[6] Tagging is therefore a kind of deictic pointing – the name 'Paul Frosh' is given referential specificity by being bound to the body shown in a photograph. Names, however, are not merely linguistic designators.[7] To name is an expression of power. This is most obvious in the *assigning* of names: 'By structuring the perception which social agents have of the social world,' Bourdieu observes, 'the act of naming helps to establish the structure of this world, and does so all the more significantly the more widely it is recognized. i.e. authorized' (1991: 105).[8] The assigning of personal names is usually undertaken by intimates (such as parents), where naming both expresses institutional power as well as interpersonal care, though it can also be undertaken by more formal and less personally invested agents (think, for example, of the renaming of migrants by immigration officials).[9]

Yet names are not *only* instruments of power. Names perform the 'entanglement' of the individual subject within the web of relationships, hierarchies, values and beliefs in a given society (Bodenhorn and von Bruck 2006), simultaneously constructing the sense of singularity attributed to the named individual while establishing their relations to others (naming is thus important in the performance of subjectivation: the social production and reproduction of subjects). Nowhere is the importance of this entanglement clearer than in rituals of name-giving and naming ceremonies, which establish the name's symbolic and socially legitimated attachment to the body of a particular person that in many cultures continues for much of their lives.[10] This entanglement of individual and group is far more significant than the assigning of an informational reference for functional or institutional use: 'The law does not care if a name "fits" the child. But it is a matter of great concern to name-givers across many cultures for whom names both express something of the child and reveal their relations to that child' (Bodenhorn and von Bruck 2006: 3). Moreover, such is their importance in bestowing, displaying and sanctioning a sense of self embedded in a particular social world, that, across cultures, personal names remain objects of profound psychological attachment and identification for the individuals they designate. Lévy-Bruhl's (1926) observation of so-called 'primitive societies' concerning the sacredness of the name as a concrete facet of one's person seems to apply much more broadly: names become almost physical appendages of the self, and to a significant extent 'some people *are* their names' (Bodenhorn and von Bruck 2006: 9; original italics). This deep self-identification with and by virtue of our names becomes even more evident through the horror of losing one's name. To deprive others of their names, or forcibly to rename them, has become a byword for dehumanization; the transatlantic slave trade and the Holocaust are among the most extreme examples.

Names therefore produce, are attached to and secure the rich specificity of individuals in complex social and cultural contexts. However, names are also units of discourse, and they enable and perform the radical *detachment* between sign and object that characterizes language generally and technologically mediated forms – such as writing – par excellence. 'Paul Frosh' can be articulated and circulated by others irrespective of my physical presence (as it is in this sentence and in this volume), as well as without my knowledge, permission or will, or indeed after my death. My name does not just fix me in place as a person; it also circulates *in place of me*, in my absence: where it travels, I need not be (this is, according to Derrida, part of the primary 'violence' of being named: 1976: 112). It refers to me, so to speak, behind my back: *in absentia*. That the authorized use of names is usually subject to regulation by law, norm or custom, and that various practices (for instance, the signature) struggle to restrain this detachment of the name from the guarantee of singular presence (Derrida 1988), only serves to emphasize the potentially radical threat to the integrity of the name-as-self that discourse promotes.

Clearly, being tagged in a photograph means that someone on a social network system like Facebook, whether they are a 'friend' or not, has used my name without my prior permission. Having our names uttered without our permission or our knowledge is an everyday, routine and unremarkable occurrence.[11] But this is not simply *any* use: there are several dimensions to this event which set it apart from ordinary conversational reference to me as a third party, whether in speech, writing or even in posts on social media. It is, first and foremost, the result of a deliberate decision to put my name *into overt circulation*. Tagging on Facebook does not occur simply when one is mentioned in a post written by someone else (though Facebook does encourage one to tag by identifying a mentioned name as someone located on Facebook and offering a tagging option). A key characteristic of tagging is that one cannot be tagged unless one is a registered user of the particular social networking system in which the tagging is performed. You can be *mentioned* on Facebook even if you are not a member of Facebook, but you cannot be *tagged*: Facebook doesn't recognize you as a system element in respect of whom operations such as tagging can be executed.

Thus tagging interpolates me in the Althusserian (1984) sense. It hails me as the subject of an institutional–ideological apparatus, specifically, as a *taggable individual*. Being tagged involves not only being addressed by others but being addressed by them *as subjects of Facebook who are hailing another of their kind*. Note the significance here of being *hailed by name*. This differs from the example given by Althusser, where being hailed is compared to turning when a policeman shouts 'Hey, you there!' in the street (1984: 48). Social networking systems, in contrast, individuate as they tag: I am not hailed by the system as 'You there!', but always as 'Paul Frosh'. In an age of increasing digital surveillance for purposes of profiling and target marketing (Turow 2012), I am more often than not already known by the apparatus hailing me as a named individual.[12] Moreover, through tagging the named person is individuated *even beyond their name*. There are many people called 'John Smith' listed on Facebook, but tagging hails only one of them. It does this not through some mystical access to the singular interior self of this or that particular 'John Smith', but according to the distinctive pattern of social connections by which each individual is distinguishable: one is individuated *through the social* as it is systemically performed, traced, calculated and patterned. While one is therefore tagged through the sociable actions of specific others, the conditions for this action are dependent on the technological infrastructure (and its own commercial commitments to datafication, network effects and economies of scale). It is not only the particular other who hails me through my name: it is the networking system itself as a constitutive social power.

Tagging, moreover, does not only address the person being tagged. As mentioned earlier, the tag is an 'operative' sign: 'the application of a tag to an image sets in motion a causal chain of physical changes to binary data that exerts influence on the structure, processing and display of information' (Rubinstein 2010: 198). Like operative writing (Krämer 2003), it possesses functionality within a technical system independent of its ostensive semantic meaning. In the case of social network sites, the tag is designed to alert others connected to both the tagger and the tagged person to the act of tagging. It executes hailing in a semi-public space, constituting the act of tagging as an observable communicative event in its own right, a performance of what Daniel Dayan calls 'monstration' (2009): the gesture of focusing attention and making visible. As in the Althusserian moment of being hailed in the street, attention is concentrated simultaneously on the one hailed and on the act of hailing itself. And yet, unlike being hailed in the street, the borders of the communicative event of tagging are radically extended in both space and time: a reverberation of responsive clicks translated into emoticons and comments from across the network, and – unless actively removed – available for perusal long after the tag has been created.

Lastly, tagging revitalizes the ancient magical power of *incantation*: the use of words to perform actions at a distance. While the performativity of language in general is often described (occasionally pejoratively) as magical (for instance, Bourdieu 1991), and the use of personal names in charms was a feature of magical practice in antiquity (Versnel 2002), contemporary social tagging seems distinctive.[13] Thanks to the technical apparatus of the digital network, social tagging gives the articulation of the name the ability *to make images of the named appear instantly before others.*

My name, tagged, is thus the given symbol of my very own self that seeks me out as an incantatory power, calling into being images of me without my willing it so. This power hails me, makes me visible and at the same time turns this hailing into a conspicuous staging of communication before numerous others. Part of the initial disturbance of being tagged, I submit, is the sudden sense of one's self being 'handled', not just by others whom one may or may not know, or by discourse as a system of language in social context but by a new techno-cultural apparatus which also assumes the guise of magic. This apparatus handles my name (and grasps my 'handle') through others: real social actors who use the social network service and call out to me as an individual within it in acts of sociability.[14] But it also makes my name utterable according to its own designs; and for these designs my name is an operative signal with no purpose except the apparatus's own functioning.

Social tagging, then, presents a new form of the power to articulate personal names. But this is only one aspect of its significance for our sense of being. It also presents a new kind of ability to give names flesh and to embody selves, repeatedly. In order to explore this further, we need to turn to the second of the two fundamental powers involved in being tagged: the power to incarnate selves through visual images; specifically, photographic images.

Photographic Incarnation

Ricoeur says of the proper name, 'singular denomination consists in making a *permanent* designation correspond to the unrepeatable and indivisible character of an entity, regardless of its occurrences. The same individual is designated by the same name' (1992: 29; original italics). Substitute the word 'visualization' for 'denomination' and 'image' for 'name', and an analogous claim could be made for the photograph's relationship to the individual body. Underpinning this analogy – though also undermining it as we shall see – is the concept of the indexical sign (Peirce 1958), which is a standard and still central claim of photography theory, even in the digital age, and even though indexicality is itself understood to be subject to ideological construction (Slater 1995).[15] Produced through contact with light emanating from the scene located in front of the camera, the photograph does not only represent me symbolically (by convention) or iconically (by resemblance) but indexically: it is a quasi-physical trace of my body's presence.

Indexicality provides a semiotic foundation for photography's epistemological and emotional power as a potential anchor of individual self-identity. In its evidentiary capacity, the photograph serves modern institutional forms of managing mobility and behaviour through the identification (and categorization) of individual bodies (Sekula 1989). Like proper names, photographs are treated as 'rigid designators' (Kripke 1980) of the person, and it is no accident that the photograph and the proper name together became central instruments by which the modern nation-state made individuals legible and recordable through documents such as passports and identity cards (Scott 1998). Additionally, personal photography has long been a primary means for the formation of autobiographical memory and identity – for picturing and narrating the self as a coherent entity along the axis of linear chronology, usually within the context of the family (Chalfen 1987; Bourdieu 1990). In this way, photographs give figural form and putative evidentiary currency to the concept of identity that Ricoeur calls 'idem', or sameness, and which is based on the principle of uninterrupted continuity or permanence in time (Ricoeur 1992: 115–17): the photographed bodies designated as 'me' are held to produce a picture of the self's own distinctive integrity and identity as it unfolds, notwithstanding physical changes to the body, differences in the content and form of the photographs, and fluctuations in the way selfhood is performed (now smiling, now scowling) in front of the camera. Contemporary shifts towards reflexive self-representation (e.g. selfies), photo sharing through social network sites (e.g. Instagram) and conversational 'live' photography (e.g. Snapchat) that have supplemented, though not replaced, the memory functions of personal photography, indicate the continued importance of photography to identity-formation (Van Dijck 2008; Hand 2012; Keightley and Pickering 2014).

However, the indexical singularity of the referent is not to be confused with the purported singularity of the self, and the photograph can also disturb the identification of distinctive self and unique body which it has been utilized to anchor. For the photograph shows my body from external perspectives which I can rarely see with my own eyes. It presents 'me' but mediated through (and from the perspective of) another, whether that other is identified as the photographer, the camera, a hybrid institutional and technological apparatus, or a generalized 'scopic regime' (Jay 1988) that makes me an object of visibility. Hence the unease which we often feel when seeing ourselves in photographs.[16]

The experience of the photographed self as other, as an estranged apparition created by an alienated gaze, is famously described by Barthes as a kind of death through duplication: in the photograph, 'I am neither subject nor object but a subject who feels he is becoming an object: I then experience a micro-version of death (or parenthesis): I am truly becoming a specter' (2000: 14–15). Photography theory frequently emphasizes that the photograph asserts its own presence through the *absence* of the body, describing the image as ghost, death-mask, even corpse.[17] And photography (or at least photography after the daguerreotype) does not simply produce a *single* 'spectre' of the depicted object. It multiplies it, detaching the individual body from its specific spatial and temporal context and replicating it again and again for unfettered circulation in the body's absence. The haunting quality of this replication of the singular is often linked to the theme of the doppelgänger in Freud's analysis of the uncanny (1955). As Gunning notes, photography in the nineteenth century, far from confirming singularity and identity over time, 'seemed to undermine the unique identity of objects and people, endlessly reproducing the appearances of objects, creating a parallel world of phantasmatic doubles alongside the concrete world of the senses verified by positivism' (1995: 64).

Anxieties over body replication and the loss of control over self-representation have thus long been connected to the reproductive and spectacular powers of photography (Frosh 2001). However, for most of photography's history, two distinctive factors constrained these anxieties. The first is that the ability to control the circulation of photographs of oneself was overtly stratified according to political and socio-economic power: privileged classes, social groups and nations exercised far more control over the creation and the circulation of images of themselves when compared to the powerless.[18] Second, until the late twentieth century, the technical, organizational and cultural divisions between domestic photography and mass-media photography (documentary, news and advertising) meant that despite the technology's replicative potential, and barring exceptional circumstances, photographs from the personal realm usually remained there.

With the ubiquity of camera technologies embedded in smartphones and other networked devices, and the importance of social network sites as forums for storing and displaying personal photographs, these constraints have been severely undermined. Thus being tagged in uploaded images magnifies the potential uncanniness of image replication and intensifies the historical anxieties already connected to photography, distributing them liberally across social groups and classes – elites included – in the name of altruistic sociability. This happens in part because digital photographs in general are almost infinitely cheaper, easier and faster to reproduce and distribute than analogue prints – and the Web and social network sites provide new arenas in which they can be publicly viewed. But it also occurs because tagging – an operative procedure, as we have seen – is an agent of replication. Tagging 'circulates' my photograph, placing it within the purview of others, not by passing it from one addressee to another but *by multiplying it as a distinct digital object*. My own name, used as a tag, becomes fastened to singular, indexical images of my body (it is me, and no other, there, then), and at the very same time replicates those images in numerous separate newsfeeds across the social network. Tagging is an act of germination, whereby the incantation of a name generates *multiple* indexical body images, making them materialize, unbidden, in heterogeneous spaces.

Being tagged also carries an imperative weight: the imperative of sociable responsiveness – of liking, sharing and commenting that is integral to interactions on social network services. In this respect, it is similar to the use of the selfie for purely sociable interaction in that it turns the photographed body into a vehicle for *phatic* interaction – communicative behaviour whose main purpose is to make and maintain sociable contact with others (Malinowski 1923; Miller 2008). Selfies, however, are acts of self-representation (see chapter 5); tagging, in contrast, treats *another's* photographed body as the substance for phatic operations, using it to send sociable signals to a relatively amorphous network of acquaintances and associates. Being tagged, one's body image is used to perform sociability on one's behalf, not only *in absentia* but according to the will of others and the logics of the apparatus. If the incantation of one's name on a social network system produces unease over one's self being 'handled' by a new social power, then the instrumental use of one's own body image for unwilled sociability creates even stronger grounds for profound ontological disturbance.

Extending the Self in the Image Stream

There is more, however. The imperative to respond to the act of tagging serves, by default, the purpose of identifying another's body image which is increasingly distributed across numerous *different* photographs. Unless overtly articulated in opposition to a particular tag (as in the query 'Is this really Paul Frosh?') or as a request to 'untag' the image, each 'like' or comment contributed by responders implicitly confirms the original tagging. If names are first attached to bodies in what Kripke (1980) calls an 'initial baptism', then – continuing the religious metaphor – being tagged is a condition of recurrent 'confirmation', where the conjunction of one's personal name with different body images is repeatedly authorized and performed in the presence of a congregation continually reassembled for that very purpose. Tagging thus fleshes out the body image associated with the named self by linking it semi-publicly with numerous photographs, while also using those photographed bodies as a medium – in the elemental sense proposed by John Durham Peters (2015) – for fleshing out the abstract schema of informational and functional connections characterizing social network systems. Tagging contributes to the palpability of social networks as sensuously experienced worlds, as *figural aggregations* of embodied individuals. It is a way of materializing and animating the social network as a connective social *body* that is populated by the continual proliferation, identification and confirmation of the named body images of its own constituent members.[19]

This systemic and social fecundity of tagging – its power of multiplication – raises an important question, as does the disturbance it can provoke. Does being tagged underscore the ideological conjunction of named person and photographed body that produces a unique unity of image and self – a potentially forced unity associated with the traditional power of photography? Or does it contribute to distributed understandings of the self, where the self extends beyond the confines of the body? The former possibility, that tagging reinforces the ideology of singular embodied personhood, seems to be the view of Daniel Rubinstein, for whom the tag 'establishes complete identity between image and text and therefore strips the photograph of its concrete and untranslatable language. The unspoken assumption behind tagging is that images can be exhausted by description' (2010: 199). Yet why isn't the very reverse the case? Why does Rubinstein assume that the attachment of the same word to innumerable *different* instantiations of a photographed body (each one in itself multiplied and dispersed across the network) produces 'complete identity between image and text', rather than a heterogeneity of figures connected to the same name? Why privilege reduction *to* the name rather than propagation and proliferation *from* the name? Why insist that tagging establishes a total identity between names and images rather than an expansive, mutable 'family resemblance' among them?

Underpinning the critique of the tag as a mechanism for suppressing visual difference is, I suspect, an implicit privileging of the power of words over images. It also seems indebted to the assumption that personal photography aggregates multiple photographs into a single embodied image of the self through chronological narrative presentation. This is a strange debt given Rubinstein's own slightly earlier claim (made with Sluis in 2008) that the 'networked image' obeys a database rather than a narrative logic (Manovich 2001): i.e. it does not follow or promote temporal sequences or hierarchies, but can be openly and variably arranged in relation to other database elements. However, even this claim requires revision: as Nadav Hochman (2014) astutely argues, the 'social media image' operates according to a dynamic logic of the transient data *stream* (think of the constantly updating Facebook news feed) rather than the more static, and less insistent, database. The consequences of this shift are compelling: 'As the data stream is a multiplicity of coexisting temporalities or "world-views" from many people and places, the experience of viewing the stream is a continuous *comparison* of temporal representations ... The effect of this comparison is the resynchronization of our own living bodies' temporality with the temporalities of others' (Hochman 2014: 2; original italics).

Social tagging is an important mechanism for inserting images into the data stream or, more precisely, for multiplying images as units of flow (the 'stream' metaphor threatens to constrain thought here: tagging does not work by treating photographs like paper boats launched on a current linking different users; it contributes to the formation of individual, idiosyncratic flows by multiplying the image particles that constitute the stream itself). These images are different from one another and are taken at different times, uploaded at different times and possibly tagged at different times, all by a variety of individuals. Given these attributes, tagging reaffirms the figural *heterogeneity* of the bodies it incarnates and the temporal thickness of their mutual intersections. There is no overriding consecutive accumulation of photographed bodies whereby each image is positioned as a component of a larger, name–body amalgam that unfolds chronologically as a unified container of the self. Rather, the name becomes distributed across diverse photographs as they shift into and out of the data stream; each one, through the tag, is socially confirmed as a unique, partial and ephemeral incarnation.

This distribution of the name across multiple photographic instantiations makes being tagged a means of routinizing and regulating the extended self (Belk 2013), whereby the self is embodied and materially distributed through objects (both digital and non-digital), and can also be recombined into aggregate formations by and with others. More specifically, being tagged fosters the heterogeneity of self-extension over four distinctive frameworks: *visual*, as the named self is extended through diverse photographs of the body; *spatial*, as the locations of these photographs – and access routes to them – are distributed beyond the proximate control of the named individual depicted; *temporal*, as the origin and performance times of images of the self and its identification through tagging are distributed across diverse temporal frameworks; and *social*, as the power to extend the self through photo-tagging is assigned to others on the network (including, through auto-tagging functions, to platform algorithms themselves), constituting 'a joint project resulting in an aggregate self that belongs as much to the others who have helped to form it as it does to oneself' (Belk 2013: 488).[20] Needless to say, this extension also makes being tagged an ongoing site of negotiation and even conflict in each of these frameworks of extension, from struggles at macro institutional levels over the nature of the photograph as a legal possession and the right to privacy (Facebook is currently being sued over the alleged privacy infringements of its 'tag suggestions' technology) to the vulnerability felt at the micro level of the single user suddenly encountering photographs of their bodies in which they have been tagged. Being tagged thus reveals a new condition in which multi-scale fluctuations of dependence between self, other, name and body are continually performed in digital media.

The Materiality of the Image and the Palpability of the Network

Yet how can tagged digital photographs be characterized as materializations or embodiments of the self if, like analogue photographs, they are understood as images of spectral absence and if, *unlike* analogue photographs, they are primarily virtual and informational entities? An initial response is that the characterization of photography as spectral tends to ignore its material dimensions. 'The potential range of material practices and material objects that comprises the category "photographs" is massive', Edwards observes, surveying a large anthropological and historical literature. 'Photographs exist as contact prints, enlargements, postcards, lantern slides, or transparencies, for example. They exist as professional formats, snapshots, art works, or the products of bazaar and street photographers. They are glossy or matte, black and white, colored or hand-tinted' (2012: 225).

This range is no less evident in the digital era than it was in the analogue, although material forms and practices have shifted. First, the continual transfer of digital images across platforms and formats frequently requires forms of adjustment (including compression, enlargement, cropping, taking screenshots of digital photographs) that alter their character – and degrade their quality – through reproduction (pixelation is one example). Consequently, and notwithstanding assertions about the perfect reproducibility of digital files, the particular materialities of digital technologies become manifest through visible changes in digital images themselves: these signs of material alteration coalesce into reflective aesthetic practices and genres such as 'the poor image' (Steyerl 2009) or 'internet ugly' (Douglas 2014). Additionally, new dimensions of materiality are evident in everyday decisions, judgements and practices regarding digital photographs. As Hand reports from his research on photo sharing:

> Not all photos had the same value, and significantly, nor did they all share the same fate. Some photographs were stored without much thought onto CDs, DVDs, memory sticks or external hard drives; others were instantly shared on Facebook or blogs and through email. 'Special' moments were often kept in additional folders and/or printed and displayed in frames, albums or scrapbooks. (Hand 2012: 174)

These differential material practices suggest that digital photographs are involved in processes of 'mattering' (Miller 1998), whereby objects do not just come to be materially perceivable and semantically significant but can become existentially valuable, giving meaning and shape to the lives of individuals and groups.[21]

All in all, then, the material attributes of photography invite us to refine, if not refute, the insistence that digital photographs are primarily software-generated data structures whose defining obedience is to computational procedures (Rubinstein and Sluis 2013). Yet photographs are not, of course, *only* material objects. They 'matter' as *mimetic* arte-facts. Taussig, developing Benjamin's concept of the 'mimetic faculty', emphasizes the duality of such artefacts: 'To get hold of something by means of its likeness. Here is what is crucial in the resurgence of the mimetic faculty, namely the two-layered notion of mimesis that is involved – on the one hand a copying or imitation and on the other, a palpable, sensuous, connection between the very body of the perceiver and the perceived' (1992: 16). Taussig links this twofold 'resurgence' of the mimetic faculty in modernity to the two types of 'primi-tive' sympathetic magic proposed by James Frazer (1950 [1922]) which create attachments and effects between things that resemble each other (the law of similarity) and between those which were once in contact (the law of contagion). Like analogue photographs before them, digital photographs possess mimetic capacities thanks to their powers of produc-ing visual likenesses (similarity), their indexical connection to depicted objects (contagion), and their appeal to viewers who do not just interpret them as images but perceive and encounter them as distinctive objects.

However, in the digital tagging of photographs, the char-acter of this encounter – the 'palpable, sensuous connection between the very body of the perceiver and the perceived' – involves something more. Sympathetic magic is a magic of attachment between objects, whether through likeness or pre-vious contact; digital tagging augments this attachment through novel kinds of technologically enabled embodied relationship. Tagging photographs, as we have seen, turns viewers into responsive congregants potentially engaged in the 'confirmation' of an image generated by an incanted name. Yet these responses – likes, comments, etc. – are more than merely verbal or symbolic performances. As I observe in other chapters (especially chapters 5 and 6), they are embodied sensorimotor actions – pressing, swiping, clicking, typing, etc. – which are performed, semi-habitually, by our gesturing hands and scrolling fingers (under the guidance of our vigilant eyes) in direct contact with touch screens or graphic user interfaces on our digital devices. These 'ways of the hand' (Moores 2014, citing Sudnow 2001) are not simply functional skills; they are principal means through which we orient ourselves to and inhabit an environment. Though tagged photographs are not primarily integrated as discrete objects into the dimensions of physical space, they *are* sensuously apprehended and manipulated through an ensemble of kinaesthetic bodily and technological interactions, further making networked digital media a 'palpable' world in which we are somatically enmeshed. If, for Christian Metz, the photograph 'cuts' the referent out of its world, then the tag re-attaches – through reference, symbol, figure and matter. To resurrect a term from film theory, tagging performs an act of *suture*: it repeatedly stitches together incanted names, incarnated images, extended selves and the bodies of viewers, turning digital networks and interfaces into entwined fabrics of existence.

Tagged Being

Being tagged, then, is not only a habitual everyday experience produced by social networking services with implications for privacy, social interaction and the political economy of digital platforms. Being tagged, hyperbolic as the claim may seem, reveals itself as an existentially significant technique for mediating the attachments of the body and the self in the face of possible unravelling and disintegration. Like the tagging technologies employed in the past and to this day in medical and military contexts, it is deeply linked to naming and figuration – powers of specification, confirmation, identification and multiplication that accompany and shape selves from birth to death, and beyond. And like these other forms of tagging, it finds expression in a shape appropriate to the material substrate of the world in which it operates.

Three things, however, make being tagged in social networking services distinctive, and perhaps even more radically indebted to naming and figuration as magical arts: first, its increasing incidence and performance among ordinary individuals in everyday circumstances as opposed to the restricted institutional contexts and extreme situations of physical tagging; second, its shift from the naming of physical bodies to the naming of mediated bodies in photographs; finally, its technologically enabled germinative capacity that proliferates vehicles of the embodied self at the same time as it multiplies attachments to them.

These three features are intertwined, their connections assuming the familiar profile of a feedback loop. Tagging has become an everyday practice as increasingly individuals live their lives in and through digital media – and hence in and through forces of replication, reconfiguration and dissemination (of discourse and images, but also of quantified data) which are fundamental to digital communication. In these conditions, self-extension shifts into high gear, raising the possibility not simply of heterogeneity and difference but also of disintegration, of an entity so over-extended, so protean, that it loses the minimal degrees of attachment needed for being experienced or recognized as a self: the advent of 'identity theft' in the digital era is one obvious expression of this vulnerability. Tagging, then, goes against the grain of the more radical accounts of distributed or 'network' models of selfhood (Banks 2017) which decentre the body as the privileged 'host' of the self.[22] Though tagging promotes a heterogeneity of body images, it returns constantly to the incarnation of the name, and the naming of the body, as central instruments in the perpetual maintenance of selfhood, a centrality it repeatedly asks its users to affirm, confirm and propagate through their own bodily responses every time they tag another or react to a tag. While tagging manages self-extension beyond the body, it is perhaps more the case that it actively extends names and bodies *into* the network, wrapping symbolic and figural flesh onto informational bones. It promotes a deeply sensuous but *parsimonious* germination of the self, channelling existential forces of mimesis, of symbolization and figuration, which were established long before the contemporary era, and reconfiguring them to shape identity and sociality in digital times. These existential forces in turn flesh out the computational and operational systems that enable tagging to be performed, animating them as multidimensional spheres of living, as palpably inhabited worlds where embodied selves are continually affirmed and confirmed.

Tagging thus enables, and constrains, the possibilities for heterogeneously extended selves in contexts that continually threaten self-dissolution, and to which tagging – as an image multiplier – itself contributes. Summoning the powers of the name and the body, hailing and individuating, incanting and incarnating, germinating and attaching, tagging invites us to rethink what constitute the 'limit situations' of our digital lives, and the remarkable techniques by which we become habituated to their systemic recurrence: how, to return to Lagerkvist, we can comprehend the mutual immanence of the extraordinary and the mundane. For while being tagged was previously a distinctive event within our existence, it is rapidly becoming a perpetual condition of our existence. We do not live in the age of being tagged; we live in the world of tagged being.

5
Selfie

The Digital Image as Gesture and Performance

Never again. On 20 January 2017, Shahak Shapira, an Israeli artist based in Berlin, launched a website in English and German called Yolocaust. An exercise in online shaming, the site was replaced a week later with a (similarly bilingual) letter that began thus:

> Dear internet,
> last week I launched a project called YOLOCAUST that explored our commemorative culture by combining selfies from the Holocaust Memorial in Berlin with footage from Nazi extermination camps. The selfies were found on Facebook, Instagram, Tinder and Grindr. Comments, hashtags and 'Likes' that were posted with the selfies are also included. (https://yolocaust.de)

The shaming exercise was apparently successful. Not only was it visited, according to Shapira, by more than 2.5 million people, and covered fairly extensively by mainstream news outlets, it also reached the twelve individuals whose 'selfies' had been exposed, leading to the extraction of confessions, expressions of contrition and regret, and apologies, along with promises to remove the offending images from their social media accounts. The message of penitence from the most egregious of the twelve offenders, who had captioned an image of himself joyfully leaping at the memorial site with the words 'Jumping on dead Jews @ Holocaust Memorial' is reproduced on the website in full. The work of shaming completed ('The Yolocaust is Over' declared an article in Israel's *Ha'aretz* newspaper's English edition: Kaplan Sommer, 21.1.2017), the images were removed from the Yolocaust site as a gesture of both generous absolution to the offenders and as a continued statement of opposition to a culture of commemoration apparently gone awry through the creation and dissemination of inappropriate images. Unfortunately, the internet is not as forgiving or as forgetful as Shapira. A postscript to the message sent by the main 'offender' adds: 'Oh, and if you could explain to BBC, Haaretz and aaaaallll the other blogs, news stations etc. etc. that I fucked up, that'd be great. ☺'. Yet the images are still available if you search for them.[1]

Yolocaust is a shockingly poetic project, by which I mean that it deliberately discloses and interposes worlds *in order* to shock. On the original site, the shock was created by using the movement of the cursor to shift between two images: the original social media 'selfie' of someone jumping, leaning, posing, smiling or otherwise appearing to have fun at the Holocaust Memorial site that Shapira had found on social media platforms, and a compositionally or thematically telling documentary photograph from the Holocaust – piles of corpses, mass graves, barracks full of emaciated survivors – which would appear as a background to the main figure, replacing the rows of giant stone slabs of the memorial as the cursor moved over the 'selfie'.[2] Hence 'Jumping on dead Jews' becomes almost literally that, as the monumental yet abstract structures of the actual site among which the jumper jumps in the original photograph are replaced by piles of dead Jews. Such substitutions give body to those commemorated by the memorial site, exchanging the material weight and heft of the stones as structures of memory and mourning with the flesh and bones, bodies and faces of photographed victims realized in a weightless, virtual medium: the digital screen. It also uses the resurrection and re-animation of the Holocaust images to destroy – or at least disrupt and erase – the social media images, a masterly act of iconoclastic replacement. Even the name 'Yolocaust' is a poetic performance, drawing attention to the palpability of the sign and the worlds it discloses through shocking conjunction. This conjunction works by combining the internet acronym 'Yolo' (which stands for 'You only live once'), whose usage is associated with acts of wacky enthusiasm, sociable idiocy and even recklessness, with the moral and historical gravity of the Holocaust and the carefully guarded solemnity that attends Holocaust memorials, museums and films. By making this juxtaposition, 'Yolocaust' reveals the true poetic gravity of 'you only live once', not as a conventional intensifier and justification for flighty and mildly risky social behaviour or extreme sports, but as a profound statement of existential limits and their appalling, brutal realization in acts of genocide. Yes, the dead Jews only lived once.

Yolocaust puts selfies in the dock and finds them guilty. Yet when we look more closely, two further characteristics of this project warrant comment. First, many of the images designated inappropriate were not actually selfies but were clearly taken by others. So 'selfies' is used as a term of moral opprobrium for all of the offending photographs. Furthermore, the non-selfies mainly depicted people doing seemingly inappropriate things – jumping, leaning, dancing – that were performed for the camera but were not acts of photography per se. The selfies, in contrast, showed little more than people posing for the camera together in a selfie: the very photographic act of taking a selfie was judged, in and of itself, to be a sufficient infringement of the sanctity of the site to deserve censure and exposure. Finally, the poetic act of conjoining and disclosing disparate worlds on the original Yolocaust site was performed through an embodied physical gesture, moving the cursor over the image to make it change.

Why are these attributes of Yolocaust significant? Because, as I will go on to argue, selfies have for good reason become connected to the performance of interactions designed to enhance sociability, and this is what in part gives them the air of de-sacralizing levity (though in fact sociability is an extremely serious matter, as we shall see at the end of the chapter). And the selfie performs sociability as a particular combination of physical actions. It is produced through bodily motions that enmesh it within an entire economy of embodied relations with contemporary media technologies, not only the mobility of the whole body as an information point, moving in surveilled and mapped physical space, but the habitual and nimble gestural movements of hands, fingers and eyes by which we navigate the interfaces of our digital devices. To understand how selfies are constituted within these embodied relations, and what the significance of their performance of sociability might be for our lives 'in' media, we need to take a closer look at the selfie as a photographic practice.

The Selfie as a Theoretical Object

Whatever else it might be, a selfie is usually a photograph, a pictorial image produced by a camera. This observation informs popular understandings of the selfie as a cultural category: 'A photograph that one has taken of oneself' (Oxford Dictionaries Word of the Year 2013: http://blog.oxforddictionaries.com/press-releases/oxford-dictionaries-word-of-the-year-2013/). Yet, despite the selfie's obvious photographic provenance, little scholarly research has drawn systematically on the intellectual resource most closely associated with the aesthetics of its host medium: photography theory.

Perhaps this is unsurprising. After all, the selfie is the progeny of digital networks. Its distinctiveness from older forms of self-depiction seems to derive from *non-representational* changes: innovations in distribution, storage and metadata that are not directly concerned with the production or aesthetic design of images. As the 2013 *Oxford Dictionaries* definition continues, the selfie is typically 'taken with a smartphone or webcam and uploaded to a social media website'. It is these innovations that are thought to distinguish the selfie, as Tifentale declares: 'Instantaneous distribution of an image via Instagram and similar social networks is what makes the phenomenon of the selfie significantly different from its earlier photographic precursors' (2014: 11).

Recent research on transformations in personal photography *in general* has been largely provoked by these non-representational developments (Gómez Cruz and Meyer 2012; Lister 2013, 2016; Gómez Cruz and Thornham 2015). And where aesthetic developments are foregrounded, they too appear to be driven by device functions not primarily concerned with image production or design. Hence the immediacy, ephemerality and incessant performativity of contemporary everyday photographs are primarily explained with reference to the combined ubiquity, mobility and connectivity of smartphone devices (Murray 2008; Van Dijck 2008; Van House 2011).

Once non-representational technological changes are made analytically pre-eminent, what role remains for an aesthetically oriented and medium-specific intellectual tradition like photography theory? In fact, the recent prominence of non-representational practices echoes a recurrent tension in photography theory that has long divided scholars, between an 'ontological' commitment to the (mainly semiotic) 'essence' of the medium, which tends to privilege the discrete photographic image as an object of aesthetic analysis, and historical conceptualizations of photography as a fluctuating constellation of different devices, material cultural practices and representational forms (Batchen 1997). This tension between aesthetic object and socio-technical practice is even evident in two of the adjective–noun compounds recently coined in contemporary photography theory itself: the networked image (Rubinstein and Sluis 2008) and algorithmic photography (Uricchio 2011).

The selfie affords a productive vantage point on this tension. On the one hand, it appears to constitute an aesthetic and representational innovation in everyday photography, potentially offering a degree of resistance to non-representational emphases (similar claims could be made for popular applications like Instagram and Hipstamatic). Moreover, as a photographic genre, it invites attention to the pictorial conventions underpinning generic identity: after all, one cannot recognize an image *as* a selfie without looking at what it represents.[3] Yet as with genre more broadly, representational criteria alone are insufficient (Mittell 2001). Understanding that a particular image is a selfie (rather than just a photograph, say, of a face) requires viewers to make inferences about the non-depictive techno-cultural conditions in which the image was created. It requires, among other things, that these viewers have been adequately socialized through having seen, taken or heard tell of selfies.

The selfie thus foregrounds representational change while putting the very term 'representation' in quotation marks as a contingent variable. This makes it a timely 'theoretical object' (Verhoeff 2009), a concrete phenomenon that is good to think with about contemporary photography and digital representation in general. The selfie prompts us to ask how it can be explained using concepts fashioned to illuminate the traditional aesthetics of photography, and how it might reconfigure those concepts to forge new directions for theorizing both photography and digital culture.

In what follows, then, I propose to animate the conceptual fecundity of the selfie by engineering some brief encounters with a number of terms in photography theory: *indexicality*; *composition*; and *reflection*. Together, these encounters will weave an argument already suggested in the discussion of Yolocaust. This argument – which is perhaps surprising, given its emergence from a visually oriented body of thought – proposes that the selfie is a 'gestural image', and that we should not understand its aesthetics purely in visual terms. Rather, the selfie inscribes the visible body into mediated, phatic interaction. Selfies conspicuously integrate still images into a techno-cultural circuit of embodied social connectivity, which I will call 'kinaesthetic sociability': this circuit links the bodies of users, their macro-spatial mobility through actual places, and the micro-bodily hand-and-eye movements employed to operate digital interfaces.

Indexicality: Trace and Deixis

Indexicality is the conceptual bedrock of traditional photography theory, as noted in the previous chapter. Based on Peirce's notion of the index as a sign that stands for its object through physical or causal connection, it designates the sense that photography is distinctive because what it depicts had, necessarily, to be located in front of the camera at the moment the photograph was taken. The photograph is described as an 'emanation' (Barthes 2000) of the referent, or a 'quotation' (Sontag 1977) from reality, since it is produced by light-sensitive material reacting to the light reflected from the spatio-temporal field exposed before the lens.

The supposed loss of photographic indexicality in a putative 'post-photographic' era of digital image simulation was loudly debated in the 1990s (Mitchell 1992; Robins 1996). Recent revisions question the simple analogue–digital binary, with claims that the substitution of photoelectronic and computational processes for photochemical and dark-room ones need not have eroded – though it may subtly have altered – photography's indexical quality (Soderman 2007).

Given this intellectual commotion, what can we learn from the selfie about photographic indexicality that has not already been said? Two things: first, that the selfie as an index is less the trace of a reality imprinted on the photograph than of an action enacted by a photographer; second, that the selfie exploits indexicality in favour of connective performance rather than semantic reference. These two things are intertwined, and they redefine photography in relation to distinct dimensions of indexicality that are often fused, which Doane (2007) calls 'index as trace' and 'index as deixis'. The former dominates traditional photography theory: the photograph is a material trace or imprint created by 'contact' with its object; it foregrounds the pastness of its original event. Yet Doane claims that 'index as deixis' is equally important. Deixis is the pointing finger directing attention onto an object: as Barthes says, 'the Photograph is never anything but an antiphon of "Look", "See", "Here it is"' (2000: 5). The connection to deictic language – 'this', 'that', 'here', 'now', and the personal pronouns 'I', 'you', etc. – is especially revealing. These terms acquire sense in reference to a present context of discourse which constantly changes: where 'here' is alters from one execution to another. The index as deixis operates in the temporality of the mutable present, rather than of the salvaged past.

Like much everyday digital photography, the selfie tips the balance between these forms of indexicality. The advent of photography as a 'live' medium, utilizing digital networks to connect interlocutors in space rather than in time, brings it closer to a conversational practice that draws images and their referents into the immediate moment of discursive interaction (which applications like WhatsApp and especially Snapchat both promote and exploit). It also turns the temporal oscillation of the photograph as trace – between the 'now' of viewing and the 'then' of the depicted scene – into a spatial oscillation between a proximal 'here' and a distal 'there'. The selfie is a form of relational positioning between the bodies of viewed and viewers in a culture of individualized movement, where one's 'here' and another's 'there' are mutually emplaced but perpetually shifting (García-Montes, Caballero-Munoz and Perez-Alvarez 2006). It continually remoulds an elastic, mediated spatial envelope for corporeal sociability.

But the selfie does more than this: it deploys both the index as trace and as deixis to foreground the relationship between the image and its producer, since its producer and referent are identical. It says not only 'see this, here, now', but 'see me showing you me'. It points to the performance of a communicative action rather than to an object, and it is a trace of that performance.

This performance is embodied. As Jerry Saltz (2014) observes: 'selfies are nearly always taken from within an arm's length of the subject. For this reason the cropping and composition of selfies are very different from those of all preceding self-portraiture. There is the near-constant visual presence of one of the photographer's arms, typically the one holding the camera.' These arms assume the role of the pointing finger: they implicitly designate the absent hand(s) and its held device as the site of pictorial production.

The selfie, then, is the culmination and also the incarnation of a *gesture* of mediation. It is an observable 'sensory inscription' (Farman 2012) of the body in and through technological means. The body is inscribed in part into an already existing order of interpersonal signification – gestures have meanings in face-to-face interactions – but it is also inscribed as a figure for mediation itself: it is simultaneously *mediating* (the outstretched arm executes the taking of the selfie) and *mediated* (the outstretched arm becomes a legible and iterable sign within selfies – of, among other things, the 'selfieness' of the image). In order to understand more about how the selfie communicates this sensory inscription, another term needs to be brought into play.

Composition and Com-position

Visual composition usually refers to the arrangement of elements within the space of a picture and their orientation to the position of the viewer (Kress and van Leeuwen 2004: 181). One key feature of conventional photographic composition that remained relatively unchanged across the analogue–digital divide is the spatial separation between photographed objects and the photographer's body. The depicted scene is produced from a position *behind* the camera, a position almost always occupied by the photographer and subsequently adopted by the viewer. Although there is a venerable history of photographic self-portraiture (Lingwood 1986), literally 'putting oneself in the picture' (Spence 1986) relies on technological 'work-arounds' like timers or remote control devices, the use of reflective surfaces or a human proxy. Taking a conventional photograph means, as a rule, not being in it.

This 'backstage' of image production generates a linear gaze through the apparatus of the camera towards those being photographed. It also encourages a directorial performance of spatial evacuation: photographers shooing unwanted objects off-frame as potential interferences. Traditional camera design and use – of both analogue and digital devices – means that the camera is not just a machine for making pictures: it is a barrier between visible photographed spaces and undepicted locations of photographing and viewing. Composition, the integration of elements together 'into a meaningful whole' (Kress and van Leeuwen 2004: 181), is thus based on a foundational *cleavage* between seeing and being seen, directing others and being (com)posed. Such compositional separation tends to underpin asymmetrical power relations between viewer and viewed (Beloff 1983 and Frosh 2001, but see Rose 2010 on the complexity of these relations), drawing its scripts from broader disciplinary 'scopic' regimes shaping social relations (Jay 1988; Tagg 1988; Sekula 1989).[4]

Three features of smartphone design enable the selfie to challenge this spatio-representational segregation: they can be held and operated relatively easily by one hand; they display an image of the pre-photographic scene large enough to be viewed at arm's length; and they include front- and back-facing cameras. The first consequence of this challenge is that the photographing self is easily integrated into the depiction. The space of photographic production/enunciation is effortlessly unified with the space of the picture itself, and *not* photographing oneself as part of an event or scene becomes an aesthetic, social, political and moral choice (Andén-Papadopoulos 2014; Becker 2013) rather than a *sine qua non* of the photographic act. Group selfies are particularly striking examples of this transformation, where the photographer is usually at the forefront of a mass of faces and bodies, visibly participating in the process of composing the image as it is taken (a famous example is Ellen DeGeneres's 'Oscar selfie' from 2014).[5]

Additionally, the unified space of production and depiction becomes a field of embodied inhabitation. The camera becomes quite literally *incorporated*, part of a hand–camera assemblage, whose possibilities and limitations are mutually determined by technical photographic parameters (available light, field of view, angle, etc.) and the physical potential and constraints of the human body. The most important embodied constellation consists of: (1) moving one's outstretched arm holding the smartphone or tablet at a calculated angle before the face or body; (2) the sensorimotor co-adjustment of those body parts which are to be photographed (frequently the face and neck); and (3) the visual and spatial coordination of these two in composing the image to be taken via the device's screen. The very term 'composition' is reconstituted through this constellation. To 'com-pose' acquires a hyphen: no longer does it refer to the arrangement of elements in a representation whose origin it hides, but to the act of *posing together*, mutually emplacing the photographing body and the depicted figure, echoing the idea of the 'com/posite' – to be situated with, alongside, in company with – outlined in chapter 2. The dominant figuration of the body shifts from the still, invisibly directed pose of others in traditional everyday photography to the dynamic, visible, self-animated gestural action of limbs and faces in selfies.

That the body is both the platform and the limitation of this new kind of self-depiction is evident from the deliberately extreme examples of photographic pyrotechnics assembled by projects like the 'Selfie Olympics' (which also include reflexive images of people taking a selfie).[6] These 'athletic' examples remind us that taking selfies is not natural to the body: it is an acquired skill and requires practice, the attainment of limbic and manual dexterity (activating the right button/icon to take the picture while often holding the device at extreme angles to maximize headspace), and the calibration of the body to technical affordances and desirable representational outcomes. The selfie is both expressive and disciplinary: this is the duality of most kinds of sensory inscription. Just as the moving body is the platform for the smartphone, so the device is the picturing agency that motivates, justifies and disciplines the body's performance. These two faces of embodied technicity are inherent, and frequently explicit, in ordinary (i.e. non-athletic) selfies, combined – as I have mentioned – in the visible arm gesture or in its implied presence.

Yet that gesture not only 'composes' technicity and embodiment in the moment of image production: it also constitutes a deictic movement of the body that draws attention to the immediate context of image viewing, and to the activity of a *viewer*. The selfie, as Zhao and Zappavinga (2018) point out, enacts intersubjective relations between photographer and viewer. The suggestive power and versatility of this deictic movement of the photographing gesture towards the viewer is vividly demonstrated in 'Around the World in 360° – 3 Year Epic Selfie' by Alex Chacon, a 3-minute video stitching together the photographer's video selfies taken as he traversed '36 countries in 600 days using 5 motorcycles' (http://www. youtube.com/user/chaiku232). A key feature of the film is the use of the outstretched arm, and especially the prosthetic limb of a stick camera mount, to create a visual–corporeal lexicon of direct kinetic relations between Alex's body and the viewer: walking alongside, hand on shoulder, moving counterbalance, circular dance, to name only a few. These (and other) gestures invite the viewer to infer and adopt a physical position in relation to the photographer. Manifested in the suggestion of bodily contact, they propose a particular kind of sociable interaction: the act of accompanying and the subject-position of companionship.

Figure 5.1: Murad Osmann, '#follow me to Times Square'.
(Courtesy of Murad Osmann.)

Murad Osmann's Instagram series 'Follow Me' (Figure
5.1) provides a converse yet parallel example of how a deictic
gesture can generate kinetic relations between viewer and
viewed (http://instagram.com/muradosmann).

In this project, every image is based on an identical formal
template, the intrusion of the photographer's arm as he (and
by implication, the viewer) is led by the hand by a young
woman, always seen from the back in a different location.
Unlike the broad lexicon of diectic and kinetic visual figures
in Chacon's film, Osmann's series demonstrates the power
of a single gesture of implied physical movement and sociable companionship sustained across multiple iterations. As
with Chacon's project, however, the outstretched arm (or

prosthetic stick mount) doesn't just show the photographer depicting himself. It also draws the viewer in as a gesture of inclusion, inviting you to look, be-with and act.[7]

Reflection and Reflexivity

Oliver Wendell Holmes famously observed that photography is a 'mirror with a memory' (1980 [1859]: 74). This may have been metaphorically apposite to photography in general, but as we have seen it was not literally applicable to most cameras. The popular iconography of the selfie literalizes Holmes's trope: rather than forming a barrier between photographer and viewed, the smartphone camera produces a reflective image for beholding oneself, apparently resembling nothing so much as a pocket make-up mirror.

It is all too easy, then, to conceptualize the selfie's gestural invitation to look through a voyeurism–narcissism model of mediated performance (Abercrombie and Longhurst 1998): as others have noted, the accusation of narcissism is one of the most common themes in public discourse about selfies.[8] While there is an enticing self-evidence to the accusation, it is often unnecessarily reductive: with important exceptions like Mendelson and Papacharissi's (2010) analysis of Face-book 'self-portraits', it tends to block further thought – regarding both selfies and narcissism – and frequently ignores its own gendered assumptions linking young women with fickle self-obsession.

Other interpretative extensions of the visual trope 'reflection' provide food for thought. The first, and most obvious, is that the selfie is a reflexive image. Reflexive texts are usually understood to direct attention to the conditions and context of their own presence, activity or efficacy: they are expressly self-referential (Stam 1992). With regard to the selfie, this observation itself has two applications. One is that the selfie is self-referential *as an image*. It makes visible its own construction as an act and a product of mediation. Losh (2014) calls this 'transparent mediation': parallel terms would include 'hypermediacy' (Bolter and Grusin 1999). Not every selfie is reflexive as an image to the same degree, though the deictic gesture manifested by the outstretched arm provides a common baseline. At the same time, the popular sub-genre employing mirrors and screens – prominent in the 'Selfie Olympics' – suggests the achievement of playful, generic self-consciousness.

Second, as vehicles of self-presentation in digital culture (Thumin 2012; Rettberg 2014), selfies are a genre of *personal* reflexivity. This is true of all selfies by definition: they show a self, enacting itself. Selfies extend the photographic grammar of everyday communication: they are an instantly recognizable visual correlate to the linguistic self-enactment routinely performed by reflexive verbs. Indeed, their ability to combine transparent mediation and personal reflexivity reveals the very instability of the term 'self' as a deictic shifter, fluctuating between the self as an image and as a body, as a constructed effect of representation and as an object and agent of representation.

Tied to techno-cultural conditions of synchronous connectivity with others, the self-enactment elicited and shown by selfies is simultaneously mediated, gestural and sociable. These three features combine in the invitation to the viewer implicitly made by the outstretched arm. They also converge through a further twist in the trope of 'reflection': the centrality of imitation and mirroring to human cognition, emotion and communication. Psychological work on imaginative projection and mental simulation (Currie and Ravenscroft 2002), neurological research on mirror neurons (Gallese 2005) and aesthetic scholarship on make-believe as the basis for mimesis (Walton 1990), despite important differences between them, connect human responses to representations with sensory and mental processes that imitate depicted states – especially, though not exclusively, the motor activity of the body. Put very crudely, responses to representations are built upon embodied simulation of what is shown: neurological and/or unconscious mental processes that perform bodily and sensory imitations 'offline'.

These ideas, though contested within their various fields, are extremely fertile for thinking about the selfie as a gestural invitation to distant others. They enable us to conceptualize the selfie as a *sensorimotor* (rather than merely sensory) inscription of a bodily gesture into a still image that summons us to do more than look. The selfie invites viewers, in turn, to make conspicuously communicative, gestural responses. Sometimes viewers respond to selfies in kind, taking reactive selfies that themselves summon further response: here, sensorimotor mirroring is almost literally achieved. In most cases, however, the action is displaced into other physical movements that execute operations via the social media platforms on which the selfies are seen: 'like', 'retweet', 'comment'. Like the selfie, such operations are also performed through sensorimotor actions – actions that are semi-conscious yet habitual to the degree that we might even call them 'reflex': fingers swiping and tapping apps on touch screens, or scrolling, moving and clicking a mouse attached to a desktop computer. In Osmann's 'Follow Me' series, for example, viewers cannot literally follow the woman's outstretched arm into the image, but the kinetic power of the gesture redirects this sensorimotor potential to a different operation of the hand, and a substitute performance of 'Follow' (circled on Figure 5.2).

As a gestural image, then, the selfie inscribes one's own body into new forms of mediated, expressive sociability with distant others: these are incarnated in a *gestural economy of*

Figure 5.2: Screenshot with Murad Osmann, '#followmeto the Camp Nou Stadium Barcelona'. (Courtesy of Murad Osmann.)

affection as the 'reflex' bodily responses by which we interact with our devices and their interfaces through the routinely dexterous movements of our hands and eyes.

The Selfie, the Phatic Body and Kinaesthetic Sociability

We have moved far from the primarily visual terms of traditional photography theory and the conventional uses of indexicality, composition and reflection. These terms have been steered towards recent conceptualizations of photography as an embodied performance and a material practice (Larsen 2005; Edwards 2012), intersecting with accounts of the corporeality of digital culture and its organization of affection (Hansen 2004). The motivation behind this rethinking of core terms is not mere theoretical whimsy. Rubbing these concepts against the grain of the selfie reveals their persistent fecundity for thinking about photography. It re-animates photography theory as an aesthetic project, in that it is concerned with the somatic and sensory dimensions of the lifeworld, and as an existential and poetic one, affirming Joanna Zylinska's claim that *'photography makes worldhood*, rather than just commenting on it' (2016: 203; original italics).

In the case of the selfie, these dimensions are fundamentally sociable. 'The impulse to sociability distils, as it were, out of the realities of social life the pure essence of association, of the associative process as a value and a satisfaction' (Simmel 1997 [1911]: 125). The selfie – deictically indexical, inclusively com-posed, reflexive and reflex – alters and deepens the relationship between photographic mediation and the impulse to sociability.

Two additional observations will clarify this claim. The first is that the selfie is, like many of the other practices and objects discussed in earlier chapters, linked to phatic communion (Malinowski 1923), whose primary purpose is the production, expression and maintenance of sociability. Miller (2008) argues that contemporary networked culture accentuates a phatic culture of non-substantive communication mediated across distances: his examples are mainly drawn from the banal verbal messages on Twitter and other social network services. The selfie represents a parallel process to this mainly verbal phenomenon: the production of the *mediated phatic body* as a visible vehicle for sociable communication with distant others, who are expected to respond.

Response is crucial: phatic exchanges stage sociability as a binding affective *energy* transferred between individuals in interpersonal settings, and response is an embodied social reflex – it is hard not to perform it. Highly ritualized and yet profoundly routinized, phatic utterances demand to be requited (Coupland, Coupland and Robinson 1992). Failure to acknowledge the nod of a passing acquaintance or her casual 'How are you?' is easily perceived as an expression of non-recognition and social exclusion. Yet how are mediated exchanges of responsive phatic energy made possible through the representational form of a still photograph?

This is where the second observation becomes important. The selfie is a pre-eminent conductor of embodied social energy because it is a *kinaesthetic* image: (1) it is a product of kinetic bodily movement; (2) it gives aesthetic, visible form to that movement in images; (3) it is inscribed in the circulation of kinetic and responsive social energy among users of movement-based digital technologies. As a kinaesthetic image, then, the selfie makes visible a broader kinaesthetic domain of digital culture that is relatively overlooked as an object of analysis. This is the limbic, gestural register, overtly apparent in games systems like Wii and Kinnect, that creates a circuit for mediating social and corporeal affective energy by intersecting with two other registers of embodied technicity: 'the mobile' – the mediated mobility of whole bodies in physical and augmented space provided by locative technologies (the body as a single moving data point), and 'the operative' – the habitually nimble coordination of hands and eyes used for navigating and operating in the virtual space of interfaces (body parts as media operators). The selfie is thus a new phatic agent in the energy flow between bodily movements, sociable interactions and media technologies that have become fundamental to our everyday, routine experience of digital life: part of what Hjorth and Pink (2014), following Ingold's work, call digital 'wayfaring'. It is a sign not only of digital photography's agency as a form of depiction but of the further transformations of figural representation itself as an instrument of mediated, embodied sociability.

The Serious Politics of Sociability

The agency of the selfie as a performance of embodied sociability, as a kinaesthetic gesture of phatic communion, has important limitations, however. This is because phatic communion in general is not unorganized or without structure. Two structural characteristics particularly stand out. The first is that phatic utterances, as linguists have noted (Laver 1975), are not as informationally empty as Malinowski suggested: 'all utterances, phatic or otherwise, mean contrastively by being differentiated from other possible utterances, as well as silence, in the context of their use' (Coupland, Coupland and Robinson 1992: 212). Their semantic content may not be salient to interlocutors, but it is not irrelevant: not anything can qualify as a recognizably phatic utterance, and not every potential phatic utterance is conventionally appropriate in every context: 'What's up?' is probably not a fitting way to greet a mourner at a funeral. This means that the distinction between connectivity and representation is not, ultimately, entirely clear cut: connectivity requires particular representations to act as its 'instruments'. Hence *which* particular instruments are selected and conventionalized (the tick of message reception in the WhatsApp interface, the gesturing body in the selfie) will be subject to a *politics* of representation. As Morley notes, in a critical commentary on Scannell's foregrouding of sociability as a principal achievement of broadcasting, 'Sociability, by definition, can only ever be produced in some particular cultural (and linguistic) form – and only those with access to the relevant forms of cultural capital will feel interpellated by it' (2000: 111). If phatic communion is conventionalized and achieved through representational forms, then its performance by individuals and groups requires levels of competence and mastery, the resources to achieve them and the authority to conventionalize certain 'utterances' – particular representations and, in the case of selfies, particular bodies – as recognizably phatic instruments.

The second structural dimension of phatic communion is the presupposition that one is recognized as a potential member of the reference group whose members can be communed with: a community. Institutional and discursive power can be brought to bear to make one sufficiently unacceptable (for instance, excommunication) or unrecognizable that one's phatic speech is shunned or is refused the status of speech at all.

Lilie Chouliaraki (2017) offers a powerful example of how the phatic sociability of the selfie can reach its limits. Analysing the self-representation of migrants and refugees in digital news, Chouliaraki outlines the distinctive ways that the mediating gesture of selfies taken by migrants arriving in Europe becomes an expression of existential affirmation:

> the selfie's locative claim ('I am *here*') also entails a strong existential dimension ('I *am* here'). Far from indexing just any random location, the deictic function of the celebration selfie goes beyond arrival to connote survival, the fact of having endured a deadly sea crossing in the Mediterranean. It is this deixis of arrival-as-survival, the selfie's 'I've made it' moment, that mobilizes its corporeal sociability, its likes, comments and shares, as an occasion of online jubilation. (Chouliaraki 2017: 85; original italics)

The 'celebration' selfies taken by migrants who have survived the crossing are, then, embodied and deictic 'vital signs' (see chapter 3), indicating to family and friends far away that one is safe, performing for and with them (via their responses on social media) relief and hope. Phatic communion in this case reaffirms one's membership not only in a community of discourse, but also in the world of the living.

Yet Chouliaraki also notes that the migrant celebration selfie is 'remediated' when reported by western news platforms, extending the term 'remediation' to signal the reframing of aesthetic content as a result of the technological embeddedness of one medium in another (2017: 79, note 1). This remediation in western news reports works, in the main, not by reproducing for viewers migrant selfies themselves (the actual pictures taken and sent), but by showing images of migrants *taking selfies*, creating forms of theatrical or spectacular estrangement from the selfie that makes it extraordinary and curious for onlookers. The act of selfie taking itself becomes the news story, inviting 'ethical appraisal, public commentary and judgement: "Who are they? Why are they owning mobile phones? Why are they taking selfies? Should they be taking them?" ... It is the fact that "they" take selfies, not their faces, that we are invited to contemplate' (2017: 86). A similarly judgemental, indeed hostile, interpretation of migrants taking selfies is discussed by Literat, who gives the example of the creation of a photographic meme showing a group of Syrian men taking an arrival selfie with a selfie stick, captioned 'You know you've been had when the "refugees" pull out a selfie stick' (2017: 4).

The sociability of the selfie, and the phatic body it circulates, are thus deadly serious as vital signs within everyday world disclosure, and yet are open to manifold, reflective disclosures – remediations – through images *of* selfies being taken. Such images neutralize the gestural invitation of the selfie form and its kinaesthetic turn to the viewer, shifting it from a first-person address ('see me showing you me') to a third-person spectacle ('see them performing for others'). Hence the selfie as a reflexive gesture of mediated sociability, and the devices which make it possible (smartphones, selfie sticks), can be presented as exhibitionist luxuries, as superfluities to a 'proper', putatively seemly image of bare life associated with the stereotype of the impoverished, fleeing (non-European) refugee. Like the word 'refugees' in the meme caption, the selfie is treated as a self-consciously citational act, placed in quotation marks as a sign that it is utterly staged, and therefore disingenuous. As a *representational* instrument of phatic sociability, then, the selfie faces a norm of performative appropriateness and 'symbolic bordering' (Chouliaraki 2017) which determines whether or not those taking it can be accepted into a wider, mediated community of the morally deserving. The celebration selfie of migrants, so significant as a first-order existential communication of survival–arrival for those undertaking it and receiving it, becomes evidence in a second-order judgement about one's right to be included in the lifeworld of strangers.

A final example will show how the selfie, as an invitational connective gesture, can itself visibly stage sociability as a habitual performance inflected by power relations. Between 20 August and 30 September 2017, Noa Jansma, a student in Amsterdam, set up an Instagram account called '#dearcat-callers'. Its 'mission statement' read as follows:

> #dearcatcallers, it's not a compliment.
>
> This Instagram has the aim to create awareness about the objectification of women in daily life.
>
> Since many people still don't know how often and in whatever context 'catcalling' happens, I'll be showing my catcallers within the period of one month.
>
> By making the selfie, both the objectifier and the object are assembled in one composition. Myself, as the object, standing in front of the catcallers represents the reversed power ratio which is caused by this project.
>
> Please join me in the fight and post your own #dearcatcallers or send me a DM

Twenty-two selfies were posted in total during the month that the account was operational, each one showing an unsmiling Noa Jansma looking into the camera, with a man or group of men, her catcallers, pictured beside or behind her, mostly smiling into the camera. The image would often be accompanied by a brief description or quotation of the catcall.

These images (Figures 5.3 and 5.4) demonstrate the poetic force of the selfie as an intervention in the world, using an act of embodied sociability aimed at distant, anonymous others to make visible the boundaries and power structures of sociability in the street. The selfie here serves, at first, as what Kompridis would call a 'decentring' form of secondary world disclosure in a number of respects, all of which trouble and disturb the routine performance of sociability as a self-evident phenomenon. First, the images are compositionally and spatially decentring: Noa Jansma's face is frequently cropped by the frame (Figure 5.3, for example), and even when it is not she is still positioned to the side of her own image. Her catcallers are usually, in contrast, depicted in full. At the same time, however, she is always in the foreground,

♡ ♀ ✈   ⊓

2,436 likes

dearcatcallers Classic 2.0 "psssst,
whoooooop, Can he have your number?"
#dearcatcallers

Figure 5.3: Noa Jansma, Classic 2.0, #dearcatcallers. (Courtesy of Noa Jansma.)

and they are usually in the background: she commands our attention and is clearly the creator and source of the image as a deictic gesture. Additionally, and against the long-standing convention of consistent expressiveness among participants in both group selfies and traditional group snapshot photographs (we all try to smile together, or we all look serious and respectable at the same time), Noa Jansma never smiles at the camera: her expression is hard to fathom precisely from the photograph alone, but it seems to combine determination and earnestness. The catcallers, in contrast, always smile and often wave or gesticulate extravagantly.

These multiple decentrings suggest that the main topic of the image is located somewhere *in between* the human figures,

Figure 5.4:   Noa Jansma, Mmmmmm beautiful sweet girl, #dearcatcallers. (Courtesy of Noa Jansma.)

in the non-figural and literally invisible relations between them, in the fact that far from the photographer of the selfie being sociably com-posed along with the male participants in the photographic scene, she – like the image itself – is thoroughly *dis*composed. A further decentring put to work here is temporal: the event of the image, its reason for being, has already happened before the selfie is taken. The selfie is a response to the catcalls but not a record of them, or for that matter a re-enactment of them (thus it is also the performance of a sensory decentring, from sound to vision). Again, the selfie presents its own centre of meaning and purpose as something out of view, hidden, incapable of disclosure except elliptically by the exposure of its very invisibility.

The final decentring is the mode of address. On the one hand, the selfie is Noa Jansma's riposte to the catcallers, her censure of their behaviour, of their inability to distinguish between sociability and harassment. Yet the image does not show her admonishing them but rather her and them addressing us, their unknown future viewers, by looking at the camera. It is not even as though they speak to each other 'through' us. Rather, the fact that the men smile and wave at us, and she does not, generates a contrast that makes visible to their unseen viewers the men's inability to distinguish photographic sociability from reproach, selfie from critique, because their understanding of sociability is not routinely put into crisis in the way that women's visibility in the streets is constantly assailed by catcalls. This is made apparent in the number of (frequently insulting) comments on the #dearcat-callers Instagram page – alongside much support for her project – that maintained, continually, that the men were 'just being friendly' (in the catcalls and in the selfies), and which blamed Noa Jansma for misunderstanding their intentions.

#dearcatcallers is profoundly, and politically, poetic. It enables the reflective disclosure of habitual, repetitive discomposure – of women by men – as a pervasive feature of the lifeworld, one that remains, to very many of those who share its public spaces (catcallers), utterly concealed behind a lived ideology of 'friendliness' and sociability. And the project performs this disclosure in the form of an *image crisis*, a discomfiting crack in the self-evident signals of com-positional harmony and apparent levity that have quickly become endemic to the selfie as a genre. The images, ultimately, are both refocusing and decentring at the same time. They continually make us, as viewers, oscillate between sociable recognition of the conventions of the selfie (the men are smiling) and critical judgement of a sociability that disguises harassment (the men are smiling), *trying* our ability to respond. Unlike Yolocaust, which puts the selfie on trial and judges it shameful, #dearcatcallers turns the selfie into a trial itself. Perhaps there is a name for this: poetic justice.

6
Interface

Remediated Witnessing and Embodied Response

The term 'interface' has become a key word in digital culture, occupying centre stage in a range of computational and design sub-disciplines concerned with managing the interactions between distinct devices. The 'user interface', more particularly, designates the system that governs relations between media technologies and their users. One specific type of user interface – the graphical user interface (GUI), which employs icons, windows and menus, along with a keyboard and a gestural input device such as a mouse or trackpad (the best-known examples are Microsoft Windows and Apple OS X) – has become almost inescapable, as well as a kind of second nature, for anyone using a personal computer. For many of us, it has established a near monopoly on the very experience and understanding of what computing is.

While user interfaces can also be said to have existed in older media (though they would not have been so labelled), digital technologies give rise to a new situation: the sheer complexity of everyday computer systems accentuates just how indispensable interfaces are to non-expert users; at the same time, the modularity and configurability of digital technologies make the interface itself available to users as an object of overt attention and potential alteration (we can frequently set our own 'preferences', changing the look, feel and functionality of many interface components). Additionally, the contemporary condition of 'ubiquitous computing' involves the extension of digital interface capacities across a range of old media (telephones, televisions, cameras), transportation technologies (car dashboards), household appliances (refrigerators, ovens, air-conditioning units) and wearable devices (watches). Interfaces, it is probably safe to say, are almost everywhere. They are a primary form through which media populate the world.

Practical questions of interface functionality and aesthetics have become important among product engineers and design professionals in fields such as human–computer interaction (HCI), and are obviously crucial for creators of devices, interface systems and media objects like websites. Solutions to these questions are frequently orientated around short-term success or profitability and are typically, though not exclusively, underpinned by assumptions regarding utility and 'task optimization', intuitive user knowledge and technological 'friendliness', and purportedly 'hard-wired' perceptual and cognitive processes. More critical and theoretical perspectives on interfaces have been offered by key theorists (e.g. Turkle 1997; Chun 2011; Galloway 2012; Manovich 2013) working within emerging areas such as 'software studies'. These perspectives all share a broad 'aesthetic' orientation to interfaces: the assumption that their design, their modes of interaction and appeal to the user's body, senses, feelings and implicit beliefs are crucial to their overall power and sociocultural significance. However, despite this recent scholarly work, it still remains true to say that 'considerable distance separates the interface design community and that concerned with critical theory' (Drucker 2014).

In chapter 2, I argued that the composite image of photography and television populates a world and enables 'indifferent' moral relations based on inattentive habituation to the non-threatening presence of multiple strangers in our intimate spaces. This composite image was the product of 'world-witnessing', a mode of perpetual presentation and poetic disclosure of inhabitable and inhabited worlds made possible through the indexical and emblematic characteristics of modern visual media. I later extended this idea to the 'hard' digital image of the screenshot and its ability to implicate, through temporal cutting, social media as poetically witnessable worlds which are profoundly interwoven with key existential conditions of life 'in' digital media.

The screenshot, however, is only one among many contemporary cultural forms (the selfie is another). As commonplace as it may be, it is by no means as ubiquitous as the 'content' it most frequently displays: the interface of the device. The question remains, then: what happens when interfaces intervene? When new kinds of screens, new embodied relationships with media devices and images, and new modulations of attention and inattention become habitual? In particular, does the introduction of graphical user interfaces, and changes in the sensuous, aesthetic and material conditions of engagement with media, potentially shift the ground of interaction with others who are made present to us, through media, as co-inhabitants of our lifeworld – especially in conditions of suffering and vulnerability? It is to these questions that I now turn.

The Aesthetics of Testimony

A central premise of interface design is that the aesthetic qualities of the interface shape user experience (Dourish 2001). This raises anxieties concerning the appropriateness of that experience when morally demanding material – such as video testimonies of Holocaust survivors – becomes widely accessible via digital devices. One ambitious solution is dramatized in a brief video clip from 2016 called 'New Dimensions in Testimony'. The video is a pilot demonstration of a broader initiative of the University of Southern California's (USC) Shoah Foundation in collaboration with the USC Institute for Creative Technologies. Filmed with 53 cameras in a special studio over five days, and employing sophisticated language processing and voice-recognition technologies, it shows a life-size 3D holographic representation of Holocaust survivor Pinchas Gutter answering questions posed by students in a classroom ('How old were you when the war ended?'), and even responding to one query by singing a Polish lullaby from his childhood.

'New Dimensions in Testimony' describes a future application of digital technologies: the technology exists but it is not yet widely available. Discursively framed by concern over the imminent death of the survivor generation, its promise is that 'long after the last survivor has left us', viewers will be able 'to engage with a survivor and ask them questions directly, encouraging them, each in their own way, to reflect on the deep and meaningful consequences of the Holocaust' (https://sfi.usc.edu/research/initiatives/new-dimensions). The project's mortality-defying rhetoric, and the spectral, uncanny quality of the holographic illusion, evokes the existential hopes and anxieties attending what Lagerkvist (2017) calls the 'digital afterlife', as well as age-old visions of the 'medium' as a bridge between the living and the dead (Peters 1999). It also points to a further shift in the orientation of testimony, facilitated by continual software-generated recalibration, towards contexts of reception in the future (Pinchevski forthcoming).[1] Moreover, the aspiration to produce a perfect simulation of co-present interaction is fuelled by an explicit contrast with film and video. 'The effect that it gives is a lot more that that person is there in the room with you than that person was filmed some time ago somewhere else,' observes Paul Debevec, Associate Director of Graphics Research at USC's Institute for Creative Technologies. 'I think it's going to be considerably more engaging and immersive and moving than if they're just up there on a video screen' (quoted in Katz 2013).[2]

Significantly, this emphasis on seemingly 'direct' engagement and immersive interaction is shared by other projects devoted to interfaces explicitly designed to bypass screens, notably various forms of 'immersive journalism' that employ technologies associated with virtual reality and virtual environments. Although interactivity with represented objects in these systems is based around the sensorimotor simulation of one's own bodily presence and movement inside a virtual space, rather than – as in the case of the hologram – the transportation of a moving virtual object into one's own physical location, these ventures share some of the underlying assumptions and accompanying rhetoric of 'New Dimensions in Testimony'. The immersive journalism projects pioneered by Nonny de la Peña (also of USC) are a case in point, the idea being to offer first-person encounters with stories and scenarios that are seemingly more direct, and less mediated, than current screen-based journalism (http://emblematicgroup. com). Prominent claims include that VR (virtual reality) technologies will not only increase viewers' sense of involvement, understanding and emotional response, but they will overcome the 'depreciation and under-representation of reality' in current audiovisual media: in comparison, immersive journalism 'constitutes a much more faithful duplication of real events' (de la Peña et al. 2010: 299).

Both 'New Dimensions in Testimony' and immersive journalism employ a familiar rhetoric of 'technological supersession' (Duguid 1996), whereby new media purportedly improve upon their predecessors. Yet whatever the validity or otherwise of this rhetoric – and there are significant counterarguments, both about the potential loss of critical and cognitive distance which *less* immersive media encourage and about the moral costs of first-person sensory engagement without first-person responsibility or shared existential risk (Robins 1996; Nash 2017) – it remains the case, at the time of writing, that the holographic prototype and even the immersive VR interfaces remain marginal to the vast majority of digitally enabled interactions with testimony.

There is, furthermore, something especially surprising about the rhetoric of supersession used by Debevec when describing 'New Dimensions in Testimony'. For today it is increasingly rare for survivor testimony to be seen 'on a video screen' *as such*. Contemporary screens for viewing these testimonies tend to be multipurpose digital displays rather than dedicated to a particular – and in this case, originally analogue – audiovisual technology. The negative comparison with video testimonies thus conceals an important omission: that current digital technologies – specifically the everyday *screen-based interfaces* of desktop and laptop computers, tablets and smartphones – have become central to user experience of filmed testimonies of Holocaust survivors. If, as the 'New Dimensions in Testimony' clip suggests, audience response is elicited through embodied encounters with technologies and their representations, then it is largely these interfaces that shape contemporary viewers' engagements with the content they view.

A deep irony accompanies this omission. Not only is the USC Shoah Foundation a principal global producer of video testimonies of the Holocaust and other genocides (Armenia, Rwanda)[3] but, following a huge digitization project, their Visual History Archive has made around 52,000 videos available for searching and viewing online (through recognized institutions like museums and universities), with 1,200 English-language testimonies open to viewing by the general public via the USC's website, as well as YouTube.[4] Hence the Shoah Foundation is already a primary remediator of survivor testimony – a key agent in the transformation of filmed accounts through their digitization and presentation via popular interfaces. It is these relatively unexamined processes of digital remediation which raise key questions concerning the aesthetics of the medium, audience engagement and moral response.

Such questions are necessarily framed by an extensive literature on the ethics of Holocaust and genocide testimony. At the risk of gross oversimplification, one can discern three broad moral priorities in this literature. The first emphasizes a moral obligation to the past and to the dead. Its ideal mode of response can be characterized as 'attending': simply being attentive to testimony, not merely in honour of the survivors who testify but in recognition of those who cannot bear witness because they perished. As Primo Levi maintained, those who survived – 'the saved' – bore witness 'by proxy', in the name of those who could not speak, 'the drowned' (1988). Merely recording and attending to the names of the dead – a key feature of memorials such as Yad Vashem's 'Hall of Names' – can be regarded as a moral act.[5] As well as forestalling historical oblivion, this obligation expresses a sense of cosmic responsibility and reparation that overcomes death. The dead may be beyond practical aid, but through attentiveness and remembrance we can return to them the individual humanity stripped from them by the impersonal ruthlessness of the Nazi genocide.

The second priority is based on a moral obligation in the present to the witness-survivor. This is underscored by the rationales developed in the analogue video-testimony projects. For instance, the filming process deployed at the Yale Archive refrained from showing the interviewers and used a sparse, uniform background and (after initial experimentation) very limited camera movement to focus entirely on the faces, gestures and voices of the survivors (Hartman 2000). This technique had reparative capacities: 'the camera, also, because it focused on the face and gestures of the witnesses, was anything but cold: in fact it "re-embodied" those who had been denied their free and human body image in the camps' (2000: 118). This obligation further required the establishment of a 'provisional community' of empathetic listeners, represented *in situ* by the interviewers, who 'become, for the survivor witness, representative of a larger community, one that does not turn away from but recognizes the historical catastrophe and the personal trauma undergone' (117). 'Engagement' – empathy for a present other and recognition of the significance of their experience – is the key mode of response to this obligation.

The third priority in relation to testimony is based on a moral obligation to the future of the survivors, the Jewish people and humanity as a whole. The relevant response mode is action-oriented, and can be specified as 'learning-watchfulness'. It privileges the acquisition and dissemination of knowledge about the Holocaust, and the derivation of historical, political and moral lessons from it and, in its universalistic version, the cultivation of values and sentiments that can prevent genocide from recurring.[6] The mantra of this obligation is 'never again'; its performance is perpetual vigilance. Both learning and moral socialization can be achieved though engagement with survivor testimony, where the potentially numbing impersonality of large-scale historical knowledge (and the sheer numbers of the dead) is ruptured by the narratives of real, identifiable individuals (Slovic 2007).

Given these moral obligations to the dead, the survivors and the future, and the associated response modes of attending, engagement and learning-watchfulness, what are the possible repercussions of mainstream actually existing digital interfaces – the kind that users of the Shoah Foundation's Visual History Archive currently rely upon – for viewers' embodied encounters with survivor testimony? And what might they entail for viewers' ability to 'reflect on the deep and meaningful consequences of the Holocaust', or to respond morally to the witnessing of suffering more broadly?

In what follows, I discuss these questions in two stages. First, I consider the digital mediation of survivor testimony and its moral ramifications in relation to the concept of media witnessing, explaining the rationale for paying special attention to mainstream, contemporary digital interfaces. Second, I focus on the aesthetics of graphical user interfaces under three key topics connected to the moral obligations outlined above: attention, engagement and action. In these sections, I sketch a phenomenology of the interface, outlining its characteristics as an embodied, sensory experience in order to review its implications for moral response among users, particularly in relation to survivor testimony. This, then, is a theoretical study in the aesthetics and ethics of digital world disclosure. But it is also an attempt to delineate conceptually what we might call the 'moral affordances' of media: the repertoire of perceptible moral responses to represented content that are made possible by the embodied, technically and culturally shaped relations between people and communication technologies.

Trajectories of Media Witnessing

The relevance to survivor testimony of embodied experience with digital devices follows directly from the technological mediation of witnessing, a topic briefly discussed in the Introduction and related to the work of the screenshot in chapter 3. If, as Peters (2001) argues, witnessing involves the transformation of experience into discourse for others, then the medium by which that discourse is rendered and received is central to the experience of the testimonial addressees, and to their ability to respond to the testimony being given.

Of course, witnessing need not be undertaken for moral purposes. The long history of the concept reveals its multifarious roles in juridical, historical, religious and scientific contexts (Peters 2001). Nevertheless, two intellectual trajectories have converged to privilege the moral dimensions of witnessing. The first understands the modern era to be morally challenging in novel ways. Thanks primarily to modern media, it is characterized by the relentless exposure of ordinary individuals to images and accounts of the horrific suffering endured by distant strangers. This exposure is performed (among other means) by journalism (Zelizer 2007; Robertson 2010; Morse 2017), humanitarian campaigns and the organization of public compassion (Sznaider 2001; Chouliaraki 2006, 2013), and memorial and pedagogical projects that promulgate accounts of previous suffering, with the Holocaust as an exemplary case (Hartman 1996; Zelizer 1998). It also raises expectations and concerns regarding the moral status of witnesses to suffering (Margalit 2002), the appropriateness and efficacy of such exposure, and the moral ramifications of the responses it elicits (or fails to elicit) among audiences (Frosh 2006; Ong 2014). For Tait (2011), the moral challenge is to turn exposure to others' suffering into responsibility for – or rather, response-ability to – that suffering: 'for the audience "response-ability" is also critical: one must be capable of empathetic response, and able to articulate that response in order to verify it' (2011: 1227).[7]

The second intellectual trajectory privileging moral aspects of witnessing accompanies but also diverges from this historical and sociocultural emphasis. It stresses the centrality of media technologies as facilitators of witnessing, if not as witnesses in their own right. Characterized broadly as 'media witnessing' (Frosh and Pinchevski 2009), this trajectory emerged from John Ellis's argument – briefly mentioned in chapters 2 and 3 – that photography, cinema and broadcasting 'brought citizens into a relationship of direct encounter with images and sounds' (2000: 9). Witnessing, for Ellis, is technically constituted by the indexical and referential excess of modern audiovisual media, the superabundance of details that they record (again, this is a superabundance that the screenshot remediates through the reproduction of extraneous details of the recorded 'screenscape'). It places distant audiences in a historically unprecedented moral position: 'You cannot say that you did not know' (Ellis 2000: 11).

Recent thinking about video-based survivor testimonies shares a similar perspective on the technical centrality of media. Pinchevski (2012) argues that the technological apparatus of video testimony generates an 'audiovisual unconscious' in survivor narratives, based on the capacity to record the silences, slippages, tics and repetitions that necessarily accompany survivors' verbal accounts. Such seemingly incidental gestural, facial and vocal epiphenomena were thus brought into significance and made amenable to retrospective diagnosis as manifestations of trauma, underpinning Felman and Laub's (1992) claim that the Holocaust engendered a 'crisis of witnessing' in survivors, whereby the events they experienced were too overwhelming to be rendered fully into discourse, resisting conscious processing and narrative integration. Hence the very capacity for interpreting these behaviours as signs of trauma depended, according to Pinchevksi, on a 'media a priori' (a concept he adapts from Kittler 1999): it was made possible by particular conditions and attributes of technological mediation.[8]

Similar concerns animate Presner's (2016) analysis of computerized database technologies and archiving techniques, such as those employed by the USC Shoah Foundation's Visual History Archive. Focusing on the infrastructure of the database rather than the user interface, Presner worries that it tends to flatten out, equalize and de-narrativize the video testimonies in the archive, eliminating precisely those contingent recorded qualities of affect and disturbance produced by the audiovisual unconscious. At the same time, computational processes offer new moral possibilities for 'distant listening' that democratize witnessing, extrapolating overarching structures, relationships and patterns from among all survivor videos in the archive, rather than focusing only on the close reading of a canonical few.

The moral dimensions of survivor testimony are heavily reliant, then, on the media technologies and cultural practices through which it is produced, organized and encountered. So far, however, most investigations of these areas have accentuated the deep logics of algorithmic processes and data organization, rather than the aesthetic qualities of embodied interaction between users and digital devices and their implications for moral response to the witnessing of suffering (important exceptions include Ashuri 2011 and Andén-Papadopoulos 2014, discussed below).

Embodied Aesthetics and the Graphical User Interface

In the case of digital media, such interactions between users and devices are mainly accomplished through the user interface: the system by which relations between a user and a device are made visible, executed and experienced (Pold 2005). The interfaces most familiar from personal computing are known generically as graphical user interfaces (GUIs), which integrate screen-based representations of windows, icons, menus, cursors and pointers, and the input devices of mouse (or trackpad) and keyboard. The more recent interfaces of mobile touch-screen devices such as tablets and smartphones are based on the same principle of 'direct manipulation' of objects located in a virtual onscreen space. Like touch-screen interfaces, the GUI constitutes a 'sensory inscription' (Farman 2012) of the body in and through technological means, combining the coordination of limbs and senses, spatial orientation in relation to a screen, and visual enframing of represented information.

There are, however, important differences between mobile interfaces and computer GUIs. Most obviously, mobile interfaces interlink two modes of bodily and semiotic 'navigation': using the touch-screen interface to navigate through the various operations of the device; and navigating with the device through physical space, a dual process that Verhoeff (2012) calls 'performative cartography'. Only the first of these navigational modes applies to computer GUIs. Other differences include physical proximity to the mobile touch screen and its handheld character.

Notwithstanding the recent popularity of mobile interfaces, there are good reasons for focusing on computer GUIs as key arenas for the aesthetic shaping of contemporary sociocultural practices, including moral response. First, computer GUIs both preceded and have co-evolved with mobile interfaces, sharing an enhanced emphasis on the direct manipulation interface as an overt aesthetic experience (Manovich 2012), as discussed below. Second, the fact that computer GUIs are principally devoted to navigation of the device's screen space, rather than physical navigation with the device, makes it possible to focus on the moral affordances of direct manipulation interface aesthetics in a relatively bounded context. Finally, the massive growth in tablet and especially smartphone usage has made mobile interfaces conspicuous objects of attention among the general public, particularly around product launches and operating system updates. It has also shifted the attention of media and cultural analysts away from computer GUIs, a turn conceivably influenced by the rhetoric of 'technological supersession' mentioned earlier. Following initial interest at the end of the millennium (for instance, Turkle 1997; Bolter and Grusin 1999; Manovich 2001), the GUI has become comparatively invisible as an aesthetic object of significant social, cultural and political consequence. Nevertheless, it remains a staple of everyday computing activities.

The continued centrality of computer GUIs to user experience does not mean that the deep computational processes and data structures of digital media – or their material, physical incarnations (chips, hard drives, etc.) – are irrelevant to the reception of survivor testimony. Indeed, Presner (2016) and others (Kirschenbaum 2012) show their significance in shaping distinct modes of encounter. However, as Chun (2011) argues, user interfaces also tend to mask many computer processes, making them invisible to the user while providing the experience of control. Moreover, Manovich (2012) makes a sharp distinction between the modernist, 'form follows function' GUIs of the early Macintosh and Windows systems of the 1980s–1990s, and those designed from the late 1990s onwards, especially the 2001 'Aqua' interface on Apple's OS X operating system. This latter group manifests a design commitment to 'the aestheticization of information tools': 'Using personal information devices is now conceived as a carefully orchestrated *experience* rather than a means to an end. The interaction explicitly calls attention to itself, with the interface engaging the user in a form of play, asking her to devote significant emotional, perceptual and cognitive resources to the very act of operating the device' (Manovich 2012: 280, italics in original).

It is thus through interface experiences that contemporary users' engagements with survivor testimonies are chiefly performed and their responses elicited. Bearing in mind that there will always be differences between operating systems and their interfaces, as well as between different software generations, we can delineate some of these experiences and their potential moral consequences through three interconnected topics, each related to a category of moral obligation to survivor testimony outlined earlier: attention, engagement and action.

Attention: From Hermeneutics to Operation

What kinds of attention to represented content are made possible when it is displayed via a computer GUI, and do they enhance or harm prospects for attending to testimony and the past of which it speaks? On my Apple iMac computer, I accessed the USC Shoah Foundation's Visual History Archive Online, and selecting – based on personal interest – video testimony from a US veteran (Kenneth Aran) involved in the liberation of Mauthausen concentration camp, proceeded to watch the interview (which was about 29 minutes long). Accessing the video involved a complex but partially routinized process of gestural input via keyboard and mouse that included selecting and clicking on a browser icon, navigating (via a Google search) to the Visual History Archive page, inputting my username and password, and navigating the archive itself – narrowing down and cross-referencing search categories – until I reached a screen offering a number of video testimonies, from which I selected one. The bulk of the surface area of the computer screen on which this video then played was in fact mainly occupied by screen space and interface features not connected to the video (Figure 6.1), including the dock at the bottom of the screen and the menu bar at the top, windows for programmes (such as Word) running behind the browser, and the iTunes mini-player displayed over the left-hand corner of the browser (kept on top of the window through an earlier iTunes settings change). In addition, the browser window contained a variety of textual and graphic elements provided by the Shoah Foundation Archive – including menu headings for navigating the archive ('About Us', 'Search', 'Search History', etc.), a Google map showing

Figure 6.1: Screenshot of default Visual History Archive web page, 3.8.2015. (Courtesy of the USC Shoah Foundation, taken from an interview with Kenneth Annan filmed in 1998. For more information: http://sfi.usc.edu.)

relevant geographical locations, and – below the video player – metadata lists connected to the film.

In order to focus on the video testimony, I clicked the icon at the bottom right-hand corner of the video player to open a full-screen display. As can be seen from the screenshot of the full-screen view (Figure 6.2), even here additional features and icons did not disappear entirely: visually and numerically represented metadata – current position in the video, video length, the picture at a particular point where my cursor was placed – as well as device and network operations, including playback, volume, settings, exit from full screen (at the bottom of the window) and a link to the video on YouTube (top right), were all made visible as soon as my hand made even the most minute movement on the mouse. The only way to get these icons and indicators to disappear was not to touch either the mouse or the keyboard at all. Of course, all of these features occupied the visual field alone. Only a premeditated intervention in my system settings could have disabled the audio pings of my computer informing me – as I watched the testimony – that new email messages had arrived.

Figure 6.2:   Screenshot of video testimony in full-screen display mode, 3.8.2015. (Courtesy of the USC Shoah Foundation, taken from an interview with Kenneth Annan filmed in 1998. For more information: http://sfi.usc.edu.)

Several significant points emerge from this somewhat pedantic verbal exposition. Although fluctuations in attention are linked to general historical shifts in modern structures of perception and representation (Crary 2002), including pre-digital screen media such as cinema, photography and television (as discussed in chapter 2), digital interfaces appear to exacerbate questions of attention in new ways (Hayles 2007; Jackson 2008). Since the purpose of a digital interface is to enable interaction with a device, the standard viewing settings usually make visible operative markers – icons, windows and menu headings, for instance, located in taskbars or docks at the edges of the screen – that remain constantly in view. The potentially distractive presence of these default markers, even at the periphery of vision, is negatively recognized by the fact that full-screen or 'focus' viewing modes are available to help screen them out (though rarely entirely).

The interface thus disperses attention among multiple, simultaneous 'hypermediated' (Bolter and Grusin 1999) interactions with the device, establishing a loop of continual alertness that is 'internal' to engagements between the user and the machine. But the interface is also geared towards forms of 'external' connectivity (via the internet, wireless infrastructures, etc.), networked exchanges with other devices designed to facilitate social relations with other people. This combination of internal interactivity and external connectivity means that digital interfaces operate in a standard context characterized by a high level of interference, encouraging, in Linda Stone's phrase, 'continuous partial attention': constant readiness to receive and respond to incoming stimuli (reminders, email and social media notifications, etc.) that makes one 'a live node on the network' (Stone 2015). Needless to say, continuous partial attention potentially undercuts the intensity and duration of viewer attentiveness to any particular item shown on a digital device.[9]

These conditions for dispersing attention are not merely cognitive. They are produced through the aesthetics and kinaesthetics of the GUI. Attention is more than a mental attribute; it is connected to action; it is physically performed (McCullough 2013). The reference to kinaesthesia – the sensation of bodily movement registered in consciousness (Noland 2009: 9–10) – emphasizes that continuous partial attention is a fundamentally embodied state that encourages certain kinds of cognitive and emotional responsiveness and potentially constrains others.

Central to this embodied regulation of attention is the emergence of a new regimen of eye–hand–screen relations. Based on the role of the mouse (and later trackpad and touch screen), this regimen recalibrates how we encounter what is screened. It oscillates between different attentive modes that combine visual, gestural and audial elements; between an 'operative' mode which constantly scans the potential functionality of the objects displayed, lingering on the surface and around the edges of the screen (and its windows) where indicators are most prominent and input most immediate; and a 'hermeneutic' mode which attends to the referential or symbolic meaning of what is shown, often moving beyond the screen surface into the virtual space behind it. Hermeneutic attention is based on the interpretive and perceptual practices of either 'taking in' informational content (for instance, textual reading) or 'immersion in' a representational schema. Operative attention – a term which draws on the idea of the 'operative sign' previously mentioned in relation to tagging

and selfies – seeks out what can be 'done to' a displayed
object, its functionality within the technical system independent of its ostensive semantic meaning, first with regard to
its general 'clickability' (does a change in cursor shape show
that it can be clicked?) and, second, to its capacities as a
hyperlink or as an interface component. Paying attention to
such operative signs involves acquiring cognitive and sensorimotor skills that fluctuate at speed between their particular
informational meanings and their responsive potentialities as
functional operators (playback, pause, full-screen, share).
Operative attention indicates a relative shift away from epistemological relations with texts or images (what do they
mean? what knowledge do they impart?) to an interactional
focus (how will this text or image respond? what connections
to the world does it enable?).

From the perspective of the three broad moral responses
to survivor testimony discussed earlier, operative attention
appears to contradict the response mode of 'attending' to the
past that honours those who testify, and through them
attempts symbolic reparation for those who cannot bear
witness. First, it is exploratory and future oriented, even if
the ostensive semantic content being accessed – such as survivor testimony – is primarily retrospective. Moreover, it is
infused with the functional possibilities of what it sees, alert
to the as-yet-undiscovered kinaesthetic potential of displayed
objects – possibilities shown by visual means, such as the
change in a cursor's shape, in the colour of a window or in
a translucent screen overlay. Operative attention is embodied
in the hand perpetually resting on the mouse and in the eye
tracking the moving cursor. It is fidgeting honed to the
promise of device responsiveness: sensorimotor restlessness
as a system requirement.

Real-time, Interactive and Haptic Engagement

Notwithstanding the potential for moral response offered to
consciousness by hermeneutic attention, the primacy of operative attention to the GUI thus seems to bode ill for 'attending' to survivor testimony as a moral act of historical

recognition. It also threatens the ability to create encounters which stimulate focused, empathetic engagement with the witness's personal trauma in the present – an original goal of video testimony as described by Hartman (2000). For even if one purposefully seeks out a particular testimony, as I did with the USC archive, simply accessing that video relies on an operative experience – with links, tabs, windows, icons – instantiated by the interface. Shifting to a full-screen view and adopting hermeneutic attention to a text in order to 'keep the survivor at the center, visually as well as verbally ... the survivor as talking head and embodied voice' (Hartman 2000: 117) appears to require an act of intense body consciousness and sensorimotor restraint. Such restraint seems discontinuous not only with the interface as an overt experience (as Manovich describes it) but with the very corporeal attention structures – the agitation of the hand on the mouse and the eye on the screen – that enabled one to locate and operate the video in the first place.

Are there, then, no aesthetic aspects of the interface that might enhance, rather than deplete, engagement with the testimonies of survivors and victims? After all, given the long, controversial history of critiques of audience passivity in media studies, it seems perverse to base a critique of digital interfaces solely on the claim that they privilege user activity. Perhaps the very embodied interactions demanded by digital interfaces also make possible varieties of moral response?

Such engagement can be conceptualized in relation to three interconnected attributes of the GUI: interactive real-time screen, haptic vision and user indexicality. Screens, whether painterly, cinematic or televisual, have long been understood in terms of a paradox. The screen depicts a world to the viewer but also separates the viewer from that world (this is implied by the screen-as-window metaphor: Friedberg 2006). The screen *screens off* (Cavell 1979), marking a distinction between representation to the audience and connectivity with the audience. Yet, unlike cinema or television, the screen of the digital device is not a barrier separating what it depicts, nor is it a window on a represented world, but a responsive surface enabling immediate sensory relations that emerge and shift in a temporal continuum of live interaction, what Manovich calls the 'interactive real-time screen' (2001). This is true of computer screens using input devices like the mouse or trackpad, as well as touch-screen displays.

This real-time integration of hand, eye and screen facilitates the transfer of sensory and affective energies between viewer and medium that can be described as 'haptic'. 'In haptic visuality,' claims Laura Marks, 'the eyes themselves function like organs of touch' (1998: 333). Haptic visuality 'spreads over the surface of the image instead of penetrating into depth' (333) and 'is more inclined to move than to focus' (338). Boothroyd further emphasizes the multi-sensory significance of movement: 'all of the senses are in a sense haptic in that they are dependent on the transmission of movement, and all movement is ultimately registered on the surfaces of "skins"' (2009: 337). The interface, too, is haptic because it coordinates the sensation and performance of movement across diverse sensory surfaces, both organic and technological: the 'skins' of the body and the device.[10]

So while operative attention seems to threaten engagement with represented content, the sensorimotor stimulation of the GUI's hand–eye–screen regimen can also create new intensities of contact between physical and virtual bodies (the body of the user, the technological device, the image of the survivor) through multi-sensory anticipation of, and sensitivity to, movement. Haptic engagement technologically instantiates both the bodily and emotional potential of 'being moved'.

Lastly, the GUI's simulation of physical causality between viewer and virtual objects allows us to link its aesthetics to heightened indexicality. As in the case of the selfie, this is not (initially, at least) the indexicality of the photographic and cinematic trace of a past event (Doane 2007). Rather, it is the indexicality of deixis, of the pointing finger (appropriately, often of the *index* finger), of a present-tense, quasi-physical connection between user and representation ('If you can point,' ran an early Apple advert, 'you can use a Macintosh'). Pointing, clicking, dragging, sliding, swiping and tapping all generate relations between the viewer and represented objects that appear simultaneously embodied and *causal*. Our gestures via the mouse or trackpad produce movements of objects in virtual space that are calibrated in direction and intensity – speed, pressure, acceleration, duration – to mimic the motion of our hands 'on' those objects and to simulate physical effects. We drag, scroll or swipe slowly, and the 'page' or video frame we are 'touching' moves slowly. We witness a transfer of kinetic energy from our own bodies to the virtual objects 'behind' or 'on' the glass screen.

This transfer of energies is experienced as a relationship of live connection, incarnated in the cursor. As 'the tangible sign of presence implying movement' (McPherson 2002: 461), the cursor references the user's haptic responsiveness – her body, its animation and participation across a mediated space that bridges both 'sides' of a screened encounter with another. It is a functional agent within the interface system, to be sure, but it is also a sign that displays the user's embodied will moving among virtual objects within the mediated realm (Engell 2013). When those virtual objects are themselves the products of media conventionally associated with 'trace' indexicality – such as photographs and films – we can postulate an 'indexical chain' of mediated bodily contiguity between users and the referents of the images, where the cursor-borne traces of users' gestures appear to make contact with the bodies of depicted others. This chain – the intersection in a single representational space of indexical signs from separate media systems – allows us to conceptualize a potential transformation from operative to moral registers: the possibility that the user's deictic act of pointing at an object can become the moral action of reaching out to another.

Perhaps the strongest figure for such an indexical chain is a user's finger touching a moving image of another's finger or face on a touch screen. However, the 'touch-blindness' of the touch screen, where the user's physical finger obscures vision of the precise point of contact, paradoxically exposes the distinctiveness of the cursor as an index of the user's body. For the cursor is continually visible to the user herself, doubling the viewer's self-location, which occurs on both sides of the screen simultaneously, thereby enhancing possibilities for self-perception and self-awareness. The cursor thus becomes a figure for functional and non-functional reflexivity concerning one's engagement with and potential obligation to depicted content, signifying and extending moral possibilities for contact.

Interactive real-time screen, haptic vision and user indexicality: together these three attributes of the GUI create a structured and integrated embodied experience for users. How might this experience support potential moral responses similar to the obligation discussed in the introduction: engagement with the witness-survivor in the present? One key prospect is that the user's experience of pointing at virtual objects provides the ground for reaching towards mediated subjects. This transfiguration works across the three attributes simultaneously: (a) from adjacency to proximity, where real-time screen interactivity not only creates an integrated space of functional adjacency between the user and interface elements but one of proximity and the promise of contact with depicted figures; (b) from objects to subjects, where haptic sensitivity to movement fills out the instrumental recognition of things into multi-sensuous apprehension of others; (c) from designation to communication, where user indexicality changes from an act of *pointing at something* into a moral gesture of *approaching an other*. Overall, this potential transition from operative to moral registers enables recognition of the represented other and engagement with their discourse. It involves bridging a critical gap: between technologically heightened sensorimotor responsiveness to stimuli and embodied moral response-ability to persons.

Co-witnessing and Communicative Action

In addition to these prospects for engagement, contemporary mainstream digital interfaces also entail possibilities for morally purposeful *action* that distinguish them from pre-digital media – including the original audiovisual format of survivor testimonies like those in the USC archive. The default condition of pre-digital media, it is worth recalling, was characterized by a sharp *dis*continuity between the encounter with depicted suffering and ensuing possible action on behalf of the sufferer.[11] This disconnection has long disturbed communication theorists, at least since Lazarsfeld and Merton's (1971 [1948]) account of the 'narcotizing dysfunction' whereby the acquisition of knowledge *about* the world, and even informed civic concern for contemporary problems, becomes a substitute for organized social action *in* the world.

In contrast, GUIs make action possible through the techno-logical framework of the device itself. They facilitate a sys-temic continuity between the interface's operative inculcation of embodied restlessness, haptic and indexical engagement with presented content, and immediate morally purposeful action. This potential has been outlined in Ashuri's (2011) analysis of the anti-occupation Israeli websites 'Breaking the Silence' and 'Machsom Watch', which she describes as 'moral mnemonic agents' (moral witnesses to the suffering of others). The moral responsibility and action of address-ees, Ashuri argues, is enabled by the interactivity of these organizations' websites, where users can freely download and/or freely disseminate testimonial texts and videos via Facebook, YouTube and other platforms. The 'moral mne-monic agent' doesn't just impart knowledge to its viewers but, 'in gathering information about injustice and suffering and passing it on to others, the agent seeks to have consumers share in the experience as well as in the responsibility for it' (2011: 455–6).

Andén-Papadopoulos makes a similar point, focusing on the mobile 'camera witnessing' of repression and suffering enabled by contemporary smartphone devices: 'In circulat-ing their (audio)visual recordings via global digital networks, people can invite others around the world to become their "co-witnesses" (Hirsch 2003: 79), to share in their act of tes-timony and working through' (Andén-Papadopoulos 2014: 761). Additionally, the aesthetic qualities of mobile camera witnessing possess a striking capacity to 'move the bodies of viewers' thanks to 'its distinctive discursive features – such as original, "raw" sound and hyper-mobilized camera-work' (2014: 761) which heighten effects of the 'realness' of depicted events and their bodily experience by those who filmed them.

The primary moral response described here is commu-nicative action: an action that takes immediate responsibil-ity for turning viewers into co-witnesses who then further widen the circle of addressees in a chain reaction of *net-worked world disclosure*. This is a compelling extension of the moral response mode of 'learning-watchfulness' outlined earlier, enabling the interpersonal promulgation of knowl-edge of suffering accompanied by the imperative to halt it, or prevent its recurrence, through the very act of getting others to watch.

However, Ashuri's use of the term 'interactivity' and Andén-Papadopoulos's observations on the aesthetic powers of digital camera witnessing both hide a significant lacuna – the assumption that the viewer's sensorimotor performance of interface operations will indeed make them morally receptive either to the website's archived content or to the video of 'live' suffering. For there is no guarantee that the operative attention elicited by the interface will proceed in directions commensurate with the hermeneutic attention demanded by such texts. Neither are users who experience live, haptic, indexical encounters with digitized video testimonies immune to being distracted – immediately as the video ends, or even beforehand – by the proximate charms of less morally significant or edifying material offering similar sensorimotor engagements. In short, there remains a necessary fissure between the interface's production of embodied responsiveness and Tait's demand for moral response-ability.

This fissure is necessary because it is the space where moral choice resides. While the gap between sensorimotor responsiveness and moral response is no doubt amenable to design interventions (for instance, in default settings) that could steer the interface experience for particular websites or apps in morally 'appropriate' directions, the challenge (and burden) of contemporary GUI usage is that moral consequences can – but need not – issue from the slightest adjustments of our hands on the mouse or trackpad. Action at a distance emanates from one of the most intimate, and banal, of bodily movements: digitality as a human–computer hybrid magnifies and glorifies the power of the digit, the human finger, as an actor in a world of vast extension. The concomitant of contemporary interface interactivity is not that moral agency has disappeared into an online virtual world of low-risk pseudo-action, as critics of 'slacktivism' might claim (Gladwell 2010), but that moral choices regarding distant strangers have been extended to the vicissitudes of our wandering gaze, the tips of our fidgeting fingers (thereby becoming truly 'digital') and the minute movements of our cursor-selves on the screen.

The Ethics of Kinaesthetics

Thanks to digital technologies, we find ourselves in a historically novel situation: the burden of our exposure to, and disclosure of, distant suffering depends on our smallest habitual and volitional gestures. This burden can be called the 'ethics of kinaesthetics'. Given what can now be done to an image or video, by my own hands and through a simple and almost cost-free movement, not attending to, engaging with or acting on it becomes a moral decision performed in minutely embodied contact with a disclosed world. It is no longer a default limitation of media technologies – technologies which, in the pre-digital era, kept me and my will at a screened distance from those bearing witness.

It is worth briefly returning to the USC Shoah Foundation's Visual History Archive 'Viewing Screen' page (Figure 6.1) to flesh out what such an 'ethics of kinaesthetics' might consist of. Continuity between responsiveness to the interface, engagement with depicted content, and immediate action are structured as sensorimotor invitations into the page design. Thanks to the browser and video interfaces, with their various save-and-share options, the page signals the downloading and dissemination functions described by Andén-Papadopoulos as 'co-witnessing'. Moreover, bodily connectivity and responsiveness are channelled into deeper exploration of this particular video narrative through clickable metadata links (biographical profile of the witness, indexing terms in the testimony, people in the testimony, relevant maps), making manifest the relations of this text to patterns, themes, places (the Mauthausen concentration camp) and the stories of other survivors and victims within the overall archive, enabling practices of 'distant listening' (Presner 2016) that move beyond – without preventing (recall the focused viewing mode) – detailed involvement with a single testimony.

As I have said, none of this is given, even though the cursor moves over the web page as a surrogate point of potentially reflexive interaction, a proxy moral compass in the interleaving of worlds. The operative characteristics of digital interfaces and their embodiment in new regimes of eye–hand–screen integration do present distinct challenges to traditional forms of prolonged, empathetic encounter with the world-disclosing narratives of survivors, constantly threatening to distract addressees whose primary sensory commitment is to the interactive aesthetics of the device rather than to any particular content, however narratively or morally compelling. At the same time, however, those very multi-sensory relations to digital screens that threaten distraction also set the stage for an alliance of sensorimotor responsiveness to the interface and moral response-ability to a world shared with depicted others. This alliance is never certain. It emerges from a new site of embodied moral agency: the interface between medium, hand and eye.

7
Conclusion

To Infinity and Beyond

The last chapter drew a distinction between the structures of attention, engagement and action associated with pre-digital video testimonies and those arising from the remediation of these testimonies via the graphical user interface. The latter, I have suggested, make available new possibilities for moral responsibility to distant and virtual others in a shared world that operate through minute, largely habitual, sensorimotor operations performed on our digital devices.

Yet within the overall framework of this book, an additional contrast presents itself between: the perpetual sensorimotor readiness for embodied interaction underpinning the 'ethics of kinaesthetics' of the contemporary interface; and the significance of inattention, non-reciprocity, transience and aggregation that characterized the 'world-witnessing' of pre-digital photography and television. These, as outlined in chapter 2, populated our lifeworlds with multiple, overlapping representations of strangers that – since they did not *demand* our attention – could be tolerated in our intimate spaces without hostility, habituating us to their perpetual presence as mediated companions and producing a fluctuating composite image of 'the human' that attends us ambiently. How does such a pre-digital framework of media poetics – of pre-reflexive world disclosure through media (photography, television) whose representational content always greatly outweighed their operative requirements for user interaction – intersect with contemporary modes that privilege operative media functionality not only as an aesthetic experience in its own right but as a new gestural repertoire, as a technologized posture of bodily agitation?

Of the many possibilities for grasping this intersection, perhaps the most tempting is provided by the narrative of 'regime change'. The age of ambient mediated companionship is past: photography and television have been replaced as cornerstones of the mediated lifeworld by digital devices and their kinaesthetic demands and possibilities. In place of the production of an extended lifeworld and its multiple mediated presences (its figures and its ground), we live in an era of the demonstrative performance of mediation as overt, continual activity. Entities that populate our immediate environment increasingly tend to be media themselves – or facets of media – and, like user interfaces, they implicitly make one basic request: continual activation.

One possible consequence of this narrative of regime change is, therefore, experiential and moral loss. Any benefit from the potential coupling of operative and moral mediated relations with others is paid for at a high price: the demise of those unnoticed structures of mass habituation to the presence of myriad strangers that are supported by traditional mass media. Yet we can also understand regime change as a gain; a reaffirmation of the intensity of the attentive encounter with the other as the apogee of moral communication, of the possibility and requirement for engagement with a particular other. Except that here it is the *distant* particular other to whom we are enabled to respond through forms of significant bodily interaction that either did not exist previously, or existed only in contexts of actual physical proximity (deictic pointing as reaching towards). This engagement with particular distant others both depends upon, and demands, physical–operative responses by individual users that circulate representations of those others to additional users in chains of co-witnessing (forwarding, posting, embedding, etc.). The encounter is not strictly dyadic but networked, with the user as a moral-operative switching point: it technologically implements Daniel Dayan's astute critique that 'focusing on the dual pair of "me and the other" is misleading. Instead of pairs, there are at least triangles ... more often than not, the other has another and this other is not me' (2007: 120).

The trope of regime change need not, therefore, be pessimistic in its consequences: ethics are back, and are more demanding of our capacity for choice than ever before by virtue of the fact that they too are *not* demanding, that it takes minimal physical, emotional and cognitive effort to act in a world so densely and deeply mediatized that the flick of a finger, like the flutter of a butterfly's wing, can have meaningful consequences far, far away. Ambience, aggregation and cohabitation are dead: long live immediacy, particularity and action.

Regime change, however, is governed by a totalizing rhetoric of supersession. This rhetoric, as mentioned earlier (Duguid 1996), offers a historical account in which one set of media technologies and accompanying behaviours replaces a previous set, and it tends to shape (some might say plague) accounts of communication 'revolutions', whether pessimistic or optimistic, and the dichotomous thinking they support. An alternative way of thinking about the shifts between media has recently been proposed by John Durham Peters. 'The advent of digital media returns us to fundamental and perennial problems of communication and civilization', he argues. 'So-called new media do not take us into uncharted waters: they revive the most basic problems of conjoined living in complex societies and cast the oldest troubles into relief' (2015: 4). Yet, while Peters is careful to avoid the hyperbolic language of media supersession and the revolutionary novelty of 'new' media, he nevertheless does promote a narrative of substitution. This narrative is based on the trope of historical (and existential) *reversion*. Understanding how media work as 'civilizational ordering devices' requires us 'to see just how *exceptional* media were in the last century' (2015; my italics).[1] For Peters, twentieth-century media, organized around telephony and especially broadcasting, were focused on distributing messages and meanings across whole communities and societies. *Content* – news, entertainment, advertising, propaganda, spectacle, the shared 'live' ceremonies of historic media events – was indeed king, and the idea of media as infrastructures of being (or indeed of social and political bodies), while definitely observed and analysed within media and communication scholarship, was nevertheless secondary and relatively inconspicuous. In contrast, with the internet,

> things have reverted back to the historical norm of a more chaotic media world. One-to-many communication on a mass scale is still around but is much less routine than in the age of 'drama for a dramatized society' that filled the airwaves in the twentieth century. We are back to the age-old modes of some-to-some, one-to-few, and even one-to-none – to a communication environment in which media have become equipment for living in a more fundamental way. (2015: 5).[2]

This narrative of reversion invites several important reflections. The first is that, in its own way, it evokes the complex etymological development of the word 'revolution' itself not as the radically new but as the *old renewed*, as the revolving of prior states of existence, knowledge, community and power. This historical model is neither one of linear continuity with the past nor of its radical rupture and replacement, but of a temporal leapfrogging over the immediately preceding era to a prior normative state; this in turn is recovered as an energizing motif in the rhetoric and performance of contemporary change.[3] The idea of digital media as a reversion to a 'chaotic media world' that constituted a 'historical norm' which antedated twentieth-century media itself tells a very modern story of the recursion of the old, even of the archaic, within the contemporary.

Another thing to note is the somewhat redemptive tenor of this recursion. The new, multidimensional communicative possibilities re-animated by digital media provide 'equipment for living in a more fundamental way' than twentieth century mass media did or do. One example of how this might be the case is through the example given by Lilie Chouliaraki (2017), discussed in chapter 5: the 'celebration' selfies taken by migrants who survived the Mediterranean crossing, and the existential affirmation ('I *am* here') they perform, are 'remediated' by western news platforms into public spectacles that turn news audiences into distant onlookers, estranged from these strangers and their life-affirming image gestures. Twentieth-century mass-media genres (news) and practices (journalism) thus promulgate a drama – for a 'dramatized society'

– of the seemingly exhibitionist selfie and the luxurious smartphone that depletes and denies the existential urgency of the migrants' condition. It also deprecates the existential consequences of the smartphone as fundamental equipment for living, part of an infrastructure of being, a phatic vehicle for the continual dissemination of 'vital signs'.

If this were the only case, Peters's narrative would be very persuasive, with the hopeful proviso that the digital reversion to a more chaotic and infrastructural media world is not continually perverted by the dramatizing machinations of mass media. Yet there are contrary examples. The most obvious case mentioned in this book is the reproduction, via the screenshot, of the last WhatsApp message from Shir Hajaj's mother to her dead daughter and its appearance as an 'about to die' image published as the main headline of a printed newspaper. In this case, the screenshot, by remediating attributes of the document and the photograph, enables the newspaper to bear public witness not only to the loss suffered by a particular mother, but to the commonly shared yet little noticed existential stakes of social media platforms as indexes of life, and death, which accompany us all the time. It is not simply that, as Peters rightly notes, one-to-many communication is still around alongside other modes; it is that the interconnectedness of our lives in these other modes through digital media, every day and every way, is itself a new 'unifying story to the society at large' (Peters 2015: 7), and one which so-called mass media can excel at telling through moments of poetic exposure and making-present. The mediated life of the one to one can and often should be dramatized, disclosing – sometimes with shocking swiftness – the givenness of its historical and human reality *for* the many *to* the many. This, too, reveals media as fundamental equipment for living.

Digital mobile devices and their infrastructures have not replaced the 'always on' of one-to-many connectivity underpinning twentieth-century broadcasting, or the framework of ambient attendance and companionship that it produced. Rather, they have *thickened* it through their intimate closeness to the individual body, *animated* it through interactive interfaces and *devolved* it to individuals, groups and technical systems through the intensive and extensive complexities of their networks. The multi-sensuous accompaniment of digital devices continually on our persons, the operative restlessness made imperative by user interfaces, the perpetual companionship of more proximate and individuated others (as well as of the apparatus itself) made visible by social media – these all take the unparalleled constancy and readiness of twentieth-century media and simultaneously expand and condense them, making the mediation of the world experientially denser and more intense than in the past.

This density – often unnoticed, sometimes intrusive and unbearable, occasionally transformative and revelatory – is, to return to this book's Introduction, given expression by the 'media manifold' (Couldry and Hepp 2017) as an image of mediated interconnectedness, amplified at both small and large scales. The manifold is a figurative-spatial emblem of the relations between a *reduced* set of actual everyday possibilities for engaging media and the 'almost infinite' range of media resources currently available in principle. 'Reduction' is of course a variable phenomenon, and one that alters historically, not necessarily in predictable stages. Yet notwithstanding this mutability, reduction is also a defining constant of human existence, especially reduction from the (almost) infinite. We are finite creatures, in so very many ways, and the more our communicative capacities are enlarged by media technologies, the more that magnification needs to be configured to human dimensions. While there is definite plasticity to these dimensions (we learn to type, to swipe, to distinguish – most of the time – between the real and 'phantom' vibrations of our devices), that adaptability is not unlimited. Ultimately, *we* are the 'bottleneck' of media.

For Couldry and Hepp, this reduction indicates the social and political ordering that patterns actual media practices at a time of exponentially expanding possibilities for mediation. Without denying the great importance of this emphasis for a renewed social theory of media, my aim has been to explore an alternate perspective and to look through the telescope from its other end. For relations of reduction can become, when the viewpoint is reversed, relations of expansion, of exposure to the energy and magnitude of mediated entanglements. This is how I have attempted to appropriate the image of the 'manifold' for media poetics, stressing the multiple enfoldings of mediated worlds and their manifest disclosure to perception and experience. Humans are indeed finite creatures: but we can think infinity, indeed a plurality of infinities, small and large. We can even make the logically perplexing but emotionally satisfying exclamation 'To infinity and beyond!', as another Pixar hero, Buzz Lightyear, does in *Toy Story*. Media increasingly saturate the world; yet, like the photograph and the screenshot, they do so not merely through their ubiquity but by being saturated in turn with the world's own plenitude. The poetics of media beckons us to stand with Simmel on the threshold of the door seeing 'life flowing beyond the limitations of isolated separate existence' (1997 [1909]: 173). Recognizing the inevitable finitude of our existence, we may still find opportunities to unfold the media manifold, making present, momentarily, 'the limitlessness of all possible directions' in our lives.

Notes

Acknowledgements

1 The most common English translation of the essay by Harry Zohn, first published in 1973 and referenced here, translates the German 'blaue Blume' as 'orchid'. I rely on Miriam Hansen's (1987: 204) reversion to 'blue flower'.

Prologue

1 It is, it should be noted, a trope patterned after the experience of western bourgeois childhood. Sleeping arrangements in other social classes, and other cultures, do not necessarily conform to the pattern conventionally depicted in this scene: a bedroom rather than a multi-purpose living space, a solitary child occupant separated at night from parents, and often also from siblings. This does not mean that non-bourgeois and non-western children do not imagine monsters at night, though the rise and expansion of solitary sleeping practices for young children in the West might have contributed to children's night-time anxiety in these societies.

2 Appearing in Book Seven of *The Republic*, Plato's parable describes – as a general allegory of human consciousness – human beings who are chained within an underground den, prevented from moving their heads, and who are unable to see anything apart from the shadows of objects and of each other cast by a light source upon a cave wall. They mistake those shadows for reality and truth.

3   The species-defining character of imagination – and especially the ability to believe in fictions – is the theme of Yuval Noah Harari's blockbuster *Sapiens* (2014). Imagination is an extraordinarily complex and historically variable concept (Brann 1991; Kearney 1994). Minimally defined here as the human ability to create new objects of perception, cognition and experience by synthesizing, but also moving beyond, prior perceptions and experiences, it is foundational to the work that media do. As Castoriadis observes, all symbolic activity presupposes an imaginary capacity, 'the capacity to see in a thing what it is not, to see it other than it is' (1987: 127).

4   The reality of the imagined and of imagination, particularly in producing and maintaining collective formations of social life, is a key theme of much recent social and political theory, including Anderson's 'imagined communities' (1991), Castoriadis's 'imaginary institution of society' (1987), Campbell's 'modern autonomous imaginative hedonism' (1987), Taylor's 'modern social imaginaries' (2002), Chouliaraki's 'humanitarian imaginary' (2013), Appadurai's imagination as 'a key component of the new global order' (1990: 5) and Orgad's 'global imagination' (2012), to name only a few.

5   For an informative journalistic account of the labour involved in creating a Pixar film, see Lane (2011).

6   This echoes the famous appeal to the audience in stagings of *Peter Pan*, where the life of Tinkerbell can only be saved through the belief of children in the existence of fairies.

7   A similar fictional account of the existential and emotional significance of adjacency between distinctive worlds is given in Phillip Pullman's *His Dark Materials* trilogy. At the end of the last book, *The Amber Spyglass* (2000), the two heroes, Lyra Belacqua and Will Parry, both from different worlds, having completed their mission of sealing the barriers between these worlds to guarantee their integrity and safety, themselves have to part, for ever. Nevertheless, they continue to 'meet' by sitting on the same bench, in the same place, at the same time, in their two different worlds. Adjacency becomes a social relationship – companionship – continually performed despite the most fundamental of separations.

Chapter 1   Introduction: Media Poetics

1   This thought experiment only works, of course, if we assume that you haven't tried to turn on the light (and that all your

other devices can run off batteries, which is admittedly unlikely for the television). Electricity too is a connective medium, an infrastructure of contemporary existence, and its total absence – coupled with the loss of connective signals to battery operated media – would also give rise to apocalyptic imaginings.

2   The overt disclosure of media's world-presencing capacities at the point of their malfunctioning parallels Sybille Krämer's insistence that media disappear in their implementation: 'the smoother media work, the more they remain below the threshold of our perception ... only noise, dysfunction and disturbance make the medium itself noticeable' (2015: 31). Error and malfunction are also important for the idea of 'the glitch' in digital art, which assumes that all media, no matter how 'noiseless' they seem, 'always possess their own inherent fingerprints of imperfection' (Menkman 2011: 12), and which celebrates the 'noise artefact' – the product of deliberate or actual technical errors – that can open up creative possibilities and reveal and reconfigure the specific materialities of digital technologies. In contrast, however, to these emphases on malfunction as noise, Barthes conceptualizes 'the rustle of language' as a 'limit-noise' of what is working well, the impossible, utopian noise of 'what, functioning to perfection, has no noise' (1986: 76–7).

3   Though the current public popularity of complex, fictional imaginary worlds that transcend their media 'vehicles' can be traced to developments in late nineteenth-century literary culture (Saler 2012).

4   The literature on the fundamental psychological, social and discursive significance of narrative, metaphor and other seemingly literary or rhetorical forms is too extensive to delineate here. Important works include Lakoff and Johnson (2003) on metaphor, Bruner on narrative (1986), Goodman on symbolization and world-making (1978), White on narrative and history (1980), Bird and Dardenne on journalism (1988), Labov and Waletzky (1997) on narrativity in everyday language.

5   The main source for this phenomenological understanding of the lifeworld is Husserl (especially 1970 [1936]) and, taken in a sociological direction, Schutz (1967 [1932]; see also Couldry and Hepp's recent discussion [2017]). Possible world theory – which comes from a very different tradition of analytic philosophy – postulates that reality is composed of a plurality of possible yet distinctive worlds, each nevertheless anchored to a central 'actual world' which grants access to them. Though much taken up in literary theory (Ryan 1991; Ronen 1994), and resonating in this book with the analysis of *Monsters, Inc.*

in the Prologue, it tends to be less concerned with the existential ramifications of the givenness of the 'actual world' and more with the semantic truth conditions of non-actual possible worlds (such as one encounters in fiction but also in metaphor: Martin 2004). At the risk of great oversimplification, one might say that it is more focused on the meaning of meaning than on the meaning of life.

6 The use of the term 'media' across all historical contexts runs the risk of anachronism: the contemporary use of the term to refer to communications techniques and technologies only emerges in the nineteenth and especially the twentieth centuries. See Peters (2015) on both the historical antiquity of media and modern understandings of the term, and Guillory (2010) for a philological-philosophical discussion of the emergence of the 'media' concept in western aesthetics and philosophy.

7 The idea of 'media logics' is usually attributed to Altheide and Snow (1979). Both Couldry (2008) and Hepp (2013) have cautioned against potentially reductive and deterministic usages of this term.

8 'Poesis' and 'poiesis' are the main English-language spellings of the ancient Greek word ποίησις, with separate entries in the *Oxford English Dictionary*. In this book, 'poesis' will be used unless the author being cited uses the alternative.

9 'The guiding question for poetics looking at a cultural text such as a television series is "how does this text work?"' (Mittell 2015: 5).

10 Bordwell's 'historical poetics', which has also been adopted and adapted by others such as Mittell, rejects the original formalist exclusivism and relates textual structures and devices to their historical, institutional and technological conditions of production.

11 Todorov's *Poetics of Prose* (1978) is principally devoted to making explicit the conventions and devices characterizing *literary* prose.

12 This famous passage is also cited by Habermas in his intervention in the controversy between Searle and Derrida over Austin's claim that theatrical, poetic and other fictional performances of speech acts are both distinctive from and parasitic upon 'normal' or 'ordinary' language use (Habermas 1998: 389). Habermas sides with Searle in support of Austin.

13 There is a rich, continuing stream of concepts relevant to this topic flowing from diverse traditions in communications and media studies. These include Lippmann's (1922) ideas of 'picturing' and stereotypes, Lazarsfeld and Merton's (1971 [1948]) 'status conferral' function, 'salience' in political

communications framing research (Entman 1993), McCombs and Shaw's (1972) agenda-setting, Dayan and Katz's (1992) account of ceremonial 'media events', Thompson's 'new visibility' (2005), Couldry's (2000) idea that '*the*' media constitute the 'frame' of the social, Dayan's (2009) concept of 'monstration', and the intense recent concern with the 'attention economy' (Goldhaber 1997; Terranova 2012). All of these very different ideas relate – either implicitly or explicitly – to the ways that modern media shape the collective attention of large-scale audiences and publics.

14   Fictionality as a distinguishing feature of literature was also rejected by others in the formalist tradition, such as Shlovsky, for whom defamiliarization, de-habituation and estrangement were key to literary effect, indeed to recovering 'the sensation of life': art 'exists to make one feel things, to make the stone *stony*' (1988 [1965]: 20). For an insightful discussion of estrangement as an effect of comparative viewing within the context of global media coverage, see Orgad 2012.

15   To complicate matters, both these meanings of the verb 'produce' – first, 'to bring forward or out, to present to view or notice; to show or provide (something) for consideration, inspection, or use; to exhibit; *spec.* to bring (a witness or evidence) before a court of law', and second, 'to bring into being or existence' – are, according to the *OED*, prevalent in English from the mid-fifteenth century to the present day.

16   I write this at the risk of grossly oversimplifying Kompridis's (2006) erudite, comprehensive and ambitious integration of phenomenological and pragmatic philosophical traditions in an attempt to enrich and re-energize (largely Habermasian) critical theory.

17   The 'hermeneutics of suspicion' perhaps echoes Ricoeur's discussion of the 'school of suspicion' and its principal 'masters', Marx, Nietzsche and Freud, though Scannell does not indicate this. For a detailed discussion of the 'hermeneutics of suspicion' in Ricouer and the term's broader travels, travails and transformations across philosophy and literary theory, see Scott-Baumann (2009), especially chs 3 and 4.

18   Scannell and Kompridis are both deeply indebted to and influenced by Heidegger, though they are also, in different ways, critical of his thought. For both of them, Heidegger's phenomenology is key to the recuperation of the everyday world as inherently significant to human experience. Here I insert an authorial full disclosure (pun intended): I am not a Heideggerian. It may not be self-serving to say so in contemporary scholarship, but there are thinkers and writers whose work

speaks to us individually and which we find productive, and those which do not and which even repel us – even if we can find many things of value in the writings of their interpreters. The cultivation of desire and attraction remains crucial to reading and thinking. Aside from a few widely cited translations of relatively short essays (on technology, the world picture), Heidegger's work (mainly *Being and Time*) has not just eluded my several attempts to read and grapple with it, but it has also pushed me away. No doubt this reflects an intellectual incapacity in me as a reader, or a weakness of the will to overcome difficulties of style, or the possibility that Heidegger should be read in German (a language I do not speak). It also perhaps expresses a semi-conscious aversion to a thinker who could show such easy enthusiasm for Nazism.

19 For Menkman, the glitch not only refers to technical malfunctions in digital media but also to breaches in cultural or social expectations (2011: 10). I am grateful to Ella Klik for suggesting the connection to glitch art.

20 An additional example, for fans of the Prologue's *Monsters, Inc.*, is the accidental entry of the child Boo into Monstropolis, thereby making unworkable the heavily regulated physical and symbolic divisions between the two worlds.

21 Other aspects that are privileged by 'presence culture' as opposed to 'meaning culture' include: the inscription of bodies into the rhythms of the world rather than the intent to dominate or change those rhythms; magic as a form of action for regulating presence and absence, and the priority of space over time as a 'primordial dimension' (Gumbrecht 2003: 83). Gumbrecht's argument also privileges 'moments of intensity', whereby presence becomes available for aesthetic experience, over the routines of everyday life (97–101).

22 One such is the following offered by media historian Lisa Gitelman: 'I define media as socially realized structures of communication, where structures include both technological forms and their associated protocols, and where communication is a cultural practice, a ritualized collocation of different people on the same mental map, sharing or engaged with popular ontologies of representation' (2006: 7). The phrase 'technological agency' is my attempt to avoid the disparaging associations that have accrued around the term 'technological determinism', which tends to result in the very thesis being denigrated in advance: see Peters for a recent discussion (2017).

23 The definition is not however 'radically minimal': this Peters associates with McLuhan and Kittler, who 'would require only

the second term of the triad – a connecting or processing device of some sort – leaving messages and people as add-ons' (Peters 2010: 266). This idea of the 'add-on' (or in a more Derridean mode, 'supplement') is of course the 'unresolvable' and inelastic performance of definitional inclusion/exclusion that Mitchell describes as endemic to the very concept of medium. Lievrouw and Livingstone (2006) provide a more complex yet also elastic definition of (new) media as 'infrastructures with three components: the *artefacts or devices* used to communicate or convey information; the *activities and practices* in which people engage to communicate or share information; and the *social arrangements or organizational forms* that develop around those devices and practices' (2006: 3). How one imagines the relations between these components is obviously crucial, however. Like Peters, Lievrouw and Livingstone are deliberately agnostic and do not specify a priori any set relationship among the three components.

24 I discuss this idea of 'fixings' in connection to their concept of the 'cut' in ch. 3 on the screenshot.

25 Marvin's work is in part dedicated to unearthing the buried historical construction of media as naturally given objects.

26 The word 'affordance' has become something of a magical term in much media and communication research, miraculously resolving contradictions between technological determinism and radical social constructionism; it is also sometimes used simply as a synonym for a 'feature' or 'characteristic' of a technology. The term is actually far more complex, emerging from Gibson's ecological psychology of perception, and used by Hutchby (2001) to counter claims regarding the radical openness of processes of social construction by arguing for a *range* of socially constructed possibilities and perceptions that are shaped by the material properties of a technology. A material characteristic of a device is only an affordance if perceived as relevant to its applications by a user (just as the ignitable properties of flint rock are only an affordance to a fire-creating species). For a recent overview, see Nagy and Neff (2015), whose notion of 'imagined affordance' attempts to reinstate user perception and expectation within the concept as used in communications and media studies.

27 The origins of 'close reading' are often associated with I. A. Richards's *Practical Criticism* (1929), which reported on and discussed his practice of soliciting written commentaries, responses and analyses from students on unidentified literary works (usually poems) which he assumed they had not

previously seen. West (2002), however, makes a strong argument that Richard's project was intended more as an experiment in the psychology of interpretation than as a new technique in literary pedagogy. See also DuBois (2003) for a discussion of close reading in relation to the rise of New Criticism in American literary studies.

28 The research literature here is truly vast, and I have not even mentioned an entire sub-field of study which takes the body's relation to technology as a core topic: human–computer interaction (HCI).

Chapter 2 Composite: The Morality of Inattention in Pre-digital Media

1 Mitchell suggests that the connection between criticism and crisis tends to result in iconoclastic hostility to images per se: 'Insofar as the very word *criticism* implies a separation of good from bad, the problem of images seems immediately to settle on evaluation, and even more urgently, on a "crisis" of value that makes true criticism seem almost by default to present itself as a kind of iconoclasm, an effort to destroy or expose the false images that bedevil us' (2005: 81).

2 This is of course a key theme in Derrida's early critique of 'logo-centric' accounts of meaning, language and writing (1976).

3 The mutual imbrications of matter and meaning are central topics in the study of material culture. See, for instance, Miller (1987), especially chs 6 and 7, and Keane (2005).

4 The vision of the cinema spectator watching this scene is in fact heavily controlled by filming techniques (close-ups of particular photographs, fade-in and fade-out, musical enhancement) and the cinematic apparatus (large screen size, darkened auditorium, relatively immobilized spectators) to reproduce the mode of attentive looking favoured by Auggie.

5 It is this 'indifference' of the photograph to the organizing perception of either artist or viewer that leads Martin Jay (1988) to classify photography as chiefly corresponding to the 'scopic regime' of 'the art of describing' rather than to 'Cartesian Perspectivalism'.

6 This of course returns us to the 'disconnection scene' at the beginning of chapter 1.

7 To disengage from connectivity would be to disable, disconnect or refuse to own or watch a television, irrespective of its

content, something which does happen among particular populations but is not a form of inattention: see Krcmar (2008) for a fascinating study.

8   Of course, there are important pragmatic differences between face-to-face civil inattention and non-reciprocal televisual face-to-face communication, not least the fact that being looked at by a co-present stranger in public is conventionally interpretable as a hostile act. This potential interpretation of personally directed hostility is diffused in television viewing.

9   My thinking on media and civil inattention has long been indebted to Natan Sznaider (2000).

10   The totemic power of the human face – and its sickening violation – can be glimpsed in the image of the totalitarian future described in Orwell's *Nineteen Eighty-Four*: a boot stamping on a human face, for ever.

11   In Barthes's case, the new, substitute idol can be found in the explicit scientism of the semiological method of his earlier work (including *Mythologies*), one in which Barthes – as 'mythologist' – needs of necessity to distinguish himself from a mere everyday 'myth-consumer': 'When a myth reaches the entire community, it is from the latter that the mythologist must become estranged if he wants to liberate the myth ... The mythologist is condemned to live in a theoretical sociality' (1993 [1972]: 156–7). Barthes's later work significantly distances itself from this scientism.

Chapter 3   Screenshot: The 'Photographic' Witnessing of Digital Worlds

1   This distinction forms the basis for Bolter and Grusin's (1999) opposition between 'transparent immediacy' and 'hypermediacy' in their discussion of 'remediation'.

2   The lack of a caption seems to have become standard practice across many news outlets, though there are exceptions. For example, a *New York Times* article also published on 31 May 2017 did caption a screenshot of Trump's tweet as 'An image of President Trump's Twitter account'.

3   The apparently unproblematic association of atoms with fixity would also be likely to raise some eyebrows among physicists.

4   In an influential article on digital documents Michael Buckland draws a parallel between using a printed logarithmic table and using a computer algorithm to compute log values: 'The table and the algorithm seem functionally equivalent. ... The

algorithm for generating logarithms, like a mechanical educational toy, can be seen as a dynamic kind of document unlike ordinary paper documents, but still consistent with the etymological origins of "docu-ment", a means of teaching – or, in effect, evidence, something from which one learns' (Buckland 1998: 7). I would claim that this argument stretches the concept of the document too far, and that its logical extension is that human teachers are also 'documents' since one (ideally) learns from them. This does not mean that an algorithm can't become a document if inscribed into documentary practices and treated as such, as Briet might argue (see below): if it is studied, for instance, as an example or specimen of algorithms.

5   For a detailed account of Briet's place within the European documentation movement, and of her 'antelope' example, see Day 2001, ch. 2, especially pp. 21–35.

6   Buckland, for instance, ends his discussion of contemporary 'documentality' with the general claim: 'We find that a shared characteristic of documents in both conventional and extended senses is that they exhibit some kind of code' (2014: 185). In contrast, the historical continuity and variation of the document as an evidentiary genre is at the centre of Gittleman's analysis, and it bears repeating that the increasing pressures of large-scale organizational coordination in modern societies – in particular the rise of state and commercial bureaucracies – contribute to the social and political importance of documents, as well as to their combined ubiquity and invisibility as a cultural form. See Hull (2012) for a useful analysis of the importance of documents not simply as bureaucratic tools but as primary means through which bureaucratic organizations cohere, function and endure.

7   Briet claims: 'From the very beginning, Latin culture and its heritage have given to the word *document* the meaning of instruction or proof. ... A contemporary bibliographer concerned about clarity has put forth this brief definition: "A document is a proof in support of a fact"' (2006 [1951]: 9).

8   Genette (1982: 127–44) is mainly credited with reintroducing into contemporary literary theory the Platonic and Aristotelian definitions of 'diegesis' (temporally plotted discourse, which, in its simplest mode, is related through the voice of a single narrator) and *mimesis* (direct imitation or enactment of speech, action or event without the voice of a narrator), usually understood to underpin the distinction between narrative and dramatic forms. The definitions and distinctions are also invoked in the telling/showing dichotomy which developed through the twentieth century (see Genette 1980: 160; Booth 1983,

especially ch. 1, as well as p. 438, note 16; see also Rimmon-Kenan 2002: 110). However, several scholars (Kirby 1991; Halliwell 2009), including Genette himself, caution against readings of the original Platonic and Aristotelian sources which make a hard and fast opposition between diegesis and mimesis as categories of narration and representation.

9   In fact, the know-show function can be recast – in the case of the screenshot but also in the case of many other subspecies of the document genre (classically, the memo: Guillory 2004) – as technical bureaucratic procedures: saving/filing and circulating/displaying.

10 Actually, the case of smartphones and tablets shows that the rhetoric of strictly rectangular frame lines is more important than fidelity to the entire screen display since some device screens have rounded edges.

11 Drucker (2014) specifies three 'basic graphic principles' of visual sign systems: '*the rationalization of a surface* (setting an area or space apart so that it can sustain signification), *the distinction of figure and ground* (as elements of a co-dependent relation of forces and tensions in a graphical field, and *the delimitation of the domain of visual elements so that they function as a relational system* (framing or putting them in relation to a shared reference)' (2014: 71, original italics; see also 202, note 84). While framing is specifically mentioned by Drucker only as an example of the third principle, here it is relevant to all three.

12 The history of the frame as device and metaphor in western visual representation is long and complex. See Friedberg (2006) for an extensive recent treatment, including in digital contexts, and Frosh (2011) on the connections between visual frames and framing as a concept in communications research.

13 *De Pictura* is usually translated into English as *On Painting*. It is also known by the name of its Italian version, *Della Pittura*, completed in 1436.

14 Derrida (1987) argues that the frame (which he identifies as a 'parergon', the name Kant gives to seeming embellishments to the work of art ['ergon']) not only makes representation possible, but achieves its greatest effectivity when it is least visible: 'There is always a form on a ground, but the parergon is a form which has as its traditional determination not that it stands out but that it disappears, buries itself, effaces itself, melts away at the moment it deploys its greatest energy' (1987: 61).

15 See Hui (2012) for a discussion of digital objects in relation to philosophical – especially phenomenological – conceptualizations of natural and technical objects.

16 This does not mean, of course, that the file *is* the document. It may be convenient for me to think of the file of this book chapter *as* the chapter: 'But it is the chapter in a meaningful and useful sense only because I assume, and can rely upon, a technical environment that includes my laptop, Microsoft Word, and a printer thanks to which I can see intelligible marks on a screen and on paper. Under such circumstances, is the file really "the document"? Or should I say that the document consists of the file plus the requisite technical environment? Or must I also include the requisite perceptible forms as well?'(Levy 2001: 157).

17 Nunberg's description of the morselization of information is also resonant of another concept developed by Manovich, though in his earlier work on *The Language of New Media* (2001): the fractal or modular character of new media objects.

18 At the time of writing, both Snapchat and Instagram have introduced mechanisms whereby the sender of a private image is notified if the recipient takes a screenshot of it. Snapchat developers seem to be playing technological cat and mouse with users who are intent on using screenshots to save images and videos that are designed to vanish. See, for instance, https://www.techadvisor.co.uk/how-to/social-networks/how-screen-shot-on-snapchat-without-them-knowing-2017-3634217/. Thanks to Tomer Frosh for this information.

19 For an extensive and important discussion of remediation, see Kember and Zylinska 2012, ch. 1.

20 Sontag is of course one of these scholars, her scepticism nicely preserved through the words 'seems' and 'passes for' in the cited sentences. In addition, and among many, many others, see: Barthes (2000), Hall (1972), Sekula (1989), Slater (1995), Tagg (1988), Zelizer (2010). See Mnookin (1998) on the complex and fascinating history of the treatment of photographs in the US legal system, and particularly their importance for the creation of a category of 'demonstrative evidence' – where demonstrative means 'addressed directly to the senses without intervention of testimony', rather than 'conclusive'.

21 Slater (1995) outlines the mutually reinforcing intersection of three realist belief structures as a basis for photography's epistemic status in the nineteenth century and beyond: *representational* realism emphasizes photography's (superior) fulfilment of conventions and standards of realism prominent in other media, especially painting; *ontological or existential* realism stresses the necessity of the real presence of the depicted object before the camera at a particular moment, and

'the presumption of a unique and privileged relation between sign and referent' (1995: 222) – a presumption other scholars, myself included, have discussed through the concept of indexicality; and *mechanical realism*, which foregrounds the production of images through a mechanized and seemingly impersonal and highly automated process.

22 Finnegan refers to Slater's three 'realisms' of photography, mentioned above, in her discussion of the 'naturalistic enthymeme' (2001: 142).

23 In her recent book (2018), Michelle Henning questions the characterization of photography as a medium of stillness and fixity and challenges its dominance in photography theory, conceptualizing photography instead as a source of mobility, as a way of setting images free by multiplying them across diverse surfaces and contexts. If Henning is right, this means that the discursive-material remediation of photographic stillness, its application to a non-photographic digital form like the screenshot, possesses a startling retrospective power: the very act of delegating a putatively 'photographic' stillness to the screenshot reinforces the belief that *pre-digital* photography was indeed a medium of fixity. Unfortunately, Henning's book was only published as my own was going to press and I am unable to pursue its important ideas any further in these pages.

24 This idea of remediation as a means for delegating states, expectations and practices from one medium to another is indebted to Lievrouw: 'People engage in communicative *practices* or action, some of which may employ those devices; practices change in an ongoing process of *remediation* of interaction, expression, and cultural works' (2014: 45; original italics).

25 However, 'screencap' is not completely synonymous with 'screenshot' since it is often used to refer to a still captured from video, whereas 'screenshot' is rarely used of video.

26 It would be simplistic to reduce all photography to the production of referential images of an external world. Abstraction – the creation of images that do not refer to physical objects or scenes – has been part of photography since its inception, from the early photograms or 'sun pictures' of Henry Fox Talbot (Rexer 2013: 27). While photography has chiefly been studied and performed as a referential practice, this emphasis on 'simulative pictures' (Lehmuskallio 2016: 245) is not the only option for a medium which can be defined more generously as a family of 'technologies for accomplishing or guiding the production of *images* on sensitized *surfaces* by means of *light*' (Maynard

1997: 20; italics in original), and which can produce a broad range of possible outcomes including conventional photographic prints, photograms, photocopies, X-rays, etc. However, while not all photographs are referential or simulative, screenshots – which are not produced on sensitized surfaces by means of light – always seem to be.

27 Even when automated through commercial screenshot services such as 'Stillio' for purposes of web archiving, the parameters of the automation are directed by human decisions.

28 'The spectator has no empirical knowledge of the contents of the off-frame, but at the same time cannot help imagining some off-frame, hallucinating it, dreaming the shape of this emptiness. It is a projective off-frame (that of the cinema is more introjective) ... excluded once and for all. Yet nevertheless present, striking, properly fascinating (or hypnotic) – insisting on its status *as excluded* by the force of its absence *inside* the rectangle of paper' (Metz 1985: 87; original italics).

29 It is in part the violence of this stasis – a violence that directs the viewer's look to the off-frame, and the location of absence – that leads Metz to conceptualize the photograph as a fetish.

30 Nevertheless, the screenshot is always of a particular device, and hence – with the partial exception of public devices – is almost always personal. Often it includes accidental clues and cues as to the identity and behaviour of the device's user. Thanks to Caroline Walsh for clarifying this point.

31 On WhatsApp, as of writing, while the default 'last seen' feature can be turned off in the system settings, the 'online' indicator cannot. Thanks to Nitzan Frosh for this information.

32 'Shiri' is the Hebrew diminutive of 'Shir'. The extra 'i' sound is a common addition at the end of Hebrew names connoting intimacy and endearment, and when used among friends and siblings is a particularly powerful indicator of parental affection.

33 There are additional forms of graphical remediation performed by this screenshot, which reinforce its connection to the fixity associated with pre-digital documents as physical objects. Particularly noticeable is the slight angle at which the screenshot seems to have been overlaid onto the news page, emphasizing the prominence of its edges and the idea that it has been physically cut and pasted onto the printed page of the newspaper.

34 The semiotics of the ✓ sign are significant here. On the one hand the tick is employed on WhatsApp as it is in many other contexts, as a marker of task completion (one might tick items bought on a shopping list). It does not seem to import

into WhatsApp the connotation of 'agreement' or 'approval' associated with the use of the tick in grading students' papers. However, the tick can also connote the presence of an individual, for instance in the ticking of a register during a roll call of pupils' names in a school classroom. This connection of the ✓, to presence also adds to the poetic palpability of this particular screenshot as a powerful 'about to die' image.

35   See Iversen (1994) for a well-known and thoughtful interpretation of Barthes's *Camera Lucida*, and the *studium–punctum* distinction, through the lens (so to speak) of Lacan's psychic registers of real, symbolic and imaginary.

36   'Whoever destroys a soul, it is considered as if he destroyed an entire world. And whoever saves a life, it is considered as if he saved an entire world' (Mishnah Sanhedrin 4:5; Yerushalmi Talmud 4:9; Babylonian Talmud Sanhedrin 37a).

37   The idea that digital media so saturate our everyday lifeworlds that they have become domains of vital connectivity with others is also important to Annette Markham's recent suggestion of 'echolocation' as a metaphor for the experience and construction of digital selfhood: 'the seemingly seamless "always on" state of connectivity is, at the more granular level, a process of continual echolocation, in the way we might think of radar, whereby the outline of an object in space is determined by sending a steady stream of sound signals and listening to the quality of the echo' (Markham 2017). One can also understand tagging on social media, analysed in chapter 5, as a practice of digital echolocation.

38   See Rosenberger (2015) for a thoughtful phenomenological analysis of phantom vibration syndrome as the calibration of the body to habitual expectations about the interactivity and connectivity of mobile devices.

39   'They give birth astride of a grave, the light gleams an instant, then it's night once more.' Pozzo, in Samuel Beckett, *Waiting for Godot* (1956), Act II.

Chapter 4 Tag: Naming Bodies and Incarnating Selves in Social Media

1   In the United States, private initiatives for military tagging of soldiers going into combat became common in the carnage of the civil war, as did demands for its compulsory state introduction (Labbe 2016). The latter occurred during the First

World War. The precise course by which military tags became known as 'dog tags' is hazy, however. Hearst applied the term in a newspaper scare campaign against plans of the Roosevelt administration to introduce social security identification, clearly drawing negative comparisons with the tagging of animals (Krajewska 2017: 99). On animal tagging, see Peters (2015: 349).

2 Findings such as Hand's are likely to vary across cultures and age groups. Miller and Sinanan, for instance, report that no teenagers in their English study (part of a comparative English-Trinidadian ethnography) opted to make private the photos they were tagged in, even if they were unlikely personally to post such images of themselves. 'So although teenagers may cull tagged pictures, they clearly feel it would be wrong to be seen as someone who has failed to share' (2017: 24–5).

3 On the perception and experience of technology as magical, particularly through its spectacular presentation, see Slater (1995). Many early anthropologists use the term 'magic' pejoratively (see, for instance, Frazer: 'magic is a spurious system of natural law as well as a fallacious guide of conduct' (1950: 11). Otto and Stausberg (2013: 1–15) provide a detailed overview of the scholarly (particularly anthropological) conceptualizations of magic and the difficulties in defining it, while Greenwood proposes an anthropological argument in favour of understanding magic as 'a universal aspect of human consciousness' (2009: 4).

4 Nevertheless, in this chapter, 'tagging' will almost always be used as a shorthand for 'tagging people in photographs on social network services'.

5 Tagging utilizing face-recognition technologies has been in use on Facebook since 2010. Facebook's 'tag suggestions' identifies faces in images based on the analysis of previously tagged images (as well as profile pictures) in the Facebook database and a personal biometric profile created from them. Facebook's default setting is that tag suggestions are made and executed unless you opt out in advance in your overall user settings; otherwise, when suggested tags appear they can only be manually removed or edited on an individual image-by-image basis: https://www.facebook.com/help/122175507864081#How-does-Facebook-suggest-tags-for-my-friends.

6 Most social scientific studies of tagging focus on the reasons individuals have for tagging others rather than on the experience of being tagged. Mainly small-scale interview-based investigations, these studies have identified a range of motivations

for tagging, such as social connectivity, gaining attention, maintaining relationships, altruism, play, status enhancement, memory and identity construction (Ames and Naaman 2007; Dhir, Chen and Chen 2017).

7   An extensive philosophical literature dealing with the nature of names and naming stretches back to classical antiquity, often characterized as a dispute over whether names work through pure 'denotative' reference and are largely devoid of semantic meaning (they endure even after losing any descriptive meaning they might have had), or whether they are 'connotative' and their meaning describes attributes of the thing they name. Modern proponents of the 'descriptive theory' include Frege, Russell and to a degree Searle. Their critics – most famously Kripke (1980) – propose an alternative 'causal theory' (Evans and Altham 1973), arguing that proper names refer to their objects by virtue of an original act of naming which creates a reference retained over time not through descriptive sense but through continued use among a community of speakers.

8   Power relations also govern the *recitation* of names, their utterance in diverse contexts. When successfully performed, assigning names and reciting names are different kinds of speech act. Assigning a name is a 'declaration' in Searle's (1975) schema – it brings into being the state of affairs to which it refers (I name you Paul Frosh; hence you are now called Paul Frosh). Uttering an already existing name rarely brings into being that to which it refers and would more often be a 'representative' (concerning the truth of a state of affairs).

9   In many cases, the seemingly 'free' naming power of intimates is ultimately underpinned by the coercive power of the state. For instance, in countries such as the United Kingdom, it is legally required to name newborn babies within a certain time period, and these names must be officially registered.

10   Butler (1993: 154) offers an important critique of the claim (proposed variously by Lacan and Zizek) that the stability of personal names produces a durable identity for the individual subject over time. She argues that this conceptualization elides the patriarchal 'social pact' that underpins naming in many cultures since it is only men's names which are stable and enduring in patronymic systems. For women, it is the obligation to change the (sur)name according to shifts in status (paternity, marriage) that is often paramount.

11   Though in certain contexts, and in certain cultures, the unauthorized use of another's given name can be considered

disrespectful (see Humphrey 2006 on Mongolian name usage) or hostile; see, for instance, Levi-Strauss (1973: 270) on the Nambikwara, and Derrida's discussion of Levi-Strauss's analysis (1976: 101–40).

12 This contrasts starkly with Wendy Chun's example of the viral YouTube video *Kony 2012*, which, she argues, imagines the viewer as simultaneously a singular and plural 'you' (2016: 36). This is closer to the Althusserian hailing scene than social tagging, but closer still to the 'anyone-as-someone communicative structure' (Scannell 2000) of traditional broadcasting, where television viewers and radio listeners are anonymous units in a vast mass audience, and at the same time are directly addressed as particular individuals (by the show host or news anchor looking directly at the camera, for instance). The singular-plural 'you' of *Kony 2012* may be a remediation of such earlier communicative structures.

13 On anthropological considerations of the magical performativity of language, including its connection to Austin's notion of performatives, see for example Tambiah (1990: 74–80), where he discusses Malinowski's analysis of magical language.

14 Lack of space prevents me from considering the connections between being named and being *grasped* by others through the etymology of the term 'handle' used on CB (citizen band) radio – and before that, according to the *OED* – as a colloquial synonym for a publicly used personal nickname. The precise origin of this sense of 'handle' is obscure, though it implies physical contact through touch, and the idea that – in a technical system where one is called upon publicly – the name is also a way of 'getting hold' of a particular individual. The word 'tag' is also associated with bodily contact through the game of tag, also called 'touch'.

15 Shifts in photographic indexicality, away from the idea of the referential 'trace' and towards the deictic performance of the photographer, will be discussed in the next chapter.

16 This unease is connected to an understanding that the body alters itself before the camera. 'I constitute myself in the process of a "posing", I instantaneously make another body for myself, I transform myself in advance into an image' (Barthes 2000: 10).

17 See Henning (2017) for an insightful analysis of the theorization of photography as a death mask, situating it in the context of a particular photographic technique ('the floating face') that emerged in the 1920s and that later became generalized to photography as such. Of course, the idea of photography as an agent in the death of bodies and matter also has an earlier

provenance. Writing in the 1850s, Oliver Wendell Holmes, for instance, provides the following triumphant view: 'Give us a few negatives of a thing worth seeing, taken from different points of view, and that is all we want of it. Pull it down or burn it up, if you please ... We have got the fruit of creation now, and need not trouble ourselves with the core. Every conceivable object of Nature and Art will soon scale off its surface for us. Men will hunt all curious, beautiful, grand objects, as they hunt the cattle in South America, for their skins, and leave the carcasses as of little worth' (Holmes 1980 [1859]: 81).

18   The power asymmetries between institutions and social groups able to control photographic representations of themselves while creating and circulating images of others is manifest across diverse episodes in the history of photography. For instance, in the power of nineteenth-century colonialism to make visible 'primitive' peoples, such as Native Americans, at the very moment of their annihilation (McQuire 1998: 125) and in the power of the liberal state to exhibit the white and black poor as part of the 1930s Farm Security Administration photographic project (Tagg 1988).

19   For a historical analogy to this aggregation of bodies into one greater social body, recall the famous 1651 frontispiece to the first edition of Hobbes's *Leviathan*, which depicts a giant monarch, bearing sceptre and crosier, whose torso and arms are composed of more than three hundred individual human figures.

20   Belk's formulation of the extended self is too complex to address in detail here. As this quotation makes clear, however, it should not be confused with a largely egotistical or narcissistic expansion of a 'core self' at the expense of otherness. Moreover, 'auto-tagging' functions – whereby the social network platform tags individuals through facial recognition technologies – mean that the 'others' who are involved in the extension of the self need not be human agents. Thanks to Gefen Frosh for clarifying this point.

21   The 'mattering' of some digital photographs is further reinforced by research on 'virtual possessions' in general – digital objects to which individuals form strong emotional attachments (not just particular photographs, but also Facebook posts, emails, game avatars, personalized music playlists, etc.). See Odom and colleagues for an illuminating discussion (2014).

22   This includes to a degree Belk's own reformulation (2013) of the extended self.

Chapter 5 Selfie: The Digital Image as Gesture and Performance

1 The faces in them are often pixelated, however.
2 See Dekel (2013) for an extensive discussion of mediation and memory at the Berlin Holocaust Memorial.
3 The need for at least basic representational criteria is evident from the sampling design of projects like 'Selfiecity': 'To locate selfies photos, we randomly selected 120,000 photos (20,000–30,000 photos per city) from a total of 656,000 images we collected on Instagram. 2–4 Amazon's Mechanical Turk workers tagged each photo. For these, we asked Mechanical Turk workers the simple question "Does this photo show a single selfie?"'
4 Significant controversies about the historical continuity of visual modes in modernity are elided here. Crary (1992) is well known for disputing any simple claim of continuity between the photographic camera, nineteenth- and twentieth-century visual regimes, and the 'camera obscura' model of vision that preceded them. Jay (1988) associates photography with two different 'scopic regimes' connected with painting, and also argues in a later essay (1995) that photography simultaneously strengthens and undermines modern 'ocularcentrism'.
5 The 'Oscar selfie' even refers to the significance of the body in the title of the tweet that accompanied its distribution on Twitter: 'If only Bradley's arm was longer. Best photo ever.' See https://twitter.com/theellenshow/status/440322224407314432? lang=en. For an analysis of this particular selfie in terms of sociability rather than (only) celebrity and commercial promotion, see the post 'The Ur-Selfie' at the Carceral Net: http://thecarceralnet.wordpress.com/2014/05/16/the-ur-selfie/.
6 First 'held' on Twitter in 2014, the 'Selfie Olympics' were widely reported in mainstream media outlets. See, for instance, https://www.huffingtonpost.com/2014/01/03/selfie-olympics-twitter_n_4538203.html. The phenomenon returned (to coincide with another winter Olympics) in 2018.
7 Purists may question whether Osmann's images are really selfies. The photographer's arm is a perpetual visual synecdoche for his presence in his own images: hence if they are not 'true' selfies, they are sufficiently close to be of relevance. Thanks to Gefen Frosh for her help in this regard.
8 An extensive and justifiable critique of the 'narcissism' accusation has emerged in recent years. See, for instance, Senft and

Baym (2015) and Burns (2015). Maddox (2017) offers an interesting reflection on selfies as 'exhibitionist' rather than 'narcissist', though she admits that this redefinition does not necessarily help counter discourses that cast the selfie (and *some* of the populations associated with it) as pathological.

Chapter 6   Interface: Remediated Witnessing and Embodied Response

1   Pinchevski (forthcoming) links the 'New Dimensions in Testimony' project to the emergence of a database logic underpinning testimony, marking 'the uncoupling of traumatic memory from the testimonial narrative as its carrier' (6). The database logic serves the purpose of making the testimony 'future proof': compatible with all possible future contexts, both technological and communicative-cultural, of interaction with viewers/interlocutors. This results, in Pinchevski's view, in an enterprise that seeks the seamless transmission of memory as data across generations, without the 'noise' of recorded disturbances, repetitions and silences that, in audiovisual narrative testimonies, came to signify trauma. 'If television and videotape were the media a priori for perceiving the impinging of trauma upon testimony, algorithm and holography are the media a priori of the removal of trauma from testimony' (forthcoming: 11–12).

2   Kansteiner (2014) suspects that audiences will perceive the hologram as a simulation which retains markers of its own historical period, thereby undermining the efficacy of synchronous interaction.

3   Other organizations undertaking large-scale video testimonies include Yad Vashem, Israel's official Holocaust memorial, research and education institute, and Yale University's Fortunoff Video Archive for Holocaust Testimonies. Older and smaller than the USC's Shoah Foundation, the Yale Archive is widely considered to have pioneered the field of video testimony.

4   Jeffrey Shandler's (2017) study of the Visual History Archive was published just as this book was in its final stages, and I was unable to consult it at the time of writing.

5   https://www.yadvashem.org/archive/hall-of-names.html.   Also see Morse's discussion of the recitation of victims' names in

relation to the concept of 'grievability, the public performance of grief and commemoration that forms communities around ethical ties' (2017: 1–2).

6 'Learning-watchfulness' also has a particularistic version, focused on the imperative to learn about the Holocaust in order to ensure no such event ever occurs again to the Jewish people.

7 Though she doesn't mention him, Tait's 'response-ability' seems to be influenced by Levinas. See Pinchevski 2005: 74–6.

8 Kittler's term is rendered as 'technological a priori'. See, for instance, Kittler 1999: notably 117–18.

9 Digital devices are also linked to systems that monitor and manage the very attention they destabilize, largely for commercial ends in an 'attention economy' (Crogan and Kinsley 2012).

10 Notwithstanding the citation from Marks, the 'haptic' is not identical to touch or to tactility. Paterson (2017) offers an intricate, sophisticated and provocative discussion of their complex interrelations. I use 'haptic' here in the sense he identifies (and to a degree, criticizes) as emerging from cinema studies, and which signals the crossing-over of sensory modalities and the augmentation of the visual rather than the specificity of touch since I am focusing on hand–eye relations engaged by the graphical user interface.

11 Interestingly, the holographic prototype of 'New Dimensions in Testimony' also suffers from the same disconnection between engagement and possible action.

Conclusion: To Infinity and Beyond

1 Peters invokes the work of Norbert Elias, in which civilization consists of 'a varying array of regimes for controlling psychic, social and biological resources' (2015: 5). Media are therefore involved in how humans order and orient relations with themselves (psychic resources), with other humans (social resources) and with the natural world (environmental resources).

2 Peters refers here to Raymond Williams's essay on 'drama in dramatized society', originally given as an Inaugural Professorial lecture in 1974, where Williams discusses the massive extension of dramatic forms, practices and frameworks across social

contexts through radio and especially television broadcasting: 'drama, in quite new ways, is built into the rhythms of everyday life .... What we now have is drama as a habitual experience: more in a week, in many cases, than most human beings would previously have seen in a lifetime' (Williams 1983: 12).

3   Think, for instance, of the inspiration, confidence and authority that the ideas – and architecture – of the ancient republics bestowed on the anti-monarchist political revolutions of the late eighteenth century. See, among other accounts, Schama (1989) on the French Revolution, notably ch. 4, section iii.

References

Abercrombie, N. and Longhurst, B. (1998) *Audiences: A Sociological Theory of Performance and Imagination.* London: Sage.

Agamben, G. (1999) *The Man Without Content.* Stanford: Stanford University Press.

Alberti, L. B. (1991 [1435]) *On Painting.* London: Penguin.

Altheide, D. L. and Snow, R. P. (1979) *Media Logic.* Beverly Hills: Sage.

Althusser, L. (1984) *Essays on Ideology.* London: Verso.

Ames, M., and Naaman, M. (2007) 'Why We Tag: Motivations for Annotation in Mobile and Online Media'. *Proceedings of the SIGCHI Conference on Human Factors in Computing Systems (CHI '07)*, pp. 971–80.

Andén-Papadopoulos, K. (2014) 'Citizen Camera-Witnessing: Embodied Political Dissent in the Age of "Mediated Mass Self-Communication"'. *New Media & Society* 16(5): 753–69.

Anderson, B. (1991) *Imagined Communities: Reflections on the Origin and Spread of Nationalism.* London: Verso.

Appadurai, A. (1990) 'Disjuncture and Difference in the Global Cultural Economy'. *Public Culture* 2(2): 1–24.

Ashuri, T. (2011) '(Web)sites of Memory and the Rise of Moral Mnemonic Agents'. *New Media & Society* 14(3): 441–56.

Bachelard, G. (1994) *The Poetics of Space.* Boston: Beacon Press.

Baker, G. (1996) 'Photography between Narrativity and Stasis: August Sander, Degeneration and the Decay of the Portrait'. *October* 76: 72–113.

Banks, J. (2017) 'Multimodal, Multiplex, Multispatial: A Network Model of the Self'. *New Media & Society* 19(3): 419–38.

Barthes, R. (1986) *The Rustle of Language*. Oxford: Basil Blackwell.

Barthes, R. (1993 [1972]) *Mythologies*. Vintage: London.

Barthes, R. (2000) *Camera Lucida: Reflections on Photography*. Fontana: London.

Batchen, G. (1997) *Burning with Desire: The Conception of Photography*. Cambridge, MA: MIT Press.

Bauman, Z. (1990) 'Effacing the Face: On the Social Management of Moral Proximity'. *Theory, Culture and Society* 7: 5–38.

Bauman, Z. (2000) *Liquid Modernity*. Cambridge: Polity Press.

Bauman, R. and Briggs, C. (1990) 'Poetics and Performance as Critical Perspectives on Language and Social Life'. *Annual Review of Anthropology* 19: 59–88.

Bazin, A. (1980) 'The Ontology of the Photographic Image', in A. Trachtenberg (ed.), *Classic Essays on Photography*. New Haven: Leete's Island Books, 237–44.

Beaudoin, J. (2007) 'Folksonomies: Flickr Image Tagging: Patterns Made Visible'. *Bulletin of the Association for Information Science and Technology* 34: 26–9.

Becker, K. (2013) 'Gestures of Seeing: Amateur Photographers in the News'. *Journalism* 16(4): 451–69.

Belk, R. S. (2013) 'Extended Self in a Digital World'. *Journal of Consumer Research* 40: 477–500.

Beloff, H. (1983) 'Social Interaction in Photographing'. *Leonardo* 16(3): 165–71.

Benjamin, W. (1992 [1936]) 'The Work of Art in the Age of Mechanical Reproduction', in H. Arendt, (ed.), *Illuminations*. London: Fontana, pp. 211–44.

Berger, J. (1982) 'Appearances', in John Berger and Jean Mohr (eds), *Another Way of Telling*. New York: Pantheon Books, pp. 85–100.

Berman, M. (1983) *All That Is Solid Melts Into Air: The Experience of Modernity*. London: Verso.

Bird, S. E. and Dardenne, R. W. (1988) 'Myth, Chronicle, and Story: Exploring the Narrative Qualities of News', in J. W. Carey (ed.), *Media, Myths, and Narratives: Television and the Press*. Newbury Park: Sage, pp. 67–86.

Bodenhorn, B. and von Bruck, G. (2006) '"Entangled in Histories": An Introduction to the Anthropology of Names and Naming', in B. Bodenhorn and G. von Bruck (eds), *The Anthropology of Names and Naming*. Cambridge: Cambridge University Press, pp. 1–30.

Boltanski, L. (1999) *Distant Suffering: Morality, Media and Politics*. Cambridge: Cambridge University Press.

Bolter, J. D. and Grusin, R. (1999) *Remediation: Understanding New Media*. Cambridge, MA: MIT Press.

Booth, W. C. (1983) *The Rhetoric of Fiction*, 2nd edn. Chicago: University of Chicago Press.

Boothroyd, D. (2009) 'Touch, Time and Technics: Levinas and the Ethics of Haptic Communications'. *Theory, Culture & Society* 26(2–3): 330–45.

Bordwell, D. (2008) *Poetics of Cinema*. London: Routledge.

Bourdieu, P. (1990) *Photography: A Middle-Brow Art*. Cambridge: Polity Press.

Bourdieu, P. (1991) *Language and Symbolic Power*. Cambridge: Polity Press.

Brann, E. (1991) *The World of the Imagination: Sum and Substance*. London: Rowman & Littlefield.

Briet, S. (2006 [1951]) *What is Documentation?: English Translation of the Classic French Text*, edited and translated by R. E. Day, L. Martinet and H. G. B. Anghelescu. Lanham: Scarecrow Press.

Brown, B. (2010) 'Materiality', in W. J. T. Mitchell and Mark B. N. Hansen (eds), *Critical Terms for Media Studies*. Chicago: Chicago University Press, pp. 49–63.

Bruner, J. (1986) *Actual Minds, Possible Worlds*. Cambridge, MA: Harvard University Press.

Bryson, N. (1983) *Vision and Painting: The Logic of the Gaze*. New Haven: Yale University Press.

Bucher, T. (2017) 'The Algorithmic Imaginary: Exploring the Ordinary Affects of Facebook Algorithms'. *Information, Communication & Society* 20(1): 30–44.

Buckland, M. (1998) 'What is a Digital Document?' *Document Numérique* 2(2): 221–30.

Buckland, M. (2014) 'Documentality Beyond Documents'. *The Monist* 97(2): 179–86.

Burgin, V. (1982) 'Photography, Phantasy, Function', in V. Burgin (ed.), *Thinking Photography*. London: Macmillan Education.

Burns, A.L. (2015) 'Self(ie)-Discipline: Social Regulation as Enacted Through the Discussion of Photographic Practice'. *International Journal of Communication* 9: 1716–33.

Butler, J. (1993) *Bodies that Matter: On the Discursive Limits of 'Sex'*. London: Routledge.

Caldwell, J. (1995) *Televisuality: Style, Crisis and Authority in American Television*. New Brunswick, NJ: Rutgers University Press.

Callon, M. (1991) 'Techno-Economic Networks and Irreversibility', in J. Law (ed.), *A Sociology of Monsters: Essays on Power, Technology and Domination*. London: Routledge, pp. 132–61.

Campbell, C. (1987) *The Romantic Ethic and the Spirit of Modern Consumerism*. Oxford: Blackwell.

Carr, C. T. and Hayes, R. A. (2015) 'Social Media: Defining, Developing, and Divining'. *Atlantic Journal of Communication* 23(1): 46–65.

Casetti, F. (2013) 'What is a Screen Nowadays?', in C. Berry, J. Harbord and R. Moore (eds), *Public Space, Media Space*. London: Palgrave Macmillan, pp. 16–40.

Castoriadis, C. (1987) *The Imaginary Institution of Society*. Cambridge: Polity Press.

Cavell, S. (1979) *The World Viewed: Reflections on the Ontology of Film*. Cambridge MA: Harvard University Press.

Chalfen, R. (1987) *Snapshot Versions of Life*. Madison: University of Wisconsin Press.

Chatman, S. (1978) *Story and Discourse: Narrative Structure in Fiction and Film*. Ithaca: Cornell University Press.

Chouliaraki, L. (2006) *The Spectatorship of Suffering*. London: Sage.

Chouliaraki, L. (2013) *The Ironic Spectator: Solidarity in the Age of Post-Humanitatianism*. Cambridge: Polity Press.

Chouliaraki. L. (2017) 'Symbolic Bordering: The Self-Representation of Migrants and Refugees in Digital News'. *Popular Communication* 15(2): 78–94.

Chun, W. H. K. (2008) 'The Enduring Ephemeral, or the Future is a Memory'. *Critical Inquiry* 35(1): 148–71.

Chun, W. H. K. (2011) *Programmed Visions: Software and Memory*. Cambridge, MA: MIT Press.

Chun, W. H. K. (2016) *Updating to Remain the Same: Habitual New Media*. Cambridge, MA: MIT Press.

Clough, P. (2008) 'The Affective Turn: Political Economy, Biomedia and Bodies'. *Theory, Culture and Society* 25(1): 1–22.

Couldry, N. (2000) *The Place of Media Power: Pilgrims and Witnesses of the Media Age*. London: Routledge.

Couldry, N. (2004) 'Liveness, "Reality," and the Mediated Habitus from Television to the Mobile Phone'. *The Communication Review* 7(4): 353–61.

Couldry, N. (2008) 'Mediatization or Mediation? Alternative Understandings of the Emergent Space of Digital Storytelling'. *New Media & Society* 10(3): 373–391.

Couldry, N. (2012) *Media, Society, World: Social Theory and Digital Media Practice*. Cambridge: Polity Press.

Couldry, N. and Hepp, A. (2017) *The Mediated Construction of Reality*. Cambridge: Polity Press.

Coupland, J., Coupland, N. and Robinson, J. (1992) '"How are You?" Negotiating Phatic Communion'. *Language in Society* 21: 207–30.

Crary, J. (1992) *Techniques of the Observer: On Vision and Modernity in the Nineteenth Century*. Cambridge, MA: MIT Press.

Crary, J. (2002) *Suspensions of Perception: Attention, Spectacle and Modern Culture*. Cambridge, MA: MIT Press.

Crogan, P. and Kinsley, S. (2012) 'Paying Attention: Towards a Critique of the Attention Economy'. *Culture Machine* 13.

Culler, J. (2002) *Structuralist Poetics: Structuralism, Linguistics and the Study of Literature*. London: Routledge.

Currie, G. and Ravenscroft, I. (2002) *Recreative Minds: Imagination in Philosophy and Psychology*. Oxford: Oxford University Press.

Daguerre, L. J. M. (1980 [1839]) 'Daguerreotype', in A. Trachtenberg (ed.), *Classic Essays on Photography*. New Haven: Leete's Island Books, pp. 11–13.

Day, R. E. (2001) *The Modern Invention of Information: Discourse, History and Power*. Carbondale and Edwardville: Southern Illinois University Press.

Dayan, D. (2007) 'On Morality, Distance and the Other in Roger Silverstone's *Media and Morality*'. *International Journal of Communication* 1: 113–22.

Dayan, D. (2009) 'Sharing and Showing: Television as Monstration'. *The Annals of the American Academy of Political and Social Science* 625: 19–31.

Dayan, D. and Katz, E. (1992) *Media Events: The Live Broadcasting of History*. Cambridge, MA: Harvard University Press.

Dekel, I. (2013) *Mediation at the Holocaust Memorial in Berlin*. London: Palgrave Macmillan.

de la Peña N. et al. (2010) 'Immersive Journalism: Immersive Virtual Reality for the First-Person Experience of News'. *Presence* 19(4): 291–301.

Derrida, J. (1976) *Of Grammatology*. Baltimore: Johns Hopkins University Press.

Derrida, J. (1987) *The Truth in Painting*. Chicago: University of Chicago Press.

Derrida, J. (1988) 'Signature, Event, Context', in: *Limited Inc.* Evanston: Northwestern University Press, pp. 1–24.

Deuze, M. (2011) 'Media Life'. *Media, Culture & Society* 33(1): 137–48.

Dhir, A., Chen, G. M. and Chen, S. (2017) 'Why Do We Tag Photographs on Facebook? Proposing a New Gratifications Scale'. *New Media & Society* 19(4): 502–21.

Doane, M. A. (2007) 'The Indexical and the Concept of Medium Specificity'. *Differences* 18(1): 128–52.

Douglas, N. (2014) 'It's Supposed to Look Like Shit: The Internet Ugly Aesthetic'. *Journal of Visual Culture* 13(3): 314–39.

Dourish, P. (2001) *Where The Action Is: The Foundations of Embodied Interaction*. Cambridge, MA: MIT Press.

Drucker, J. (2014) *Graphesis: Visual Forms of Knowledge Production*. Cambridge, MA: Harvard University Press.

DuBois, A. (2003) 'Close Reading: An Introduction', in F. Lentricchia and A. DuBois (eds), *Close Reading: The Reader*. Durham: Duke University Press, pp. 1–40.

Duguid, P. (1996) 'Material Matters: The Past and Futurology of the Book', in G. Nunberg (ed.), *The Future of the Book*. Berkeley: University of California Press, pp. 63–101.

Edwards, E. (2012). 'Objects of Affect: Photography Beyond the Image'. *Annual Review of Anthropology* 41: 221–34.

Ellis, J. (1982) *Visible Fictions*. London: Routledge.

Ellis, J. (2000) *Seeing Things: Television in the Age of Uncertainty*. London: I. B. Tauris.

Engell, L. (2013) 'The Tactile and the Index: From the Remote Control to the Hand-held Computer: Some Speculative Reflections on the Bodies of the Will'. *NECSUS* 2(2): 323–36.

Entman, R. M. (1993) 'Framing: Toward Clarification of a Fractured Paradigm'. *Journal of Communication* 43(4): 51–8.

Erlich, V. (1973) 'Russian Formalism'. *Journal of the History of Ideas* 34(4): 627–38.

Evans, G., and Altham, J. E. J. (1973) 'The Causal Theory of Names'. *Proceedings of the Aristotelian Society. Supplementary Volumes* 47: 187–225.

Farman, J. (2012) *Mobile Interface Theory: Embodied Space and Locative Media*. New York: Routledge.

Felman, S. and Laub, D. (1992) *Testimony: Crises of Witnessing in Literature, Psychoanalysis and History*. London and New York: Routledge.

Finnegan, C. A. (2001) 'The Naturalistic Enthymeme and Visual Argument: Photographic Representation in the "Skull Controversy"'. *Argumentation and Advocacy* 37(3): 133–49.

Fox Talbot, W. H. (1844–6) *The Pencil of Nature*. London: Longman, Brown, Green and Longmans. Guttenberg Project Ebook version (2010): http://www.gutenberg.org/ebooks/33447.

Francke, H. (2005) 'What's in a Name? Contextualizing the Document Concept'. *Literary and Linguistic Computing* 20(1): 61–9.

Frazer, J. (1950 [1922]) *The Golden Bough: A Study in Magic and Religion*. London: Macmillan.

Freud, S. (1955) 'The Uncanny'. *The Standard Edition of the Complete Psychological Works*, Vol. XVII. London: Hogarth Press and the Institute of Psycho-Analysis, pp. 219–52.

Friedberg, A. (1993) *Window Shopping: Cinema and the Postmodern*. Berkeley: University of California Press.

Friedberg, A. (2006) *The Virtual Window: From Alberti to Microsoft*. Cambridge, MA: MIT Press.

Frosh, P. (2001) 'The Public Eye and the Citizen Voyeur: Photography as a Performance of Power'. *Social Semiotics* 11(1): 43–59.

Frosh, P. (2003) *The Image Factory: Consumer Culture, Photography and the Visual Content Industry*. Berg: Oxford.

Frosh, P. (2006) 'Telling Presences: Witnessing, Mass Media, and the Imagined Lives of Strangers'. *Critical Studies in Media Communication* 23(4): 265–84.

Frosh, P. (2007) 'Penetrating Markets, Fortifying Fences: Advertising, Consumption and Violent National Conflict'. *Public Culture* 19(3): 461–82.

Frosh P. (2011) 'Phatic Morality: Television and Proper Distance'. *International Journal of Cultural Studies* 14(4): 383–400.

Frosh, P. and Pinchevski, A. (2009) 'Why Media Witnessing? Why Now?', in P. Frosh and A. Pinchevski (eds), *Media Witnessing: Testimony in the Age of Mass Communication*. London: Palgrave Macmillan, pp. 1–19.

Gallese, V. (2005) 'Embodied Simulation: From Neurons to Phenomenal Experience'. *Phenomenology and the Cognitive Sciences* 4: 23–48.

Galloway, A. R. (2012) *The Interface Effect*. Cambridge: Polity Press.

García-Montes, J. M., Caballero-Munoz, D. and Perez-Alvarez, M. (2006) 'Changes in the Self Resulting from the Use of Mobile Phones'. *Media, Culture & Society* 28(1): 67–82.

Genette, G. (1980) *Narrative Discourse: An Essay in Method*. Ithaca: Cornell University Press.

Genette, G. (1982) *Figures of Literary Discourse*. New York: Columbia University Press.

Ginzburg, C. (2004) 'Family Resemblances and Family Trees: Two Cognitive Metaphors'. *Critical Inquiry* 30: 537–56.

Gitelman, L. (2006) *Always Already New: Media, History and the Data of Culture*. Cambridge, MA: MIT Press.

Gitelman, L. (2014) *Paper Knowledge: Toward a Media History of Documents*. Durham: Duke University Press.

Gladwell, M. (2010) 'Small Change: Why the Revolution Will Not Be Tweeted'. *The New Yorker*. 4 October, http://www.newyorker.com/magazine/2010/10/04/small-change-malcolm-gladwell.

Goffman, E. (1963). *Behavior in Public Places: Notes on the Social Organization of Gatherings*. New York: The Free Press.

Goldhaber, M. (1997) 'The Attention Economy and the Net'. *First Monday* (2)4. http://firstmonday.org/article/view/519/440.

Gómez Cruz, E. and Meyer, E. T. (2012) 'Creation and Control in the Photographic Process: iPhones and the Emerging Fifth Moment of Photography'. *Photographies* 5(2): 203–21.

Gómez Cruz, E. and Thornham, H. (2015) 'Selfies Beyond Self-Representation: The (Theoretical) F(r)ictions of a Practice'. *Journal of Aesthetics and Culture* 7(1).

Goodman, N. (1978) *Ways of Worldmaking*. Indianapolis: Hackett Publishing.

Greenwood, S. (2009) *The Anthropology of Magic*. Oxford: Berg.

Guillory, J. (2004) 'The Memory and Modernity'. *Critical Inquiry* 31: 108–32.

Guillory, J. (2010) 'The Genesis of the Media Concept'. *Critical Inquiry* 36(2): 321–62.

Gumbrecht, H. U. (1994) 'A Farewell to Interpretation', in Hans Ulrich Gumbrecht and K. Ludwig Pfeiffer (eds), *Materialities of Communication*. Stanford: Stanford University Press, pp. 389–402.

Gumbrecht, H. U. (2003) *Production of Presence: What Meaning Cannot Convey*. Stanford: Stanford University Press.

Gunning, T. (1995) 'Phantom Images and Modern Manifestations: Spirit Photography, Magic Theater, Trick Films, and Photography's Uncanny', in P. Petro (ed.), *Fugitive Images: From Photography to Video*. Bloomington: Indiana University Press.

Habermas, J. (1998) *On the Pragmatics of Communication*. Cambridge, MA: MIT Press.

Hall, S. (1972) 'The Determinations of News Photographs'. *Working Papers in Cultural Studies*. Birmingham, UK, pp. 53–87.

Halliwell, S. (2009) *The Aesthetics of Mimesis: Ancient Texts and Modern Problems*. Princeton: Princeton University Press.

Hand, M. (2012) *Ubiquitous Photography*. Cambridge: Polity Press.

Hansen, M. (1987) 'Benjamin, Cinema and Experience: "The Blue Flower in the Land of Technology"'. *New German Critique* 40: 179–224.

Hansen, M. B. N. (2004) *New Philosophy for New Media*. Cambridge, MA: MIT Press.

Hansen, M. B. N. (2006) *Bodies in Code: Interfaces with Digital Media*. London: Routledge.

Harari, Y. N. (2009) 'Scholars, Eyewitnesses, and Flesh-Witnesses of War: A Tense Relationship'. *Partial Answers: Journal of Literature and the History of Ideas* 7(2): 213–28.

Harari, Y. N. (2014) *Sapiens: A Brief History of Humankind*. London: Harvill Secker.

Hariman. R. and Lucaites, J. (2007) *No Caption Needed: Iconic Photographs, Public Culture and Liberal Democracy*. Chicago: University of Chicago Press.

Hariman. R. and Lucaites, J. (2016) *The Public Image: Photography and Civic Spectatorship*. Chicago: University of Chicago Press.

Hartman, G. (1996) *The Longest Shadow: In the Aftermath of the Holocaust*. Bloomington: Indiana University Press.

Hartman, G. (2000) 'Tele-Suffering and Testimony in the Dot Com Era', in B. Zelizer (ed.), *Visual Culture and the Holocaust*. London: The Athlone Press, pp. 111–24.

Hayles, N. K. (2007) 'Hyper and Deep Attention: The Generational Divide in Cognitive Modes'. *Profession* 13: 187–99.

Henning, M. (2017) 'The Floating Face: Garbo, Photography and Death Masks'. *Photographies* 10(2): 157–78.

Henning, M. (2018) *Photography: The Unfettered Image*. London: Routledge.

Hepp, A. (2013) *Cultures of Mediatization*. Cambridge: Polity Press.

Highmore, B. (2011) *Ordinary Lives: Studies in the Everyday*. London: Routledge.

Hirsch, M. (2003) 'I Took Pictures: September 2001 and Beyond', in J. Greenberg (ed.), *Trauma at Home: After 9/11*. Lincoln, NE: University of Nebraska Press, pp. 69–86.

Hjarvard, S. (2008) 'The Mediatization of Society: A Theory of the Media as Agents of Social and Cultural Change'. *Nordicom Review* 29(2): 105–34.

Hjorth, L. and Pink, S. (2014) 'New Visualities and the Digital Wayfarer: Reconceptualizing Camera Phone Photography and Locative Media'. *Mobile Media & Communication* 2(1): 40–57.

Hochman, N. (2014) 'The Social Media Image'. *Big Data and Society* 1(2).

Hoelzl, I. and Marie, R. (2015) *Softimage: Towards a New Theory of the Digital Image*. Bristol: Intellect.

Holly, M. A. (1995) 'Past Looking', in Stephen Melville and Bill Readings (eds), *Vision and Textuality*. London and New York: Macmillan.

Holmes, O. W. (1980 [1859]) 'The Stereoscope and the Stereograph', in A. Trachtenberg (ed.), *Classic Essays on Photography*. New Haven: Leete's Island Books, pp. 71–82.

Hopgood, S. (2006) *Keepers of the Flame: Understanding Amnesty International*. Ithaca, NY: Cornell University Press.

Horton, D. and Wohl, R. (1956) 'Mass Communication and Para-Social Interaction: Observations on Intimacy at a Distance'. *Psychiatry* 19: 215–29.

Hui, Y. (2012) 'What is a Digital Object?' *Metaphilosophy* 43(4): 380–95.

Hull, M. S. (2012) 'Documents and Bureaucracy'. *Annual Review of Anthropology* 41: 251–67.

Humphrey, C. (2006) 'On Being Named and Not Named: Authority, Persons, and Their Names in Mongolia', in B. Bodenhorn and G. von Bruck (eds), *The Anthropology of Names and Naming*. Cambridge: Cambridge University Press, pp. 157–76.

Husserl, E. (1970 [1936]) *The Crisis of European Sciences and Transcendental Phenomenology*, trans. D. Carr. Evanston: Northern University Press.

Hutchby, I. (2001) *Conversation and Technology: From the Telephone to the Internet*. Cambridge: Polity Press.

Iversen, M. (1994) 'What is a Photograph?' *Art History* 17(3): 450–64.

Jackson, M. (2008) *Distracted: The Erosion of Attention and the Coming Dark Age*. Amherst, NY: Prometheus Books.

Jakobson, R. (1960) 'Linguistics and Poetics', in T. Sebeok (ed.), *Style in Language*. Cambridge, MA: MIT Press, pp. 350–77.

Jameson, F. (1991) *Postmodernism, or the Cultural Logic of Late Capitalism*. Durham: Duke University Press.

Jay, M. (1988) 'Scopic Regimes of Modernity', in Hal Foster (ed.), *Vision and Visuality*. Seattle: Dia Art Foundation Discussions in Contemporary Culture, Bay Press, pp. 2–23.

Jay, M. (1995) 'Photo-unrealism: The Contribution of the Camera to the Crisis of Ocularcentrism', in S. Melville and B. Readings (eds), *Vision and Textuality*. Durham, NC: Duke University Press, pp. 344–60.

Jenkins, H. (2006) *Convergence Culture: Where Old and New Media Collide*. Cambridge, MA: MIT Press.

Jenkins, H., Ford, S. and Green, J. (2013) *Spreadable Media: Creating Meaning and Value in a Networked Culture*. New York: New York University Press.

John, N. (2016) *The Age of Sharing*. Cambridge: Polity Press.

Johnson, D. (2013) *Media Franchising: Creative License and Collaboration in the Culture Industries*. New York: New York University Press.

Kansteiner, W. (2014) 'Genocide Memory, Digital Cultures, and the Aesthetization of Violence'. *Memory Studies* 7(4): 403–8.

Katz, L. (2013) 'Holograms of Holocaust Survivors Let Crucial Stories Live On'. *CNET*. 11 February, http://www.cnet.com/news/holograms-of-holocaust-survivors-let-crucial-stories-live-on.

Keane, W. (2005) 'Signs Are Not the Garb of Meaning: On the Social Analysis of Material Things', in D. Miller (ed.), *Materiality*. Durham, NC: Duke University Press, pp. 182–205.

Kearney, R. (1994) *The Wake of Imagination*. London: Routledge.

Keightley, E., and Pickering, M. (2014) 'Technologies of Memory: Practices of Remembering in Analogue and Digital Photography'. *New Media & Society* 16(4): 576–93.

Kember, S. and Zylinska, J. (2012) *Life after New Media: Mediation as a Vital Process*. Cambridge, MA: MIT Press.

Kern, S. (1983) *The Culture of Time and Space 1880–1918*. Cambridge, MA: Harvard University Press.

Kirby, J. T. (1991) 'Mimesis and Diegesis: Foundations of Aesthetic Theory in Plato and Aristotle'. *Helios* 18(2): 113–28.

Kirschenbaum, M. G. (2012) *Mechanisms: New Media and the Forensic Imagination*. Cambridge, MA: MIT Press.

Kittler, F. A. (1999) *Gramophone, Film, Typewriter*. Stanford: Stanford University Press.

Koch, G. (1995) 'Nähe und Distanz: Face-to-face Kommunikation in der Moderne', in Gertrud Koch (ed.), *Auge und Affekt*. Frankfurt am Main: S. Fischer Verlag, pp. 272–91.

Kompare, D. (2005) *Rerun Nation: How Repeats Invented American Television*. London: Routledge.

Kompridis, N. (1994) 'On World Disclosure: Heidegger, Habermas and Dewey'. *Thesis Eleven* 37: 29–45.

Kompridis, N. (2006) *Critique and Disclosure: Critical Theory Between Past and Future*. Cambridge, MA: MIT Press.

Krajewska, M. (2017) *Documenting Americans: A Political History of National ID Card Proposals*. Cambridge: Cambridge University Press.

Krämer, S. (2003) 'Writing, Notational Iconicity, Calculus: On Writing as a Cultural Technique'. *MLN* 118(3): 518–37.

Krämer, S. (2015) *Medium, Messenger, Transmission: An Approach to Media Philosophy*. Amsterdam: Amsterdam University Press.

Krauss, R. (1986) *The Originality of the Avant-garde and Other Modernist Myths*. Cambridge, MA: MIT Press.

Krcmar, M. (2008) *Living Without the Screen: Causes and Consequences of Life without Television*. London: Routledge.

Kress, G. and van Leeuwen, T. (2004) *Reading Images: The Grammar of Visual Design*. London: Routledge.

Kripke, S. (1980) *Naming and Necessity*. Cambridge, MA: Harvard University Press.

Labbe, S. A. (2016) 'The Evolution of the Military Dog Tag: From the Civil War to Present Day'. *The Gettysburg Compiler: On the Front Lines of History* 176. Available at: http://cupola.gettysburg.edu/compiler/176.

Labov, W. and Waletzky, J. (1997) 'Narrative Analysis: Oral Versions of Personal Experience'. *Journal of Narrative & Life History* 7(1–4): 3–38.

Lagerkvist, A. (2017) 'Existential Media: Toward a Theorization of Digital Thrownness'. *New Media & Society* 19(1): 96–110.

Lagerkvist, A. and Andersson, Y. (2017) 'The Grand Interruption: Death Online and Mediated Lifelines of Shared Vulnerability'. *Feminist Media Studies.* http://dx.doi.org/10.1080/14680777.2017.1326554.

Lakoff G. and Johnson M. (2003) *Metaphors We Live By.* Chicago: University of Chicago Press.

Lane, A. (2011) 'The Fun Factory: Life at Pixar'. *The New Yorker,* 16 May: 74–87.

Lanham, R. A. (1993) *The Electronic Word: Democracy, Technology and the Arts.* Chicago: University of Chicago Press.

Larsen, J. (2005) 'Families Seen Sightseeing: Performativity of Tourist Photography'. *Space and Culture* 8(4): 416–34.

Latour, B. (1992) 'Where Are the Missing Masses?', in W. Bijker and J. Law (eds), *Shaping Technology.* Cambridge, MA, MIT Press, pp. 225–58.

Laver, J. (1975) 'Communicative Functions of Phatic Communion', in A. Kendon, R. M. Harris and M. R. Key (eds), *The Organization of Behavior in Face-to-Face Interaction.* The Hague: Mouton, pp. 215–38.

Lazarsfeld, P. and Merton, R. (1971 [1948]) 'Mass Communication, Popular Taste and Organized Social Action', in W. Schramm and D. E. Roberts (eds), *The Processes and Effects of Mass Communication.* Urbana: University of Illinois Press, pp. 459–80.

Lehmuskallio, A. (2016) 'The Camera as a Sensor: The Visualization of Everyday Digital Photography as Simulative, Heuristic and Layered Pictures', in E. Gómez Cruz and A. Lehmuskallio (eds), *Digital Photography and Everyday Life: Empirical Studies on Material Visual Practices.* London: Routledge, pp. 243–66.

Levi, P. (1988) *The Drowned and the Saved.* New York: Summit Books.

Levi-Strauss, C. (1973) *Tristes Tropiques.* London: Penguin Books.

Levy, D. (2001) *Scrolling Forward: Making Sense of Documents in the Digital Age.* New York: Arcade Publishing.

Lévy-Bruhl, L. (1926) *How Natives Think.* London: George Allen & Unwin.

Lievrouw, L. A. (2014) 'Materiality and Media in Communication and Technology Studies: An Unfinished Project', in T. Gillespie, P. Boczkowski and K. Foot (eds), *Media Technologies: Essays on Communication, Materiality, and Society.* Cambridge, MA: MIT Press.

Lievrouw, L. and Livingstone, S. (2006) *Handbook of New Media: Social Shaping and Social Consequences of ICTs,* updated student edn. London: Sage.

Lingis, A. (1994) *The Community of Those Who Have Nothing in Common*. Bloomington and Indianapolis: Indiana University Press.

Lingwood, J. (ed.) (1986) *Staging the Self: Self-Portrait Photography 1840s–1980s*. London: National Portrait Gallery.

Lippmann, W. (1922) *Public Opinion*. London: Allen & Unwin.

Lister, M. (2013) 'Introduction', in M. Lister (ed.), *The Photographic Image in Digital Culture*. Abingdon: Routledge, pp. 1–21.

Lister, M. (2016) 'Is the Camera and Extension of the Photographer?', in E. Gómez Cruz and A. Lehmuskallio (eds), *Digital Photography and Everyday Life: Empirical Studies on Material Visual Practices*. London: Routledge, pp. 267–73.

Literat, I. (2017) 'Refugee Selfies and the (Self-)Representation of Disenfranchised Social Groups'. *Media Fields Journal* 12: 1–9.

Livingstone, S. (2009) 'On the Mediation of Everything: ICA Presidential Address 2008'. *Journal of Communication* 59: 1–18.

Losh, E. (2014) 'Beyond Biometrics: Feminist Media Theory Looks at Selfiecity'. http://selfiecity.net/#theory.

Luckmann, B. (1978) 'The Small-Life Worlds of Modern Man', in T. Luckmann (ed.), *Phenomenology and Sociology: Selected Readings*. Harmondsworth: Penguin Books, pp. 275–90.

Lund, N. W. (2010) 'Document, Text and Medium: Concepts, Theories and Disciplines'. *Journal of Documentation* 66(5): 734–49.

Maddox, J. (2017) '"Guns Don't Kill People. . .Selfies Do": Rethinking Narcissism as Exhibitionism in Selfie-related Deaths'. *Critical Studies in Media Communication* 34(3): 193–205.

Madianou, M. and Miller, D. (2012) *Migration and New Media: Transnational Families and Polymedia*. London: Routledge.

Malinowski, B. (1923) 'The Problem of Meaning in Primitive Languages', in C. K. Ogden and I. A. Richards (eds), *The Meaning of Meaning*. London: Routledge & Kegan Paul, pp. 296–355.

Manovich, L. (2001) *The Language of New Media*. Cambridge, MA: MIT Press.

Manovich, L. (2012) 'The Back of our Devices Looks Better than the Front of Anyone Else's: On Apple and Interface Design', in P. Snickers and P. Vonderau (eds), *Moving Data: The iPhone and the Future of Media*. New York: Columbia University Press, pp. 278–86.

Manovich, L. (2013) *Software Takes Command*. New York: Bloomsbury.

Margalit, A. (2002) *The Ethics of Memory*. Cambridge, MA: Harvard University Press.

Markham, A. (2003) 'Metaphors Reflecting and Shaping the Reality of the Internet: Tool, Place, Way of Being'. Paper presented at the conference of the *Association of Internet Researchers (AOIR)*.

Toronto, Canada, October 2003. https://annettemarkham.com/writing/MarkhamTPW.pdf.

Markham, A. (2017) 'Echo-Locating the Digital Self. Blog Entry'. September 2017. https://annettemarkham.com/2017/09/25844/.

Marks, L. U. (1998) 'Video Haptics and Erotics'. *Screen* 39(4): 331–48.

Marlow, C., Naaman, M., boyd, d. and Davis, M. (2006) 'HT06, Tagging Paper, Taxonomy, Flickr, Academic Article, to Read'. *Proceedings of the Seventeenth Conference on Hypertext and Hypermedia (HYPERTEXT '06)*, pp. 31–40.

Martin, T. (2004) *Poesis and Possible Worlds*. Toronto: University of Toronto Press.

Marvin, C. (1988) *When Old Technologies Were New: Thinking About Electric Communication in the Late Nineteenth Century*. Oxford: Oxford University Press.

Massumi, B. (2002) *Parables for the Virtual: Movement, Affect, Sensation*. Durham: Duke University Press.

Maynard, P. (1997) *The Engine of Visualization: Thinking Through Photography*. Ithaca: Cornell University Press.

McCombs, M. and Shaw, D. (1972) 'The Agenda-Setting Function of Mass Media'. *Public Opinion Quarterly* 36(2): 176–87.

McCullough, M. (2013) *Ambient Commons: Attention in the Age of Embodied Information*. Cambridge, MA: MIT Press.

McLuhan, M. (1994) *Understanding Media: The Extensions of Man*. Cambridge, MA: MIT Press.

McPherson, T. (2002) 'Reload: Liveness, Mobility and the Web', in N. Mirzoeff (ed.), *A Visual Culture Reader*. London: Routledge.

McQuire, S. (1998) *Visions of Modernity*. London: Sage.

Mendelson, A. and Papacharissi, Z. (2010) 'Look at Us: Collective Narcissism in College Student Facebook Photo Galleries', in Z. Papacharissi (ed.), *A Networked Self: Identity, Community and Culture on Social Network Sites*. New York: Routledge, pp. 251–73.

Menkman, R. (2011) *The Glitch Moment(um)*. Amsterdam: Network Notebooks, Institute of Network Cultures.

Metz, C. (1985) 'Photography and Fetish'. *October* 34: 81–90.

Meyrovitz, J. (1986) *No Sense of Place: The Impact of Electronic Media on Social Behavior*. Oxford: Oxford University Press.

Miller, D. (1987) *Material Culture and Mass Consumption*. Oxford: Basil Blackwell.

Miller, D. (1998) 'Why Some Things Matter', in D. Miller (ed.), *Material Cultures: Why Some Things Matter*. London: University College London Press, pp. 3–21.

Miller, D. and Sinanan, J. (2017) *Visualising Facebook: A Comparative Perspective*. London: UCL Press.

Miller, V. (2008) 'New Media, Networking, and Phatic Culture'. *Convergence* 14(4): 387–400.

Mitchell, W. (1992) *The Reconfigured Eye: Visual Truth in The Post-Photographic Era*. Cambridge, MA: MIT Press.

Mitchell, W. J. T. (1994) *Picture Theory: Essays on Verbal and Visual Representation*. Chicago: University of Chicago Press.

Mitchell, W. J. T. (2005) *What Do Pictures Want? The Lives and Loves of Images*. Chicago: University of Chicago Press.

Mittell, J. (2001) 'A Cultural Approach to Television Genre Theory'. *Cinema Journal* 40(3): 3–24.

Mittell, J. (2015) *Complex TV: The Poetics of Contemporary Television Storytelling*. New York: New York University Press.

Mnookin, J. L. (1998) 'The Image of Truth: Photographic Evidence and the Power of Analogy'. *Yale Journal of Law and the Humanities* 10(1): 1–74.

Moeller, S. (1999) *Compassion Fatigue: How the Media Sell Disease, Famine, War and Death*. London: Routledge.

Mole, C. (2011) *Attention is Cognitive Unison: An Essay in Philosophical Psychology*. Oxford: Oxford University Press.

Moores, S. (2014) 'Digital Orientations: "Ways of The Hand" and Practical Knowing in Media Uses and Other Manual Activities'. *Mobile Media & Communication* 2(2): 196–208.

Morley, D. (2000) *Home Territories: Media, Mobility and Identity*. London: Routledge.

Morse, T. (2017) *The Mourning News: Reporting Violent Death in a Global Age*. New York: Peter Lang.

Murray, S. (2008) 'Digital Images, Photo-Sharing, and our Shifting Notions of Everyday Aesthetics'. *Journal of Visual Culture* 7(2): 147–63.

Nagy, P. and Neff, F. (2015) 'Imagined Affordance: Reconstructing a Keyword for Communication Theory'. *Social Media + Society* 1(2).

Nancy, J.-L. (2000) *Being Singular Plural*. Stanford: Stanford University Press.

Nancy, J.-L. (2005) *The Ground of the Image*. New York: Fordham University Press.

Nash, K. (2017) 'Virtual Reality Witness: Exploring the Ethics of Mediated Presence'. *Studies in Documentary Film*.

Neale, S. (1990) 'Questions of Genre'. *Screen* 31(1): 45–66.

Noland, C. (2009) *Agency and Embodiment: Performing Gestures/Producing Culture*. Cambridge, MA: Harvard University Press.

Norval, A. and Prasopoulou, E. (2017) 'Public Faces? A Critical Exploration of the Diffusion of Face Recognition Technologies in Online Social Networks'. *New Media & Society* 19(4): 637–54.

Nunberg, G. (1996) 'Farewell to the Information Age', in G. Nunberg (ed.), *The Future of the Book*. Berkeley: University of California Press, pp. 103–36.

Odom, W., Zimmerman, J. and Forlizzi, J. (2014) 'Placelessness, Spacelessness, and Formlessness: Experiential Qualities of Virtual Possessions'. *Proceedings of the 2014 Conference on Designing Interactive Systems* (DIS '14), pp. 985–94.

Ong, J. C. (2014) '"Witnessing" or "Mediating" Distant Suffering? Ethical Questions Across Moments of Text, Production, and Reception'. *Television & New Media* 15(3): 179–96.

Orgad, S. (2012) *Media Representation and the Global Imagination*. Cambridge: Polity Press.

Otto, B. and Stausberg, M. (2013) (eds) *Defining Magic: A Reader*. London: Routledge.

Oxford English Dictionary Online (March 2018), Oxford University Press.

Panofsky, E. (1972 [1939]) *Studies in Iconology: Humanistic Themes in the Art of the Renaissance*. Boulder, CO: Westview Press.

Paterson, M. (2017) 'On Haptic Media and the Possibilities of a More Inclusive Interactivity'. *New Media & Society* 19(10): 1541–62.

Peirce, C. S. (1958) 'The Icon, Index and Symbol', in C. Hartshorne and P. Weiss (eds), *Collected Papers of Charles Sanders Peirce, Volume II: Principles of Philosophy and Elements of Logic*. Cambridge, MA: Harvard University Press, pp. 274–307.

Peters, J. D. (1999) *Speaking Into the Air: A History of the Idea of Communication*. Chicago: The University of Chicago Press.

Peters, J. D. (2001) 'Witnessing'. *Media, Culture & Society* 23(6): 707–24.

Peters, J. D. (2010) 'Mass Media', in W. J. T. Mitchell and M. B. N. Hansen (eds), *Critical Terms for Media Studies*. Chicago: University of Chicago Press.

Peters, J. D. (2015) *The Marvellous Clouds: Towards a Philosophy of Elemental Media*. Chicago: The University of Chicago Press.

Peters, J. D. (2017) '"You Mean My Whole Fallacy Is Wrong": On Technological Determinism'. *Representations* 140: 10–26.

Pettman, D. (2016) *Infinite Distraction: Paying Attention to Social Media*. Cambridge: Polity Press.

Pfister, D. S. and Woods, C. S. (2016) 'The Unnaturalistic Enthymeme: Figuration, Interpretation, and Critique after Digital Mediation'. *Argumentation and Advocacy* 52(4): 236–53.

Pinchevksi, A. (2005) *By Way of Interruption: Levinas and the Ethics of Communication*. Pittsburgh: Duquesne University Press.

Pinchevski, A. (2012) 'The Audiovisual Unconscious: Media and Trauma in the Video Archive for Holocaust Testimonies'. *Critical Inquiry* 39(1): 142–66.

Pinchevski, A. (forthcoming) *Transmitted Wounds: Media and the Mediation of Trauma*. Oxford: Oxford University Press.

Pold, S. (2005) 'Interface Realisms: The Interface as Aesthetic Form'. *Postmodern Culture* 15(2).

Presner, T. (2016) 'The Ethics of the Algorithm: Close and Distant Listening to the Shoah Foundation Visual History Archive', in C. Fogu, W. Kansteiner and T. Presner (eds), *Probing the Ethics of Holocaust Culture*. Cambridge, MA: Harvard University Press, pp. 175–202.

Price, D. (1997) 'Surveyors and Surveyed: Photography Out and About', in L. Wells (ed.), *Photography: A Critical Introduction*. London: Routledge, pp. 55–102.

Pullman, P. (2000) *The Amber Spyglass*. London: Scholastic Press.

Reckwitz, A. (2002) 'The Status of the "Material" in Theories of Culture: From "Social Structure" to "Artefacts"'. *Journal for the Theory of Social Behaviour* 32(2): 195–217.

Rettberg, J. (2014) *Seeing Ourselves Through Technology: How We Use Selfies, Blogs and Wearable Devices to See and Shape Ourselves*. London: Palgrave Macmillan.

Rexer, L. (2013) *The Edge of Vision: The Rise of Abstraction in Photography*. New York: Aperture.

Richards, I. A. (1929) *Practical Criticism: A Study of Literary Judgment*. London: Kegan Paul.

Ricoeur, P. (1992) *Oneself as Another*. Chicago: The University of Chicago Press.

Rimmon-Kenan, S. (2002) *Narrative Fiction: Contemporary Poetics*, 2nd edn. London: Routledge.

Ristovska, S. (2016) 'Strategic Witnessing in an Age of Video Activism'. *Media, Culture & Society* 38(7): 1034–47.

Robertson, A. (2010) *Mediated Cosmopolitanism: The World of Television News*. Cambridge: Polity Press.

Robins, K. (1996) *Into the Image: Culture and Politics in the Field of Vision*. London: Routledge.

Ronen, R. (1994) *Possible Worlds in Literary Theory*. Cambridge: Cambridge University Press.

Rose, G. (2010) *Doing Family Photography: The Domestic, the Public and the Politics of Sentiment*. Farnham: Ashgate.

Rosler, M. (1989) 'In, Around and Afterthoughts (on Documentary Photography)', in R. Bolton (ed.), *The Contest of Meaning: Critical Histories of Photography*. Cambridge, MA: MIT Press, pp. 305–42.

Rosenberger, R. (2015) 'An Experiential Account of Phantom Vibration Syndrome'. *Computers in Human Behavior* 52: 124–31.

Rubinstein, D. (2010) 'Tag, Tagging'. *Philosophy of Photography* 1(2): 197–9.

Rubinstein, D., and Sluis, K. (2008) 'A Life More Photographic: Mapping the Networked Image'. *Photographies* 1(1): 9–28.

Rubinstein. D. and Sluis, K. (2013) 'The Digital Image in Photographic Culture: Algorithmic Photography and the Crisis of Representation', in M. Lister (ed.), *The Photographic Image in Digital Culture*, 2nd edn. Routledge: London, pp. 22–40.

Ryan, M.-L. (1991) *Possible Worlds, Artificial Intelligence and Narrative Theory*. Bloomington: University of Indiana Press.

Saler, M. (2012) *As If: Modern Enchantment and the Literary Prehistory of Virtual Reality*. Oxford: Oxford University Press.

Saltz, J. (2014) 'Art at Arm's Length: A History of the Selfie'. Vulture. com. 27 January. Retrieved from: http://www.vulture.com/2014/01/history-of-the-selfie.html.

Scannell, P. (1996) *Radio, Television and Modern Life*. Oxford: Blackwell.

Scannell, P. (2000) 'For-Anyone-as-Someone Structures'. *Media, Culture & Society* 22(1): 5–24.

Scannell, P. (2014) *Television and the Meaning of 'Live': An Enquiry into the Human Situation*. Cambridge: Polity Press.

Schama, S. (1989) *Citizens: A Chronicle of the French Revolution*. New York: Knopf.

Schulz, W. (2004) 'Reconstructing Mediatization as an Analytical Concept'. *European Journal of Communication* 19(1): 87–101.

Schutz, A. (1967 [1932]) *The Phenomenology of the Social World*. Evanston: Northwestern University Press.

Scott, J. (1998) *Seeing Like a State: How Schemes to Improve the Human Condition Have Failed*. New Haven: Yale University Press.

Scott-Baumann, A. (2009) *Ricoeur and the Hermeneutics of Suspicion*. London: Continuum.

Searle, J. R. (1975) 'A Taxonomy of Illocutionary Acts', in K. Gunderson (ed.), *Language, Mind and Knowledge*. Minneapolis: University of Minnesota Press, pp. 344–69.

Sekula, A. (1989) 'The Body and the Archive', in R. Bolton (ed.), *The Contest of Meaning: Critical Histories of Photography*. Cambridge, MA: MIT Press, pp. 342–88.

Senft, T. M. (2008) *Camgirls: Celebrity and Community in the Age of Social Networks*. New York: Peter Lang.

Senft, T. M. (2015) 'The Skin of the Selfie', in A. Bieber (ed.), *Ego Update: The Future of Digital Identity*. Dusseldorf: NRW Forum Publications.

Senft, T. and Baym, N. (2015) 'What Does the Selfie Say? Investigating a Global Phenomenon'. *International Journal of Communication* 9: 1588–1606.

Shandler, J. (2017) *Holocaust Memory in the Digital Age: Survivors' Stories and New Media Practices*. Stanford: Stanford University Press.

Shlovsky, V. (1988 [1965]) 'Art as Technique', in David Lodge (ed.), *Modern Criticism and Theory: A Reader*. London: Longman, pp. 16–30.

Silverman, K. (2015) *The Miracle of Analogy: Or, The History of Photography Part 1*. Stanford: Stanford University Press.

Silverstone, R. (1994) *Television and Everyday Life*. London: Routledge.

Silverstone, R. (2007) *Media and Morality: On the Rise of the Mediapolis*. Cambridge: Polity Press.

Simmel, G. (1997 [1903]) 'The Metropolis and Mental Life', in David Frisby and Mike Featherstone (eds), *Simmel on Culture*. London: Sage, pp. 174–85.

Simmel, G. (1997 [1909]) 'Bridge and Door', in David Frisby and Mike Featherstone (eds), *Simmel on Culture*. London: Sage, pp. 170–4.

Simmel, G. (1997 [1911]) 'The Sociology of Sociability', in D. Frisby and M. Featherstone (eds), *Simmel on Culture: Selected Writings*. London: Sage, pp. 120–30.

Slater, D. (1995) 'Photography and Modern Vision: The Spectacle of "Natural Magic"', in C. Jenks (ed.), *Visual Culture*. London: Routledge, pp. 218–37.

Slovic, P. (2007) '"If I Look at the Mass I Will Never Act": Psychic Numbing and Genocide'. *Judgment and Decision Making* 2(2): 79–95.

Soderman, B. (2007) 'The Index and the Algorithm'. *Differences* 18(1): 153–86.

Sontag, S. (1977) *On Photography*. New York: Doubleday.

Spence, J. (1986) *Putting Myself in the Picture*. London: Camden Press.

Stam, R. (1992) *Reflexivity in Film and Literature: From Don Quixote to Jean-Luc Godard*. New York: Columbia University Press.

Stewart, S. (1984) *On Longing: Narratives of the Miniature, the Gigantic, the Souvenir, the Collection*. Baltimore: The Johns Hopkins University Press.

Steyerl, H. (2009) 'In Defense of the Poor Image'. *E-flux Journal* 10: http://www.e-flux.com/journal/10/61362/in-defense-of-the-poor-image/.

Stone, L. (2015) 'Continuous Partial Attention'. http://lindastone.net/qa/continuous-partial-attention/.

Strömbäck, J. (2008) 'Four Phases of Mediatization: An Analysis of the Mediatization of Politics'. *International Journal of Press/ Politics* 13(3): 228–46.

Sudnow, D. (2001) *Ways of the Hand: A Rewritten Account*. Cambridge, MA: MIT Press.

Sznaider, N. (2000) 'Consumerism as a Civilizing Process: Israel and Judaism in the Second Age of Modernity'. *International Journal of Politics, Culture and Society* 14(2): 297–314.

Sznaider, N. (2001) *The Compassionate Temperament: Care and Cruelty in Modern Society*. Lanham: Rowman & Littlefield.

Tagg, J. (1988) *The Burden of Representation: Essays on Photographies and Histories*. London: Macmillan.

Tait, S. (2011) 'Bearing Witness, Journalism and Moral Responsibility'. *Media, Culture & Society* 33(8): 1220–35.

Tambiah, S. J. (1990) *Magic, Science, Religion and the Scope of Rationality*. Cambridge: Cambridge University Press.

Taussig, M. (1992) 'Physiognomic Aspects of Visual Worlds'. *Visual Anthropology Review* 8(1): 15–28.

Taylor, C. (2002) 'Modern Social Imaginaries'. *Public Culture* 14(1): 91–124.

Terranova, T. (2012) Attention, Economy and the Brain. *Culture Machine* 13. https://www.culturemachine.net/index.php/cm/article/view/465/484.

Thompson, J. B. (1995) *The Media and Modernity: A Social Theory of the Media*. Cambridge: Polity Press.

Thompson, J. B. (2005) 'The New Visibility'. *Theory, Culture & Society* 22(6): 31–51.

Thorburn, D. and Jenkins, H. (2003) *Rethinking Media Change: The Aesthetics of Transition*. Cambridge, MA: MIT Press.

Thumin, N. (2012) *Self-Representation and Digital Culture*. London: Palgrave Macmillan.

Tifentale, A. (2014) 'The Selfie: Making Sense of the "Masturbation of Self-Image" and the "Virtual Mini-Me"'. 14 February, http://selfiecity.net/#theory.

Todorov, T. (1978) *The Poetics of Prose*. Ithaca: Cornell University Press.

Todorov, T. (1981) *Introduction to Poetics*. Minneapolis: University of Minnesota Press.

Tolson, A. (1996) *Mediations: Text and Discourse in Media Studies*. London: Arnold.

Tomlinson, J. (1999) *Globalization and Culture*. Chicago: The University of Chicago Press.

Turkle, S. (1997) *Life on the Screen: Identity in the Age of the Internet*. New York: Phoenix.

Turow, J. (2012) *The Daily You: How the New Advertising Industry is Defining Your Identity and Your Worth*. New Haven: Yale University Press.

Uricchio, W. (2011) 'The Algorithmic Turn: Photosynth, Augmented Reality and the Changing Implications of the Image'. *Visual Studies* 26(1): 25–35.

Van Dijck, J. (2008) 'Digital Photography: Communication, Identity, Memory'. *Visual Communication* 7(1): 57–76.

Van Dijck, J. (2014) 'Datafication, Dataism and Dataveillance: Big Data Between Scientific Paradigm and Ideology'. *Surveillance & Society* 12(2): 197–208.

Van House, N. A. (2011) 'Personal Photography, Digital Technologies and the Uses of the Visual'. *Visual Studies* 26(2): 125–34.

Verhoeff, N. (2009) 'Theoretical Consoles: Concepts for Gadget Analysis'. *Journal of Visual Culture* 8(3): 279–98.

Verhoeff, N. (2012) *Mobile Screens: The Visual Regime of Navigation*. Amsterdam: Amsterdam University Press.

Versnel, H. S. (2002) 'The Poetics of the Magical Charm: An Essay in the Power of Words', in P. Mirecki and M. Meyer (eds), *Magic and Ritual in the Ancient World*. Lieden: Brill, pp. 105–58.

Walton, K. (1990) *Mimesis as Make-believe: On the Foundations of the Representational Arts*. Cambridge, MA: Harvard University Press.

Webster, J. (2011) 'The Duality of Media: A Structurational Theory of Public Attention'. *Communication Theory* 21: 43–66.

West, D. W. (2002) 'Practical Criticism: I. A. Richards' Experiment in Interpretation'. *Changing English* 9(2): 207–13.

White, H. (1980) 'The Value of Narrativity in the Representation of Reality'. *Critical Inquiry* 7(1): 5–27.

Winston, B. (1984) 'Television at a Glance'. *Quarterly Review of Film Studies* 9(3): 256–61.

Williams, R. (1983) *Writing in Society*. London: Verso.

Williams, R. (1990 [1975]) *Television: Technology and Cultural Form*. London: Routledge.

Wolf, M. J. P. (2012) *Building Imaginary Worlds: The Theory and History of Subcreation*. New York: Routledge.

Zelizer, B. (1998) *Remembering to Forget: Holocaust Memory Through the Camera's Eye*. Chicago: The University of Chicago Press.

Zelizer, B. (2007) 'On "Having Been There": "Eyewitnessing" as a Journalistic Key Word'. *Critical Studies in Media Communication* 24(5): 408–28.

Zelizer, B. (2010) *About to Die: How News Images Move the Public*. Oxford: Oxford University Press.

Zhao, S. and Zappavigna, M. (2018) 'Beyond the Self: Intersubjectivity and the Social Semiotic Interpretation of the Selfie'. *New Media & Society* 20(5): 1735–54.

Zylinska, J. (2016) 'The Creative Power of Nonhuman Photography', in K. Kuc and J. Zylinska (eds), *Photomediations: A Reader*. London: Open Humanities Press, pp. 201–24.

Index